Positive Atheism

Positive Atheism
Bayle, Meslier, d'Holbach, Diderot

Charles Devellennes

EDINBURGH
University Press

Edinburgh University Press is one of the leading university presses in the UK. We publish academic books and journals in our selected subject areas across the humanities and social sciences, combining cutting-edge scholarship with high editorial and production values to produce academic works of lasting importance. For more information visit our website: edinburghuniversitypress.com

© Charles Devellennes, 2021, 2022

Edinburgh University Press Ltd
The Tun – Holyrood Road
12(2f) Jackson's Entry
Edinburgh EH8 8PJ

First published in hardback by Edinburgh University Press 2021

Typeset in 10/12 Goudy Old Style by
Servis Filmsetting Ltd, Stockport, Cheshire,
and printed and bound by CPI Group (UK) Ltd, Croydon, CR0 4YY

A CIP record for this book is available from the British Library

ISBN 978 1 4744 7843 4 (hardback)
ISBN 978 1 4744 7844 1 (paperback)
ISBN 978 1 4744 7846 5 (webready PDF)
ISBN 978 1 4744 7845 8 (epub)

Contents

Introduction:
The Birth of Positive Atheism

The history of atheism begins with an injustice. Plato, in his *Apology*, describes the trial of his teacher and mentor Socrates during which the latter is accused by his fellow citizen Meletus of being a 'complete atheist' (τό παράπαν άθεος).[1] The epithet of atheism is consubstantial with the history of philosophy, as those with unorthodox views about the gods get labelled 'atheists' and face death sentences – even from a democratic polity such as Athens. Studies of the history of atheism inevitably begin with looking at the accusers, those who impose the term on others, for such a focus forms the backbone of the first two millennia of the concept.[2] The case of Socrates, as the one of the second-century Christian apologist Justin Martyr,[3] or the better-known cases of Descartes, Spinoza and Hume, all fall under this category of considering atheism from the point of view of its enemies. For Socrates, as for the others, the accusation soon proves shallow if not completely empty. Socrates will easily dispel Meletus' case, yet he was arguing as a philosopher and not as a defence attorney. The potency of the Socratic philosophical critique, resting on the argument that he could not both believe in oracles and prophecies while simultaneously be a complete atheist, earned him a logical victory but cost him his life. Indeed, he further clarified that since the oracles had ordered him to question everything, he was not about to stop the activities that led to his second accusation: that he corrupted the youth.

This introductory chapter will provide three arguments before detailing the content of the subsequent chapters. In the first place, it will argue, against much of the existing literature on modern atheism, that starting with the accusers of 'atheists' is counter-productive to the study of atheism as a phenomenon, and that a history of positive atheism is desperately needed. The second argument will be that atheism itself is a radical doctrine, and that a study of this radicalism needs to unpack the multiple meanings of the concept itself. This will allow me to engage with other works on radical thinkers in the Enlightenment, notably those of Jonathan Israel and his critics. Third, this introduction will argue that its methodical approach is one of critical history and hermeneutics, and that such approaches – shared in part by the authors investigated in this book – provide an important angle in the history of atheism. Finally, this chapter will introduce the four authors discussed in this volume: Pierre Bayle, Jean Meslier, Paul-Henri d'Holbach and Denis Diderot. Out of these, only two are outright atheists (in the sense that they self-identify as such), while the other two have more nuanced attitudes towards their self-identity, but nonetheless all are unwavering in their defence of an understanding of atheism as a positive doctrine.

Modern Atheism

Two excellent scholars have already thoroughly researched the perception of atheism by theists and their use of it as epithets of accusation. In 1990, Michael Buckley[4] and Alan Charles Kors[5] both published their respective works on the origins of modern atheism in France. Both share a similar outlook that I wish to move past. Their scholarship, historiographical work and attention to the details of historical narrative are not questioned here (and in many ways, they have informed my own work). Nevertheless, their initial theoretical starting point is not the only valid one, and it will become clear that their work needs to be supplemented by new scholarship that bypasses the limitations inherent in their method. Both authors spend most of their energy on the accusers of atheists; that is, on those who throw the epithet 'the atheist' at others. Buckley, for example, is explicit about his method:

> Perhaps the first instance of coherence in any attempt to under-stand atheism is this: the central meaning of atheism is not to

be sought immediately in atheism; it is to be sought in those gods or that god affirmed, which atheism has either engaged or chosen to ignore as beneath serious challenge.[6]

This is equivalent to saying that any description of Christianity is incoherent if it does not study the pagan cults and Jewish religion it was built on. The possibility of modern atheism's rise, for Buckley, is to be sought in the failure of theologians of the period to be convincing enough for their contemporaries. Why were they unsuccessful? Because, for Buckley, theologians attempted to become philosophers to combat the *philosophes*, and they ended up giving up aspects of their theology (such as Christology) in order to do so.[7] Since they were weaker at philosophy than their adversaries, the atheists won and the rest is history. Kors is equally clear about his method: although he started by looking at the atheists themselves (his work on Holbach is testament to his scholarship on the matter[8]), his *Atheism in France* worked backwards in time towards the sources of disbelief.[9] Equating his work to a detective novel, he focused on the orthodox sources of disbelief, an approach he has recently expanded upon with even greater detail and scholarship.[10] As a historian of ideas, I find the work of these two authors indispensable and praiseworthy, and have certainly used many of their insights here. As a theorist, however, I find their strict historiographies limiting. Fundamentally, I reject their methodical approach – starting with theology to understand atheology – as there is an obvious alternative that has at least equal validity and coherence: starting with the atheists. The precise nature of the historical method and contribution of this book will be detailed later in this introduction, but for the moment the reader should bear in mind that this theoretical contribution comes from taking positive atheism as a starting point, and unpacking the radical elements within its various formulations, focusing on four authors – Bayle, Meslier, Holbach and Diderot – who provide an important theoretical contribution to social and political theory.

The first argument made in this book is that starting with the accusation of atheism is to begin from precisely the wrong point of view – that is, if one is concerned with taking atheism seriously and understanding it as a phenomenon of importance. It is the wrong approach, because since the end of the seventeenth century and in particular with the work of Bayle, we have the first *positive* formulation of atheism, which snowballed into a complex set of theories about the nature of the phenomenon. Ironically perhaps, this first defence of atheism, this first formulation of a positive atheism, comes from someone who was (most probably) not an atheist himself, and for whom the problem was a serious intellectual, practical and political one, as he certainly believed there were atheists living around him, but not a personal problem. Nevertheless, a positive understanding of atheism emerges during the Enlightenment, and it has a particularly French flavour for the first hundred years of its history. Despite the fact that Bayle was a Frenchman who lived and wrote in the Netherlands, and that the baron d'Holbach was of German origins and naturalised as a Frenchman, all four major thinkers of positive atheism between the late seventeenth to the late eighteenth centuries were French, and writing in that language. One could speculate why that is – the absolute nature of the French monarchy may have sparked more radical ideas, the intransigent Catholic Church doctrine during that century could have triggered a more aggressive response – but the precise national character of this doctrine is not the message to remember here. For all we know, it could be historical contingency that meant that we have texts from four French authors defending atheism at the time, and scholars may yet unearth more texts of which I am not aware from outside the French-speaking world.[11]

The essential message of this book is quite different from these national Enlightenments, as all four thinkers depended massively on other European (and in some sense, global) debates, as will become clear in the following chapters. What is important here is that there is a conceptual shift from atheism as an epithet of accusation, which had existed since the fifth century BCE at the very least, to a positive doctrine of atheism which began in the seventeenth century. This point in itself is not original and has been noted by many before me.[12] The great Hegel himself had understood the emptiness of the negative conception of atheism, a charge made against 'an individual whose ideas about God differ from those of other people', and noted the true shift into 'materialism, atheism and naturalism' in the philosophy of Frenchmen, especially in 'Mirabaud [the *nom de plume* of Holbach], to whom the *Système de la Nature* is attributed'.[13] This book follows the Hegelian insight here and treats atheism within this dialectic. We will see that for early atheists themselves, atheism was thought to have existed for a long time, and perhaps even to predate theism, and even to predate the gods of pagan worshippers. If they are correct, the dialectic proposed here is that a form of atheism existed, was largely though never entirely displaced by a variety of beliefs and religious practices, and then re-emerged in modernity. We will see more precisely how this is formulated later in individual chapters on the four thinkers, but it is clear that the emerging global nature of travel facilitated the rise of this dialectic, as encounters with 'primitive' atheists by travellers played a key role in contemporary debates about the existence of atheists. In other words, the atheist was no longer a hypothetical person, built up and destroyed again as a philosophical exercise to strengthen one's faith, but was thought of as a real, existing person either living in the distant past of humanity, or on the edges of the known world. The veracity of this claim is not analysed here – anthropologists and archaeologists may be better suited to assess it – but it certainly served as a conceptual tool to understand the nature of modern atheism.

Negative Atheism in Context

Let me turn to the changing landscape of atheism in France in a very long eighteenth century, stretching from 1618 to 1789. On 2 August 1618, Lucilio Vanini was arrested in Toulouse. What were the ignominies this Neapolitan medical doctor in his thirties, recently arrived in the city, was accused of? Atheism, blasphemy, impiety, and other crimes, a lethal combination worthy of the worst of punishments. After a six-month trial, the court found him guilty, and the sentence fell: Vanini was to be burnt at the stake. The precise sentence states that Vanini:

> was condemned to be dragged on a plank to the St Étienne church, where he will be undressed to his shirt, will hold a

brazen torch in his hand, wear a rope around his neck, and, kneeling in front of the church's door, will seek the forgiveness of God, the King, justice. Following custom, he will be driven to Salin square where, seated at the stake, his tongue will be cut out, he will then be strangled, his body burnt and reduced to ashes.[14]

The sentence was carried out faithfully. For the next two centuries, the story of Vanini's condemnation and sentence acted as a stark warning to all potential atheists, and until 1789 was a constant reminder of the *ancien régime*'s cruelty and arbitrariness.

The supreme irony here is that Vanini was not an atheist, at least in the sense that he denied the existence of God. In fact, in his writings he had been at pains to defend a conception of God, or Providence, and had argued against atheism. Vanini's work is certainly an attack on the Catholic orthodoxy of his day, but he admits ignorance when it comes to the nature of God: 'You ask me what God is; if I knew it I would be God, for no one knows God, and no one knows what he is, but God himself.'[15] Vanini even finished his argument about the existence of God with a submission to the Pope's authority on matters of faith – probably too little too late for many of his readers, who had understood too well that his conception of God as the universe could not be reconciled with the Church's doctrine.[16] During his long trial, Vanini attempted to use this argument against the accusations of atheism, for example by arguing that a piece of straw he had found on the ground was enough of a proof for the existence of God.[17] But what he did not realise was that atheism, in the early seventeenth century, was not about the denial of any conception of God, but about the denial of the God of the accuser. Vanini was being accused of negative atheism – or negating the God of the theologians. He died a philosopher for these crimes and refused to repent or take consolation from the Franciscan friar who accompanied him in his last moments. He, of course, succumbed to his ordeal in agony when, having refused to submit his tongue to the knife, it was forced out with pincers before being cut off with a knife.[18]

But perhaps Vanini's belief in Providence was not in vain: his

example acted as a reminder to future generations of unorthodox believers, deists, pantheists and atheists alike that the erring
conscience of the philosopher was not free, and that if caught off
guard, it would lead them to a similar fate. Far from eradicating
'atheism', we see then a radicalisation of unorthodox religious
positions that led to avowed atheism by the time Meslier wrote his
Memoirs. That is not to say that Vanini is the only source of inspiration for these thinkers, and that his death is the sole cause of
the emergence of atheism as we know it; but it is a stark reminder
of the milieu within which positive atheism emerged – a hostile,
dangerous and cruel world where ideas could see you burnt at the
stake. A century and a half later, in 1766, a similar fate will befall
on the Chevalier de La Barre, for impiety and blasphemy. He will
have his tongue cut out, his head severed from his body, and his
body burnt at the stake, to the horror of even the most moderate
of Enlighteners, such as Voltaire.

This negative conception of atheism, as a denial of God,
Providence, or even of the particular God of a particular Church,
is powerful to this day. Many who would not call themselves atheists are labelled as such by those for whom any disagreement with
their orthodoxy constitutes a lack of belief in the very existence
of God. Even Bayle, as we will see, is guilty of this generalisation.
Atheists are, for him, those who deny Divine Providence and the
immortality of the soul. He could not quite conceive that someone who denies these two essential truths of religion could be
anything but an atheist. And atheists are not immune from similar
labelling. Meslier, the first self-avowed atheist, was unaware of his
own originality. For him, he was merely putting in his particular
context arguments that he believed to have been eternal – or at
least going to the roots of Greek philosophy. Alan Charles Kors
has demonstrated very well, in the recent volume of his trilogy,
Epicureans and Atheists in France, 1650–1729, that it is constant
references to the ancients that unite many of the authors he looks
at.[19] Even Holbach atheises other authors, who are not themselves
atheists. Out of the four authors studied in this book, only Diderot
is careful not to attribute the label to others who would have disagreed with it, probably because he was uncomfortable with the
label being applied to himself.

But negative atheism is not merely a label imposed on others. It can also be a powerful critical tool to dispel some of the so-called myths of theological systems, religious beliefs and practices, and secularised theological concepts. From Bayle onwards, it is clear that atheists bring about a fundamental challenge to believers and theologians: the question of whether we need scripture, religion, or God for ethical action. The negative critique of the atheist, whether it is a fictional atheist or a real person, is all the more poignant if they otherwise have lived good lives, been law-abiding citizens and performed good actions around them. The first challenge was thus not rational, in the sense that it did not rest on the particular arguments of philosophers, but rather ontological, as it became increasingly clear that good atheists existed, which went against orthodox beliefs about the source of moral action. It seems that the first atheists were not the philosophers we will discuss in this book, but rather the atheists of the past or the atheists of the new world. Part of the challenge for modern Europe was increased exposure to beliefs that were not those of the three religions of the Book, which medieval Europe was used to. Travel accounts, such as those of Bougainville on which Diderot commented at length, had been challenging European thought since at least the sixteenth-century conquest of the Americas.[20] The precise nature of this challenge remains to be seen, and is beyond the scope of the present work, but it surfaced in all four of our thinkers as an important source of early or primitive atheism, and it is clear that it is of vital importance for the overall picture of a history of atheism writ large. Atheism appeared as a fait accompli in modern Europe – partly because of encounters with new beliefs and people due to European colonial enterprises.

Added to this was the rise of increasingly provocative philosophical accounts that moved closer and closer to the outright denial of God. Spinoza's metaphysics had certainly shocked many of his contemporaries, and Bayle was among those who spilled much ink trying to refute his system. Spinozism also became a synonym for atheism, and although this was to change when Holbach's *System of Nature* came out in 1770, the association between a Spinozist philosophy and the denial of God remained strong throughout the Enlightenment, and still has resonance today.[21] Apart from

Bayle, however, there is little evidence of in-depth knowledge of Spinoza's work in Meslier, Holbach or Diderot. But perhaps that is to misrepresent the way in which ideas spread in early modern times. Unconcerned with academic referencing styles, attribution of ideas to their authors, or even remaining faithful to an author's intentions, the authors we will be looking at often pillaged, plagiarised, altered or otherwise took for their own ideas that they had read. For Bayle and Holbach, it was essential to share their ideas with a wider public, sometimes at great personal cost, participating in and overstepping what Voltaire dubbed 'écrasez l'infâme'. Meslier's *Memoirs* certainly had a similar sentiment, though his limited access to books, libraries and learned societies circumscribed his efforts in that regard. Diderot went further with his dedication to the *Encyclopédie*, taking great personal risks (as he was the named editor of the work) to share up-to-date knowledge of technical, physical and social phenomena with his contemporaries, even if this meant compromising on the radicalism of the publications. His personal works of a political nature, many remaining unpublished during his life, point to his goal of enlightening posterity and future generations. Some men, he believed, are simply born ahead of their time.

Voltaire himself, who spent most of his life fighting against the abuses of the Catholic Church and superstition, was an opponent of the new philosophy spreading atheistic ideas. Ever a deist, Voltaire could not accept that atheism should be extended to the masses. In his *Le philosophe ignorant* of 1766, Voltaire attacked Spinoza's atheism, preferring the critique of Bayle to the geometrical system of the Dutch philosopher.[22] Favouring a theory of the supreme artisan of nature, Voltaire opted for defending ignorance over theological systems. Instead of Spinoza's all-too-systemic philosophy, Voltaire preferred adoring God without knowing precisely who he is. Voltaire also spent much time trying to refute Holbach's system, culminating in his formal response: *Dieu, Réponse de Mr. de Voltaire au Système de la nature*. Voltaire's argument against Holbach is poignant: if, as Holbach argued, the idea of God has held some men back from crimes, it is sufficient reason for keeping the illusion alive, even if God turned out to be our greatest deceit.[23] Voltaire uses utility against Holbach, in other words, and argues that negative atheism simply removes a necessary spring in the regulation of passions of certain men – by which he meant *le vulgaire*, the least educated and poorest in society. The question then remains whether an atheism that destroys the values that had hitherto served as a moral restraint on people can replace those values with others that work at least as well as previous ones. For that, a positive notion of atheism needed to supplement the negative conception of it as that which destroys. Destruction is always a necessary first step, but it is not itself sufficient and needs to be supplemented by a quest for meaning.

La Mettrie provided the strongest challenge to Holbach and Diderot in particular, but also to any who wished to provide a more positive theory of atheism. La Mettrie's materialism, as he espoused it in *L'homme machine*, largely denied the existence of the soul and expanded Descartes' claims about the souls of animals to humans. Though La Mettrie was accused of atheism because of his position, he never openly rejected the existence of God. He had, however, attacked Diderot's early deistic writings, which leads contemporary scholars such as Ann Thomson to conclude that his atheism is 'clear enough'.[24] La Mettrie himself prefers to claim that he is 'taking no sides'[25] in the debate, though he may well have been motivated by caution. What troubled Diderot and Holbach was the lack of positive system coming out of La Mettrie's work. Himself a doctor, he had little if anything to say about morality and politics, and the consequences of his materialism for these areas of knowledge. In his *Discours preliminaire*, he points towards the veracity of Bayle's claims about the compatibility of virtue and atheism. But he also defends sensuality and the free exercise of passions and voluptuousness.[26] This was too much, too fast, and a strong defence of a system of morals that was not only still compatible with atheism, but rather derived from it directly, was needed for those trying to build an atheology that went beyond reaction and negation.

Positive Atheism

It is worth noting here that the sense in which I employ the notions of negative and positive atheism differ slightly from the

sense in which these terms are used in religious definitions of atheism. The *Catholic Encyclopedia*, for example, describes negative
atheism as a philosophical system which does not include God
within its reasoning (such as some forms of atheism), and defines
positive atheism as a doctrine that actively denies the existence of
God.[27] This definition, however, is hopelessly dated, as it would be
difficult to differentiate between the variety of works that do not
mention God as part of their system. In other words, the Catholic
definition makes it impossible to distinguish between a deist, a
pantheist, an agnostic or an atheist – or, even worse, would cate-
gorise most writings today as atheistic on the basis that they make
no mention of God. Jacques Maritain, himself a Catholic apologetic, made a much more fruitful contribution to the debate. He
differentiated between negative atheism as a 'destructive process
of casting aside the idea of God, which is replaced only by a void',
and positive atheism as 'a desperate, I would say heroic, effort to
recast and construct the whole human universe of thought and the
whole human scale of values according to that state of war against
God'.[28] This distinction, between a destructive negative atheism
and a constructive positive atheism, though still cast in terms that
make atheism appear to be merely reactive to theism, is already
closer to the definition used in this book, though I will introduce
a slight subtlety to it that will help recast the debate over negative
and positive atheism away from the Christian apologetic bias.

In order to reconceptualise the notions of negative and positive
atheism, it is useful to cast a wider net in the history of ideas. In his
essay *Two Concepts of Liberty*, Isaiah Berlin distinguished between
two different traditions of liberty, one negative, which answers
the question of how much a person or group of persons should be
left to do what they wish without interference, for the negative
conception, and who is the source of control or interference, for
the positive sense.[29] Berlin's distinction between negative and
positive versions of the same concept is helpful for the distinction
between negative and positive atheism made here. This is because
the two versions of the concept are not evaluated in terms of their
respective moral worth (Berlin indeed favoured negative liberty
over positive liberty), but in respect to the linguistic properties
of the two concepts. Negative freedom can thus be understood as

freedom *from* (interference), and positive freedom as freedom *to* (do something). The same linguistic distinction applies to atheism. Negative atheism is a negation of the gods it reacts against, and is thus negative in its orientation, while positive atheism is an affirmation of self-sustaining philosophical outlook, independently of the gods that have historically provided foundations for so many philosophical systems. Just as negative liberty can be characterised as the wish to free oneself from the rule of a master, negative atheism is an attempt to show the limitations of the power of the gods and seeks emancipation from religious systems. And just as positive liberty is concerned with issues of self-mastery and how much one is free to follow the dictates of one's own reason, positive atheism seeks to set philosophical bases for a life without gods. *Pace* Maritain, negative atheism is no longer exclusively understood as destructive of atheism (though of course an element of destruction is present within it), but rather as a movement of emancipation from pre-existing modes of thought that supposed the existence of gods. Positive atheism, in its turn, is also recast no longer as merely a constructive movement of a war against God, but as a potentially independent mode of thought, seeking self-mastery and autonomy. We will return to these concepts in the conclusion, and also show that they are not the last step in the dialectic of atheism, and that already in the eighteenth century, particularly with Diderot, there were attempts to overcome their limitations.

This notion of positive atheism is a relatively new development in the history of ideas. In Chapter 1, we will see that Bayle was the first advocate of a form of positive atheism, arguing that atheists can indeed have a positive philosophical outlook, although he restricted this sphere to the field of ethics. The four authors discussed in this book, Bayle, Meslier, Holbach and Diderot, all share a similar outlook in this respect, each defending the existence of positive atheists, and at least for two of them, Meslier and Holbach, each defending themselves as positive atheists.[30] The selection of these four authors has been based on this notion of positive atheism as a philosophical system seeking independence from theological notions. There were, of course, other choices available. This book could have covered self-avowed atheists (and on that basis excluded Bayle and Diderot, but potentially including others such as Sade or La Mettrie), but the focus on self-identity as an atheist is quite problematic for a number of reasons. As David Wooton argues, there were good reasons for these authors to hide their own identity, and it is not illegitimate to read between the lines.[31] Certainly, then, the question remains as to whether Spinoza, Hobbes, Vico or others were in fact hidden atheists, and a focus on self-avowed atheism obscures this. Hobbes, for example, can be equally read as a hidden atheist[32] or an unusual Christian,[33] with more or less equally compelling arguments on either side. The persuasiveness of an argument in favour of or against an author's hidden atheism will likely rest on a number of factors that cannot fully settle the issue, such as the strength of the arguments in defence of religion, the compatibility of the philosophy of the author with an atheistic worldview, and the possibility of unorthodox religious belief that is not necessarily atheistic. When it comes to the authors interpreted in this book, I will not shy away from these questions. The controversy over the question of Bayle's atheism, which still rages today, will be discussed in Chapter 1. But the selection of authors made here was not based on their own atheism, either hidden or avowed, but rather on their philosophical defence of a positive sense of atheism. This was done, despite Bayle's own rejection of atheism, and despite Diderot's attempt to move past the limitations of atheism he saw, particularly in the philosophy of his friend Holbach, as we will see in Chapter 4. What becomes increasingly evident when looking at the notion of positive atheism is that it not only proposes a radical rethinking of philosophical foundations in the late seventeenth to late eighteenth centuries, but rather that it also challenges the political foundations of the societies in which these authors lived. This social and political radicalism is, I will show, an integral part of positive atheism, and an exploration of what this radicalism might mean is warranted here.

Four Radicalisms

The existence of primitive atheists, either in the distant past or on the shores of the new worlds discovered by European explorers, lent legitimacy to atheists for their beliefs (or lack thereof). It allowed them to make a *radical* claim, in the Latin sense of the word *radix*: it gave positive atheism *roots*. This is the first sense of radicalism explored here. If the first message of this book is that positive atheism is worth considering on its own as an important historical and contemporary phenomenon, the second claim of this book is that this modern atheism is radical at its very core. This, of course, was recently argued by Jonathan Israel and before him by Margaret Jacob, and I will come back to these two important contributions in a moment. But the first sense in which I wish to convey the radical nature of atheism is simpler than the one these authors propose. The first sense in which positive atheism is radical is that is makes a claim about the roots of humanity as a whole, some of which at least are thought to ignore the gods entirely.

The second sense in which atheism is radical is that proposed by Holbach himself, which he makes in the conclusion of his infamous *System of Nature*. Atheism will only take hold, he argues, if one 'pulls out all the way down to the roots the poisoned tree that has for so many centuries overshadowed the universe'.[34] This tree, for Holbach, is religion in its present form in the eighteenth century, but also in its various superstitious forms in preceding centuries. The radical act of positive atheism will thus be to uproot all beliefs and superstitions that have come from a theological past, and to rethink all of our concepts in an atheological manner. The new, modern atheism which emerges dialectically from the interaction of primitive atheism and modern theism is a radical political theology – or perhaps a radical political atheology. Despite what some critics of the radical Enlightenment have said, the term is not foreign and superimposed upon the period. At the very least, one of the thinkers discussed in this book conceived his own atheism as radical in this sense – as uprooting previous beliefs and re-examining all beliefs in the light of his new positive atheistic doctrine.

This brings us directly to a third sense of radical, which is the one advocated by Jacob and Israel, and it merits more detailed attention.[35] Jonathan Israel's trilogy of the 'radical Enlightenment' has stirred some debates among historians and philosophers as to what constitutes the appropriate methods of study of this time period, and what we can say about the Enlightenment as a whole. In many ways, Israel's reinterpretation of the Enlightenment has revived the grand Enlightenment theories, reminiscent of Peter Gay's seminal studies of the 1960s.[36] What is Israel's 'grand Enlightenment' thesis, and why has it been so controversial in some circles? One must start with what the Enlightenment is not, according to Israel, before what can say what it is. Contrary to many interpretations, the Enlightenment is *not* a national move-ment. There is no opposition, according to Israel, between the French *Lumières*, the German *Aufklärung*, the Italian *Illuminismo* or the English and Scottish *Enlightenment*. It is a more unified version of the Enlightenment that Israel proposes, where the dif-ferences do not lie in one's national allegiance, nor even in the language in which one writes. On the contrary, the focus is on bringing together cross-national debates. Many of the philoso-phers of this Enlightenment were multilingual and cosmopoli-tan, and travelled to other countries to spread their ideas – even between nations at war. There are good historical reasons to take this first point seriously, and to be much more sceptical of the national Enlightenments theory. Israel, in the third volume of his theory, pushed this even further: the Enlightenment is not even *European*! With impressive historical research to back up this claim, Israel shows us that the Enlightenment was spread far and wide, in North America among Native American popu-lations, in colonial Latin America, in Haiti, in China, in Japan, in India, and in European lands not explored by other historians, notably eastern Europe and Russia. Israel thus proposes a *universal* history of the Enlightenment, where the nuances are no longer to be thought of in terms of national schools. Rather, it is the *political* and *social* dimensions of the Enlightenment that take priority in Israel's thesis.

What, then, are the differences between various strands of this unified Enlightenment? Israel proposes a *political* typology of the Enlightenment, between the *moderate* thinkers of the move-ment, such as Locke or Hume, and the *radical* wing, with Spinoza, Bayle and Meslier, among others. The unity of the Enlightenment retains its potent appeal in Israel's thought, as both these moderate and radical wings share much in common and are often attacked indiscriminately by their common enemies. In particular, the apologists (Catholic or Protestant) put themselves to the task of refuting the Enlighteners' philosophical systems. Yet important differences persist between the two wings, notably on the role that the privileges of the *ancien régime* should play in society. The moderate Enlightenment, often motivated by a theological interpretation of social order based on a strict hierarchy and on ecclesiastical authority, clashes with the radicals' emphasis on universality and equality.[37] Based on preference for one's fellow nationals, the defence of a social hierarchy based on an aristocracy and clergy, the defence of a (constitutional) monarchy, the fear of atheism for the masses (thought to lead them to moral corruption), the moderate Enlightenment is the right wing of the Enlightenment movement. While the moderates are still progressive when measured against the intolerant, feudal, absolutist and orthodox thought of the apologists, they are nonetheless prepared to compromise with the regime. Preferring deism to atheism, constitutional monarchy to revolution, aristocratic patronage rather than educational reform, political influence rather than opposition, the moderates are ready to accommodate some of the regime's worst aspects to achieve incremental progress without upsetting social structures radically. It is a left/right spectrum that is proposed here by Israel, a *political* thesis of the radical Enlightenment that is explicitly made only in the third volume of the trilogy when Israel is concerned with the question of democracy since 1750.[38] The right, even the moderate right, is monarchist while the radical left is democratic. The right believes in Divine Providence that guides progress, while the left, whilst not always atheistic, disagrees that the divine has any role to play in human affairs. Where the right wishes to enlighten the middle classes, the left believes that all the people deserve enlightenment, and that every social policy must have the greatest number in mind.

This third meaning of radicalism, which foregrounds the concepts of democracy, universality and equality, proved too much for Israel's many critics. A comprehensive review of Israel's critics would require a book of its own,[39] hence I only wish to stress one aspect here: the political critique. If the battle of the moderate and radical Enlightenment culminated with a political distinction between right and left, what are the shades and currents within this broad picture? As I will argue in individual chapters, while each of the theorists of positive atheism discussed is radical in one sense illustrated here, some are more radical than others. Bayle who defended the legitimacy of an absolute monarch is contrasted with Meslier whose name would appear on an obelisk erected in Moscow in 1918 as a forerunner of communism. What this book will aim to do is to paint a diverse picture of this atheistic radicalism, and this will at times show that Israel's focus was misplaced by making all radicals defenders of modern, liberal, egalitarian democratic values. There are positions defended in that period that will be shown to be on the left of what Israel wanted to defend; and there are also positions on his right. Radicalism is not a monopoly of the left, and neither is it a monopoly of the liberal left. It is of little surprise that the reception of some of these authors was warmest on the far left of the political spectrum, and the bourgeois nature of the atheistic rebellion of the period was seen by many, most notably Marx, as possessing the seeds of even more radical reform.

A fourth meaning of radicalism needs to be considered here: a philosophical radical position. If atheism itself is not philosophically radical enough to begin with, the possibility of thinking matter was surely the singular idea that pushed the boundaries of the possible. Ann Thomson has provided a thorough study of these early ideas of thinking bodies, and demonstrated just how philosophically radical those ideas were at the time.[40] For those unfamiliar with the debates, here is a contemporary example to illustrate how radical this idea (that a body could think) was at the time. Imagine, as Jane Bennett does,[41] that there is a power cut during a storm which cuts off an entire population from its regular supply. Now, imagine that this power cut was the result of a complex assemblage of agencies, from users of electricity to energy providers and regulatory frameworks – but also, and importantly, of non-human actants. That is, imagine that such a power cut, which occurred in the eastern United States in 2003, was the result of acts by material bodies such as electricity. The thought that electricity is an actant (a being that can act) is just as alien to us today as the

thought that a body could think was to a seventeenth-century educated person. It is no stranger to suggest, for someone who believes
that thought lies in the soul, that it may actually be situated in the
brain, than it is to suggest, for someone who believes that action is
the exclusive characteristic of sentient beings, that matter also acts
independently of sentience. Such philosophical radicalism, however, does not necessarily lead to political radicalism. La Mettrie,
who shocked his contemporaries in the middle of the eighteenth
century by suggesting that man is a machine, had little to say about
the political consequences of his thought.[42] Yet he certainly was a
radical in the philosophical sense. Equally, one of the most radical
philosophers of the period had little political radicalism. David
Hume's critique of induction, where he suggests 'that there can be
no *demonstrative* arguments to prove, *that those instances, of which
we have had no experience, resemble those, of which we have had experience*', is still baffling to his readers today. As if this was not radical
enough, Hume continues by stating that 'We can at least conceive
a change in the course of nature; which sufficiently proves, that
such a change is not absolutely impossible.'[43] The idea that we
can never be sure of necessity because nature itself could change
its course has been challenging philosophers of science ever since,
and has sparked radical philosophical debates in recent years.[44]
Yet Hume himself was shocked by the radicalism of the atheistic
position of Holbach and Diderot, while visiting them in Paris, and
his own philosophical extravagance did not match their political
challenge. There is no necessary connection between philosophical radicalism and political radicalism – La Mettrie and Hume
provide two clear examples of this. The only necessary connection
between radical philosophical ideas and politics lay in the minds of
their opponents, who tended to destroy the reputation of authors
by arguing that their speculations led to atheism and thus to social
collapse. In actuality, there is an element missing in the recipe for
political radicalism, and what this book argues is that this element
is a form of *critique* which emerges, develops and grows in the
period analysed.

  These four types of radicalism (about the roots, performing an
uprooting, politically radical, and philosophically radical) testify
to the plurality of term. We will see in the four chapters that

follow that Bayle, Meslier, Holbach and Diderot's radicalisms are quite distinct from one another. That is not to say that they share nothing in common, and the task of this book is to shed some light on what this shared radicalism is, despite the obvious differences of the four authors. In particular, we will see that the idea of critique is common to all four thinkers, and that this critique can help us conceptualise the history of atheism as a threefold movement (negative, positive and meta) which we will come back to in the conclusion. Atheism will thus not only be critical of theism, as it was in its beginning, but also be critical of itself and its attempts to build itself as a positive, stand-alone philosophy. Critique as a method runs throughout this movement and unites radical atheists in their philosophies.

Critical History

Bayle changed something forever when he started working on his historical and critical dictionary: he spread the already thriving field of critique from the narrow confines of Talmudic and biblical criticism to the fields of history and, by extension, politics. Critique acquired with him a positive epistemological status that we will discuss in Chapter 1, and which made it an essential duty for the critic to overturn every claim to truth, every judgement and every prejudice he or she comes across. The first critical claim of this book, thus, is to overturn the history of critique, which all too often starts with Kant at the end of the period we are considering here. Critique was an essential part of the entire Enlightenment (however one defines it), as even critics of Bayle's project could not escape the powerful drive of the concept. Meslier's social and political commentary, Holbach's detailed complaints against the association of Church and state, and Diderot's subtle dialectic all owe much to that initial movement of critique that acquires a positive meaning of its own. If critique had been confined to the texts themselves, as it had been under biblical criticism, Bayle's project would not have been so successful. It was successful exactly because it dealt with social, ethical and political issues that his contemporaries were concerned with. Dispelling myths and misunderstandings on topics in the Old Testament, thoughts on Epicureans and Manicheans or on Protestants' hopes of over-throwing the King of France, Bayle managed to marry history with contemporary concerns. Bayle's critical history was a way to speak to the present, and I hope that this book does the same, inspired as so many have been before me by the work of this magnificent thinker.

A critical history will do a number of things. It will be attentive to context, fitting in very well with contextualist approaches to the history of ideas.[45] It will be attentive to the variety of differ-ent aspects that may have influenced an author's thought and the development of their ideas. It will not shy away from looking beyond the text to examine the lives of the authors, the social and political context within which they were writing, the economic relations around the authors' lives, the geopolitical context of their thought, the controversies they were responding to, and the literary climate within which the works are situated. But there is one thing a critical history will refuse to do, following Bayle's precepts. It will refuse to assign to authors views that they explic-itly deny and will refuse to speculate about their religious views beyond what they told us themselves – in their works, correspond-ence or otherwise. I will thus not side with those who see Bayle as a secret atheist (it is possible, but it contradicts the method that he himself applies to authors he analyses), nor will I side with those who see Diderot as an atheist – he is far too ambiguous and complex to neatly fit the title. This book, which is dedicated to a positive theory of atheism, will begin with a self-defined Protestant, and end with an ambiguous non-believer, and have two self-avowed atheists in the middle. This is because what this critical history tells us is that you do not need to be an atheist to contribute to a positive theory of atheism. This critical history can be thought as a counter-history of political thought, an alter-native to the dominant theories which tower over other historical approaches, while drawing strength and inspiration from their detailed analyses. There is little doubt, for example, that Buckley and Kors are correct in their assessment that particular weakness in theology facilitated the rise of atheism. But this does not make atheism parasitic any more than it makes Christian theology par-asitic on pagan sacrifices. It only means that modern atheism has a history, and the importance of a critical history is to show why this matters to us, in the present.

To achieve this dual purpose of a critical history – to achieve historical accuracy and to be useful to the present – I have drawn on the work of Hans-Georg Gadamer. Gadamer is critical of the objectification of the past, of treating it as an object *out there* that must be preserved and studied without the historian putting any of his or her own prejudices into it. Instead a 'false objectification',[46] Gadamer promotes a hermeneutical ontology that recognises that the human sciences do not study objects in themselves,[47] but rather explicate that 'the object of historical understanding is not events but their "significance"'.[48] The centrality of method, Gadamer shows, dates back further than the objective historiography of the nineteenth century. Gadamer's critique remains potent today. Historicism is guilty of forgetting its own historicity, because it hides behind its method,[49] and considers itself unaffected by history. This, according to the hermeneutics of Gadamer, is a fallacy since one is always already affected by history, even when one is conscious of one's historicity.

While there is no neutrality in the study of history for both Heidegger and Gadamer, understanding is still possible through a foregrounding of one's prejudices.[50] Whereas the French Enlightenment gives a negative connotation to the concept of prejudice, German Romanticism reacts against this *prejudice against prejudice*, and rehabilitates the role of prejudices in understanding. For Gadamer, '[t]he recognition that all understanding inevitably involves some prejudice gives the hermeneutical problem its real thrust'.[51] It is, in Gadamer's thought, one of the problems with the Enlightenment in that its prejudice against prejudice 'denies tradition its power'.[52] Tradition, as a source of authority, is thus replaced by *reason* in Enlightenment philosophy. But what they failed to grasp, and what Romanticism failed to grasp as well when it tried to rehabilitate tradition over reason, is that there does not need to be an antithesis between reason and tradition.[53] Reason, Gadamer further says in what sounds like a Humean parody, 'is not its own master but remains constantly dependent on the given circumstances in which it operates'.[54] If reason belongs to history itself, if it loses its claim to independence that the Enlightenment granted it, then subjection to the authority of tradition can be perceived, as Gadamer does, as 'an act of reason, though an inconspicuous one'.[55] Adding some nuance to Gadamer's critique of reason, I will show in following chapters that reason is not as straightforward in the Enlightenment, and that it may be subjected to critique – precisely through this movement he analyses between reason and tradition. Reason, when it recognises its own historicity, thus opens itself to critique, and this forms an essential movement of the metatheology I will identify in Chapter 5.

Hermeneutics can be a radical method, although it does not quite have this shape in Gadamer's own works. The radical hermeneutics I propose here has at least two major differences with that of Gadamer. The first major difference is that I do not focus on a specific tradition – let us call it the German tradition for lack of a better word – which Gadamer largely focuses on. Instead, I am interested in counter-traditions, multiple competing ideas and concepts, and their authors. It is certainly not the Tradition with its capitalised importance, or the mainstream of philosophy or indeed political theory. Few, even in specialist circles in political thought, would have heard of all four of the authors studied here, and those outside these circles have little hope of having heard those any of these names – apart perhaps from Diderot, whom I was fortunate enough to read in secondary school, and who is still widely taught in France. Of course, Israel in the English-speaking world has done much to bring these names to the eyes of his eaders, and a philosopher in France, Michel Onfray, has popularised (somewhat) the names of Meslier and Holbach.[56] Because they are so little known, however, and because of the methodical reasons given above relating to understanding the whole in its context, I have opted for providing short biographical introductions to all of these authors. These are not merely cosmetic, however, and I defend them on the grounds that they provide insights into their thought, which I use later in these chapters. Others have used these biographical introductions at length, and I also follow their lead in this respect.[57] Perhaps these four authors will form the backbone of a new tradition – of scepticism, materialism and atheism – but this remains to be developed further, and it is beyond the scope of this book.

Structure of the Book

After this brief introduction, which has clarified at least three things – the importance of studying atheism as a positive historical phenomenon; the meanings of the term 'radical' and the tensions between them; and the methodical aspirations of the book – I will move on to individual thinkers. The order of these thinkers is not quite chronological – Bayle precedes Meslier who preceeds the other two, but Diderot was a decade older than Holbach and began writing before him. Additionally, they were close friends and it is clear that Diderot spent a lot of time proofreading Holbach's works, so questions of influences are still important between the two, as we will see. The reason why Diderot comes after Holbach in this book is a theoretical one: Diderot in many ways completes (and to an extent critiques) the work of Holbach. This will become clear in Chapter 4 and the reader will have to wait until then to be fully convinced of the order of things here.

In Chapter 1, we begin by discussing Pierre Bayle's complex life: his childhood in southern France among Huguenots, the famous conversion to Catholicism and the return to Protestantism, the meanderings of exile in Geneva, then northern France, and the final exile to Rotterdam in the United Provinces. Bayle's scholarship is so vast that it is daunting even for the most avid of his readers. His *Dictionary*, a best-seller of its time despite being banned in numerous countries, is over two million words long, or three times the size of the King James Bible. And there are numerous other works of his to consider! We will navigate through his works all too quickly, with the task of understanding his political theory at its fullest, and to explain why his thinking about atheism was so radical to begin with. Notions of toleration will become extremely important not only for himself, but for later thinkers discussed, and the figure of the virtuous atheist will be shown to play a fundamental role in his political thought. His support for the legitimacy of Louis XIV's absolute rule will challenge certain preconceptions of Bayle as a supporter of democracy, but they will be placed in their polemical and historical contexts, to show that Bayle's position on the issue is still a radical one. Finally, the chapter will show that Bayle should be considered as one of the (if not the) first critical theorist, because of the centrality that the notion of critique plays in his thought, and the method that he introduces to the study of history. As I have already discussed in this introduction, his method certainly inspired this book, and Bayle's sharp mind and works radiate through the ages.

In Chapter 2, Jean Meslier is shown to be a remarkable figure of the Enlightenment, despite having lived most of his life in the isolation of his small village in the Champagne region of France. A Catholic priest, he was to become – not without irony – the first self-avowed atheist of history. In his memoirs, he tells his parishioners of his deepest thoughts that he had hitherto kept hidden from them: that there is no god, that religion has perverted our lives and corrupted politics, and that a revolution is necessary – all of this by the time of his death in 1729, a full sixty years before the French Revolution. In Israel's definition of the radical, Meslier is certainly the most radical of all: a fervent democrat, a true believer in equality and a revolutionary, he is the poster child of the radical Enlightenment. Yet many aspects of his thought are underplayed: his development of a proto-utilitarian ethic – that Holbach will certainly pick up and expand on – and his defence of animal rights. We will expand on these, before considering the most influential interpretation of Meslier to date: that he was a forerunner of communism. I will show that despite some obvious overlaps, the anachronism is not helpful to understanding Meslier and his politics, and that instead we should think of him as a radical republican thinker. While I will shy away from making a direct link and a necessary connection between atheism and radicalism in political thought in this book, it is in Meslier that this link is the strongest. *Ni Dieu, ni maître,* neither God nor master, could have been his motto, and if one seeks a strong critique of the alliance of Church and state, it is in Meslier's work that one must delve.

In Chapter 3, Paul-Henri Thiry, baron d'Holbach's exciting Parisian salon life will be shown to have had a profound importance on his contemporaries, as well as a lasting impact on the history of atheism. Born in the Holy Roman Empire, in the Palatinate, Holbach benefited from the financial success of an uncle, who made a fortune in the Parisian stock market and bought his nobility as a result. Holbach went to study in Leiden in the Netherlands, and later established one of the longest-lasting salons of the century. Entertaining some famous historical figures such as Benjamin Franklin and David Hume, as well as many others, for a period of nearly forty years, he was to share his ideas with his guests and work tirelessly towards their clandestine publication. Author of more than a dozen books, countless translations of other works into French, and around four hundred articles in the Encyclopaedia of Diderot and d'Alembert, Holbach was a relentless intellectual that only illness could stop from working. Well known for his systematic atheism, but little known for his political thought, Holbach deserves a much larger share in the history of ideas than he has at present. His fully fledged theory of materialism will be shown to impact on his ethical, social and political thought of the 1770s, where he not only built an entire utilitarian system, decades before the more famous utilitarians, notably Bentham, but also drew the political consequences of his moral doctrine. His complex republicanism will be addressed in great detail, including his defence of citizenship for women, defence of material safety which includes the provision of basic needs, and the development of a new unit of political analysis: the ethocracy or the governing of a polity through ethics.

In Chapter 4, Denis Diderot's religious thought will be shown to be the culmination of modern atheism. In many ways, the sceptical philosophy of the editor of the *Encyclopédie* is the most complex of the four thinkers I discuss in this book, because Diderot can be conceptualised both as an atheist and as a thinker that attempted to move past atheism. I will show that Diderot never quite settles his religious thought and maintains the possibility of the existence of God even in his most atheistic moments. But this God is never outside the realm of materialism, and Diderot will be unwavering in his defence of an interpretation of the universe in purely material terms. This will apply equally to his political thought, always conceived materially as providing the conditions for human flourishing and emancipation. Diderot will be shown to be an important social contract theorist, pushing his thought towards a critique of the notion of the state of nature from a critical colonial perspective. His economic thought will also further ground the materialism of his politics, defending an early version of a labour theory of value, and showing that the wealth of nations lies in the emancipation of the lowest classes of society. A radical position indeed.

Finally, in the Conclusion, I will draw together the consequences of this nascent tradition of political atheism for us today. What can Bayle, Meslier, Holbach and Diderot, as diverse as they are, teach us about the impact of atheism on political thought and its future development? I will argue that three important movements can be identified in the history of atheism as a concept: a negative phase, where atheism needs to distance itself from theism and belief in God more generally; a positive phase, where atheism builds itself as a positive doctrine, worthy of independent evaluation and capable of surviving even without reference to previous doctrines it reacted against; and finally, what I have come to call a metatheism, encompassing both the movement past theism (meta-theism) and past atheism (meta-atheism), in a dialectical movement towards another type of atheism. It has been the aim of this book to show that this triple movement is not new, but rather that it is internal to the history of atheism itself, particularly through the four authors we have discussed. It provides both a descriptive account of the types of theories developed between the late seventeenth and late eighteenth centuries on the matter, and a normative model for us to follow, expand on and adapt today.

Notes

1. Plato, *The Apology*, 57.
2. Whitmarsh, *Battling the Gods*.
3. Roberts, *Justin Martyr and Athenagoras*, 11.
4. Buckley, *At the Origins of Modern Atheism*.
5. Kors, *Atheism in France*.
6. Buckley, *At the Origins of Modern Atheism*, 14–15.
7. Ibid. 33.
8. Kors, *D'Holbach's Coterie*.
9. Kors, *Atheism in France*, 3–4.
10. Kors, *Naturalism and Unbelief in France*; Kors, *Epicureans and Atheists in France*.
11. For an analysis of later atheists in England, see Budd, *Varieties of Unbelief*.

For an example of atheism in Sweden, see Jansonn, "'A Swedish Voltaire'".

12. See, for example, Paganini, 'Pour une histoire de l'athéisme à part entière'.

13. Hegel, *Lectures on the History of Philosophy*, III, 387. Comment in brackets is my addition.

14. Cousin, 'Vanini', 721–2.

15. Ibid. 687.

16. Ibid. 694.

17. Ibid. 714.

18. Ibid. 725.

19. Kors, *Epicureans and Atheists in France*.

20. Las Casas, *An Account, Much Abbreviated*.

21. Israel, *Radical Enlightenment*.

22. Voltaire, *Le philosophe ignorant*.

23. Voltaire, *Dieu. Réponse de Mr. de Voltaire*, 27.

24. Thomson, 'Introduction', in La Mettrie, *Machine Man and Other Writings*, 1996), xciii.

25. La Mettrie, *Machine Man*, 25.

26. La Mettrie, *Preliminary Discourse*, in *Machine Man and Other Writings*, 160.

27. Aveling, 'Atheism'.

28. Maritain, 'On the Meaning of Contemporary Atheism', 268.

29. Berlin, *Four Essays on Liberty*.

30. It is of little surprise that Mitchell Stephens's history of atheism from Ancient Greece to today takes Meslier, Holbach and Diderot as exemplars of Enlightenment atheism. See Stephens, *Imagine There's No Heaven*.

31. Wooton, 'New Histories of Atheism', 34.

32. Berman, *A History of Atheism from Hobbes to Russell*.

33. Mortimer, 'Christianity and Civil Religion in Hobbes's *Leviathan*'.

34. Holbach, *Système de la nature*, 642, my translation.

35. Jacob, *The Radical Enlightenment*.

36. Gay, *The Enlightenment: An Interpretation*, 103.

37. Israel, *Radical Enlightenment*, vi.

38. Israel, *Democratic Enlightenment*.

39. Just of few of the best critiques include: Jacob, 'Radical Enlightenment: Philosophy and the Making of Modernity, 1650–1750 (review)'; Kors, 'Radical Enlightenment: Philosophy and the Making of Modernity, 1650–1750 (review)'; Connolly, 'The Radical Enlightenment: Faith, Power, Theory'; Chisick, 'Interpreting the Enlightenment'; La Vopa, 'Radical Enlightenment: Philosophy and the Making of Modernity, 1650–1750 (review)'; and many others.

40. Thomson, *Bodies of Thought*.

41. Bennett, *Vibrant Matter*, ch. 2.

42. See Thomson, 'Introduction', in La Mettrie, *Machine Man and Other Writings*.
43. Hume, *A Treatise of Human Nature*, 62 [1.3.6], emphasis in original.
44. See, for example, Meillassoux, *Après la finitude*.
45. Skinner, 'Meaning and Understanding in the History of Ideas', 3–53.
46. Gadamer, *Truth and Method*, 312.
47. Ibid. 285.
48. Ibid. 325.
49. Ibid. 299.
50. Ibid. 271.
51. Ibid. 272.
52. Ibid. 273.
53. Ibid. 282.
54. Ibid. 277.
55. Ibid. 282.
56. Onfray, *Les ultras des Lumières*.
57. For example, see Rosemboim, *The Emergence of Globalism*.

1

Bayle and Virtuous Atheism

Few in the seventeenth and eighteenth centuries would have contested Bayle's radical potential, at the very least as a fervent and
consistent critic of all things political, or doubted his commitment to a particular vision of society that was largely at odds with
that of his contemporaries. His critical influence on important
thinkers of his centuries is well documented, and many in the
nineteenth century would have had their intellectual formation
influenced by Bayle – most notably Bentham, John Stuart Mill,
Hegel, Feuerbach and Marx.[1] Today, however, few outside the
specialist literature of the period have heard of Bayle's political
thought, and it is a tragedy that despite huge scholarly interest and
controversy around this great author, his arguments have not pen-
etrated the wider imaginary, while those of often less convincing
and less radical authors have – as is the case of Locke's defence of
toleration, a weaker and less convincing version than that which
Bayle had published prior to Locke. To familiarise the reader
with Bayle the man, a short biographical introduction will detail
important aspects of his life, from his childhood in the south-west
of France to the émigré life he led in the Netherlands. No study
of Bayle's oeuvre could avoid the question of the author's religion,
and in the second section I will show that I err on the side of
caution, and follow Bayle's own method of not ascribing religious
beliefs (or lack thereof) to authors who have explicitly argued
they do not have them. I will paint a portrait of a complicated,
troubled and struggling Calvinist, who maintains the importance
of faith to his last days and attempted to convince the world that

faith and reason were compatible, even though they sometimes clashed with each other. Beyond this personal faith, however, lies the most radical argument of Bayle: that there can be such a thing as a virtuous atheist, and that toleration should be extended as widely as possible, including toleration of atheists. This vision of the world is motivated by Bayle's defence of the erring conscience, a troublesome concept even for him, as it led him to consider whether the fanatic (whose conscience also errs) can also be tolerated. We will see that Bayle provides a complex defence of toleration that will deny the compulsion to enter a faith, but only by suggesting the radical proposal of a right to exit that faith. Not without its echoes in contemporary political theory, this solution is elegant, consistent and ingenious, and Bayle will be shown to be its inceptor. Finally, this chapter will look at Bayle's ideal of the republic of letters. By analysing his method of critique, I will show that his work is inherently political in a number of ways, notably by insisting on the public nature of reason, and by using critique as a radical method for political thought, but also for the art of governing – for the politics of politicians.

Biographical Introduction

Pierre Bayle was born in 1647 in the small village of Carla (that has since been renamed Carla-Bayle) in the south-west of France. With less than half the population it had in the seventeenth century, Carla is now a small village – although back then it was a small town possessing its own bourgeoisie, in the sense of town-dwellers with small income from their lands. Bayle was born into one such family, and as the son of a Calvinist – Huguenot – minister, he received a good education at the hands of his father and the town's school. He spent his days farming the family lands, hunting quail or 'hurrying the grape growers' – testifying to his family's relative wealth since they were able to hire manual labourers.[2] But there was little money going around in this region of France in the seventeenth century, and Pierre had to wait for his older brother to finish his studies before he could begin his own at the Protestant academy at Puylaurens in 1668 – the cost of books, candles and tuition was prohibitive even for his family of the small bourgeoisie.

Unimpressed by his 'debauched' fellow students, who spent their days skipping lessons rather than learning, Bayle spent his time reading the religious controversy that animated the academy: a refutation of Richelieu's *Method*, the treatise written by this minister of Louis XIV that aimed to convert Protestants back to the Catholic faith.[3] Not convinced by his teacher André de Martel's *Response to the Method*, he sought answers to his doubts, and moved to Toulouse where he converted to Catholicism. As Élisabeth Labrousse points out, this episode should not surprise us. Driven by his studies in logic, his quest for truth and the relative poverty of the Protestant argument he was exposed to, he 'logically, the next day' (*postera die iterum Logicus*) 'converts', as he himself noted in his diary.[4] But this was not a 'conversion' as we understand it; this was not an utter and complete change of the young Bayle's religious outlook. It was a rectification of trajectory in his quest for true Christianity, and it is thus not surprising that it ended up being short-lived, once he came know the Catholic Church better.

His re-conversion back to Calvinism occurred after only seventeen months in the Catholic faith. Once again, it is to be conceptualised more as a rectification of his trajectory than as a total overhaul of his beliefs. Having been exposed to controversies within the Catholic Church (plagued by the Jansenist question in his day), Bayle found its answers to be inadequate, as he had found Calvinist answers to controversies inadequate a year previously. In the absence of an authoritative judge to tell these controversies apart, he concluded that the responsibility lay with each person's conscience to determine their own path. This put him directly at odds with the Catholic Church's claim to infallibility, and his concept of the 'erring conscience', which we will come back to, has strong biographical overtones.[5] But this return to the faith of his forefathers, even if it can be understood by us as a fruit of this wandering between doctrines, had legal consequences which Bayle could not ignore. Converting back to the reformed religion was strictly forbidden, and by such an act Bayle became an outlaw in his own country. He quickly decided to leave his native region, never to return to the warm and sunny climate of the south-west of France, and emigrated to Geneva. In Geneva began a new period of his life, where he took various positions as tutor to wealthy

Protestant households. First entering the service of Friedrich von Dohna, a German aristocrat who served the Dutch provinces for much of his life, he stayed in Geneva for three years where he was able to finish his studies in his spare time. In the spring of 1674, under the disguise of a pseudonym to avoid detection by the authorities, Bayle returned to France and headed for Rouen, where he served other Protestant households, before spending a brief period in Paris in 1675, after which he left the capital for the Protestant academy of Sedan later that year.

Bayle secured a professorship at Sedan, partly thanks to the support of Pierre Jurieu, the academy's professor of theology. But the salary for the position was inadequate to cover living costs, and for some time Bayle depended on personal financial support from Jurieu himself, who had independent wealth. The relationship between the two men was to change significantly over the years, from an initial position of friendship to bitter rivalry, from a position of inferiority and financial dependence of the young Bayle to its reversal once in the Netherlands, as we shall see. Initially very demanding, Bayle's position at Sedan required him to teach five hours a day in addition to preparing lectures, and, at least for the first few years, it took most of his time. During the following years at Sedan, particularly from 1679, Bayle read widely the texts he could get his hands on, including among many others Spinoza's *Tractatus Theologico Politicus*.[6] However, the academy faced increasing pressure from royal authorities, and its privileges were finally revoked in 1681: the Protestant centre of learning closed down and its professors had to seek employment elsewhere. Having been aware of the precarity of his employment, Bayle had already started looking for an alternative, and after the closure of the academy he decided to move to Rotterdam in the United Provinces. Already the centre of a French-speaking Walloon community that had emigrated from the southern Netherlands during the war with Spain, it was a welcoming town for French Calvinists. Bayle's situation in the Netherlands was almost immediately a significant improvement on his position during his time at Sedan. Not only did he secure employment at Rotterdam's École Illustre, where he became professor of philosophy and history, but he also immediately became acquainted with an editor who took an interest in an unpublished text he had written just before leaving France. His professorship was much less demanding than the position in Sedan, asking of him only two to three hours of public lectures a week, and left him with ample time to write, thus beginning his literary career.

It is in this context that Bayle published his first works, the *Various Thoughts on the Occasion of a Comet* and the *General Criticism of M. Maimbourg's History of Calvinism*, both published in 1682. These books immediately gave Bayle a wide literary audience, and were quickly condemned and publicly burned in France, taking away any hope Bayle may have had of returning quickly to his native land. In 1684, he began his monumental *News from the Republic of Letters*, one of the first literary journals in history, which was extremely well received both in the Netherlands and in France. In 1685, two tragedies punctuated Bayle's life. Identified as the author of the *General Criticism* of 1682, Bayle became the target of French authorities. Unable to reach him, they detained his brother, who died after a short time in the prison's squalid conditions. As if in immediate succession to this personal tragedy, Louis XIV then revoked the edict of Nantes, forcing many more Calvinists to seek refuge throughout Protestant lands, notably in the Netherlands. Bayle wrote a direct response to the revocation, *The Condition of Wholly Catholic France Under the Reign of Louis the Great*, as well as a text dealing with the issue of forced conversion, *A Philosophical Commentary on These Words of the Gospel, Luke 14.23, 'Compel Them to Come In, That My House May Be Full'*, both published in 1686. This prolific period of writing, immediately following the two biggest tragedies of Bayle's life – one personal, one political – was followed by a long illness, lasting almost two years, during which Bayle had to abandon his journal, and stop writing. It is only after the Glorious Revolution of 1688–9, and the hope it gave to French Huguenots of a return to France under a Protestant monarch backed by the rest of Protestant Europe, that Bayle resumed his writings, first in the *Réponse d'un nouveau converti à la lettre d'un réfugié* (1689), and then in the notorious *Avis aux réfugiés* (1690).

This period was marked by the famous controversy with Jurieu, during which the growing gulf between the two thinkers turned into bitter rivalry.[7] A political disagreement in its beginnings, the struggle between the two thinkers revolved around the possibility of overthrowing the French King and placing a Protestant monarch in his stead. Jurieu advocated the revolutionary position here, defending the rights of oppressed citizens against a tyrannical monarch, while Bayle defended the conciliatory position, defending absolute rule over violent revolution. Beyond these intellectual positions, the conflict between the two thinkers quickly escalated beyond reason, and Jurieu was fond of name-calling his adversary, accusing him of being a Socinian, a deist and an atheist.[8] During a period of nearly three years, the controversy raged on and consumed much of Bayle's attention. By 1693, Jurieu had successfully lobbied the Walloon Church of Rotterdam, and managed to get Bayle's professorship at the École Illustre revoked, and to get Bayle banned from teaching. This was to be a blessing in disguise for Bayle, who by then earned enough from his publications to sustain his modest lifestyle. He was able to dedicate himself fully to his next project, his magnum opus: the *Historical and Critical Dictionary*. For the rest of his life, Bayle was to write article after article for this enormous project of over two million words – about three times the length of the King James Bible. The first two volumes of the *Dictionary* came out in 1696 and were an immediate success – quickly followed by its official ban in France. Leibniz was to call it the 'most beautiful of dictionaries',[9] and for the next century it was an item that any good library would have acquired. Bayle then spent years finishing the dictionary as well as revising the contents of the first edition, culminating in a second edition by 1701. In 1706, the year of his death, Bayle published his *Réponse aux questions d'un provincial*, and left his *Entretiens de Maxime et de Thémiste* unfinished. Feeling himself weakening, he wrote to a friend, almost as a confession: 'I die a Christian philosopher, convinced and touched by God's goodness and forgiveness.'[10]

Bayle's Religion

When it comes to interpreting Bayle's religious thought, there is still, to this day, no consensus on the matter and there are bitter debates still going on in scholarly journals to that effect.[11] Bayle has been labelled in a variety of different ways. He has been accused of being an atheist, an agnostic, a secularist, a fideist, a Calvinist, an Arminian, a secret Catholic, a Socinian, a Manichean, a Cartesian, an existentialist positivist, a Judaising Christian, a Judeo-Christian, or even a secret Jew.[12] It is thus a daunting task to put this complex thinker into a box and assign him a label, but my argument here rests on the claim that there is not enough evidence to contradict what he himself says about his religion – that is, that he remains a Christian and a Calvinist. On this question I thus side with Labrousse, and most recently Thomas Lennon (and others) who have argued that Bayle must be understood in terms of his fideism and be considered a sincere if unorthodox Calvinist.[13] I will show later that the opposing view – that championed by Jonathan Israel, Gianluca Mori and Antony McKenna – is not without its merits.[14] The *rationalist* Bayle does exist, and when it comes to the interaction between religion and politics, Bayle is unscrupulous in his attacks on all forms of superstition, including against his own brethren.

The debate about Bayle's religious views is not even eased by looking at his vast correspondence. As Antony McKenna notes, the correspondence itself, as is the case everywhere in Bayle's lifetime, is not a private affair but rather to be considered as a semi-public body of letters. In these letters, Bayle plays a role, depending on who the correspondent is, that does not offer clear answers and revelations regarding his personal views. Bayle, concludes McKenna, 'is secret'.[15] Not even to his friends does he divulge information in writing, and there are simply no traces of his innermost thoughts available to us. Even though his correspondence is filled with allusions to his own religiosity, it will fail to convince a sceptic of Bayle's religious sincerity, such as McKenna himself, that these are conclusive proofs of Bayle's inner beliefs. I will need to introduce a hermeneutic argument in favour of Bayle's religious views to justify my own position.

Briefly, I want to give four sets of reasons why Bayle can be considered a sincere believer, which together should go some way to convince the reader that given the consequences of attributing to him the label of atheism, it is best to err on the side of caution

and accept Bayle's own self-characterisation. I will give biographical, philosophical, epistemological and hermeneutic arguments
in favour of this view. In the first instance, there are biographical
elements that point to Bayle's continued religion. His conversion
back to Calvinism, after a brief conversion to Catholicism, is
certainly a sign of his commitment. This relapsing act, as he must
have been aware at the age of twenty-two, made him a permanent
exile. He was never to see his parents again, and he was to spend
the rest of his life in the cold climates of Switzerland, northern France and the Netherlands. His correspondence, moreover,
reveals constant references to his continued religious practice, his
use of prayers, attendance in church, and engagement with his
local religious community, which eventually cost him his chair at
the École illustre. Yet taken on its own, this evidence in inconclusive either way. Many of his letters that we have (for most
have been lost) are to his parents, and he could be using religious
language in order not to displease them. His exterior signs of religiosity may be deceiving, as he has a vested interest in appearing
to be religious during his long controversy with Jurieu, who was
trying to discredit Bayle precisely on the grounds that he was a
secret atheist.

Let me now turn to philosophical reasons why Bayle's secret
atheism is not a convincing argument. The clearest illustration of
his opposition to what he considers as one of the strongest atheistic positions is his article on Spinoza in his *Dictionnaire*.[16] The
article, the longest in the entire work, denounces the impiety of
Spinoza, and the contradictions within his thought. But Bayle's
attack is not solely on Spinoza, whom he sees as the most recent
incarnation of an old immanent philosophy that has existed since
antiquity. In the first edition of the dictionary, Bayle's critique
parallels Bernier's critique of Spinoza: 'if God is the same thing
as Nature, the unity of God is lost in the diversity of the world', a
critique made more potent by the argument that Spinoza confuses
two terms, 'similar' and 'identical', and that Spinoza's monistic
philosophy cannot save the identity of God if it confuses him
with the world. In other words, Spinoza's monadology, where
matter exists as a whole, only consisting of various modifications
of itself, is unconvincing for Bayle. In particular, it is the notion

that matter can think of its own accord that Bayle finds problematic: for it is not clear who is thinking if matter is unified in just one substance.[17] Spinoza, Bayle tells us, even if he has no doubt ridiculed the mystery of the Trinity, in fact proposes a much more absurd notion: that God is but one substance, but that there are not three, but an infinite number of persons within it. It is better to stick to what custom tells us, Bayle concludes, than to adopt a new system that has at least as many problems with it than our previous one. At least we will take solace in the promise of eternal happiness, have confidence in our prayers, and that other men will follow the dictates of their conscience, rather than to follow Spinoza for whom none of these guarantees exist. Interestingly, Bayle is not providing *proofs* for the superiority of belief in God over atheism, he is merely pointing out that most involve mysterious movements and claims, and that if one is to accept a mystery, one should stick to the one that provides the greatest benefit. It is ultimately a rather utilitarian argument for belief, not far from Pascal's wager.

This philosophical argument points to the limits of our knowledge – and to Bayle's sceptical background. Adam Sutcliffe has shown that what differentiates Bayle's thought from Spinoza's is the emphasis on doubt over certainty. During his eulogy of Bayle, his friend Jacques Basnage noted that the philosopher of Rotterdam used his genius with great efficacy 'as to find difficulties' in all things.[18] As Sutcliffe elaborates, 'Nothing perturbs Bayle more than the hubris of certainty',[19] against which Bayle proposes a radical sceptical position. This radical doubt is defined by its ability to penetrate scepticism itself: a true sceptic must also 'doubt if it is necessary to doubt'.[20] The potency of Baylian scepticism was not lost on his readers. Holbach will later praise him for teaching so well how to doubt, Mendelssohn will later use Bayle's treatment of Diogenes' cynical philosophy,[21] and the influence of Bayle on Hume has been well documented.[22] In the midst of the wars of religion of the sixteenth century, Catholic and Protestant theologians alike had unleashed the arguments of Pyrrhonism to discredit their heretic adversaries, a critique that was still active in the late seventeenth century. For Bayle, the challenge remained, and it was clear to him that one could not rely on reason alone to understand some of the mysteries of the universe. The problem of evil, for example, or the logic of the Trinity, are two examples where Bayle is clear about his approach. Unlike later thinkers, like Holbach, who will draw atheistic conclusions when faced with the same problems, Bayle turns to faith to help explain these mysteries. When reason cannot square the circle, one must not dismiss the existence of circles, but have faith that their existence is real, if beyond our comprehension. What follows from this position is a strong opposition to a philosophical system in Bayle's thought, unlike what he found in Spinoza, or what was later to be formulated by self-avowed atheists. This limit to reason, particularly when it comes to matters of religion, does not, however, mean that reason has no role whatsoever to play in human knowledge. Bayle may not have a rationalist *foundation* in the strong sense of the word – his scepticism is a much more important, foundational approach – but reason remains important in matters of historical record, and most importantly, in political matters. Reason, in other words, has its (important) place in human affairs; it is, however, too limited to be able to grasp the mysteries of religion. Faith, here, is a much safer bet – Pascal was right to put the demands of faith as a wager.[23] Religion, properly understood, is not opposed to reason; it is beyond reason, which must nonetheless keep its place in the worldly affairs of men.

Finally, there are hermeneutic arguments that favour erring on the side of caution when it comes to Bayle's religiosity. Bayle himself argued that to attribute religious views to others can be an act of great violence and should never be taken lightly. If hermeneutics is the art of interpretation, it is not without difficulties and hazards. The Gadamerian method that guides this book, which I have briefly discussed in the introduction, demands the interplay of the whole with the part, of the entire body of work of the author with the detail of its parts. Taken as a whole, Bayle's work is full of ambiguities and difficulties of interpretation. He at times advocates for reason, at times for faith. He often sides with the atheists, and at times attacks authors for their lack of piety and their religious views. He writes under the cover of characters whose views are not obviously his but certainly contain elements of his own reflections. In order to understand his most political suggestions, it is important to keep in mind that his particular vision of the positive nature of atheism, which I will detail below, functions even if Bayle himself is a sincere believer. His arguments for toleration and the erring conscience, in other words, are fully compatible with his own personal faith, described in his correspondence. The virtuous atheist can exist, says Bayle, and whether he is himself a secret atheist, or a sincere if unorthodox believer, the consequences of having atheists in society remain the same. This is perhaps why Bayle is so widely read, particularly in the eighteenth century: atheists, deists, as well as unorthodox and more traditional believers could see merit in his argumentation.

The Virtuous Atheist

Part of the debate about Bayle's religious views is driven by his defence of atheism. This defence, which he will continue to espouse from his earliest works of the 1680s to the last works of 1706, is an important part of Bayle's philosophy and the most radical religious position to be found in his thought. In his *Various Thoughts on the Occasion of a Comet* of 1682, his philosophical debut, Bayle already puts his position forward on atheism. Arguing against the role that comets play in human affairs, Bayle puts forward a series of responses and objections to eight 'reasons' put forward by those who oppose his view.[24] The seventh reason, called the theological reason, states that God is meant to have made use of comets to introduce pagans to the idea of Divine Providence, and thus prevent their fall into atheism.[25] Bayle will argue against this, and one facet of his conception of atheism becomes immediately clear: atheists are defined as those who deny Divine Providence. Irrespective of their own conception of God, all those who deny the very idea of Providence can be classified as atheists. A second aspect of his thought on atheism comes just a little later in the work, when he provides objections to the theological reason for comets. God cannot have used comets to drive pagans away from atheism and into idolatry, for it would just chase them from one crime into another crime.[26] Atheism is thus clearly not defended as a doctrine that Bayle agrees with, let alone identifies with, or as an ideal, but as a crime that needs to be fought and argued against. The confusion comes from Bayle's then oft-repeated assertions that idolatry is a worst crime than atheism. Among the reasons why atheism is preferable to idolatry, Bayle cites that the Demon prefers idolatry to atheists who deny his very existence; that it is a worse crime to give wrong attributes to God than to deny His existence; that idolatry and a strong belief in God make the idolater's crimes even worse; that idolaters are more difficult to convert than atheists; and that neither the idolater nor the atheist has a better heart than the other.[27] In other words, Bayle gives theological arguments for the superiority of atheists to idolaters, an affective argument (that their heart is as capable of emotions), and a moral argument. The conclusion from these arguments in the *Thoughts on the Comet* is that his use of theological arguments reinforces the view that Bayle was a convinced Christian, while the affective argument puts him in the intellectual legacy of Spinoza's *conatus*.

The moral argument was to become the most famous of Bayle's arguments, and he spends much time developing it throughout his literary career. Bayle spells out this moral argument for atheists: 'Atheism does not necessarily lead to the corruption of morals.'[28] While he may have had Spinoza in mind when he discusses this possibility of a virtuous atheist, there is also evidence that he thought of the Chinese as an example of virtuous atheists.[29] This thesis of the virtuous atheist, which directly opposes that put forward by Jurieu, was to become the signature of Bayle's moral philosophy. Jurieu's position, that atheism is a crime worthy of death, is opposed as a 'false prejudice', and its reasoning, that the lack of belief in Divine Providence will open the doors to all sorts of unspeakable crimes, exposed as erroneous. Bayle's argument against Jurieu is quite simple: experience shows us that we do not act according to our principles. Why not? Because our actions are not driven by general principles, such as piety, belief in God, charity and so forth, but rather we are driven by our dominant passions (*la passion dominante du cœur*), our temperament, our habits or our sensibility.[30] Belief in God thus adds nothing of significant weight when it comes to preventing crimes. The idolater, and supposedly the Christian believer as well, has no advantage over the atheist, for they are all subject to the same passions that drive our actions. In fact, Bayle continues, a society of atheists can be just as virtuous as any other type of society. All it needs is to be able to punish crimes to provide a counterweight to the passions, and to introduce ideas of honour and infamy.[31] Atheists are just as susceptible of praise and blame, including in their afterlife: they may not believe in the immortality of the soul, but they still want their name to acquire said immortality. And Bayle cites numerous historical examples of atheists who cared deeply about morality and their reception in posterity. Among the ancients, he cites Diagoras, Theodorus of Cyrene, Euhemerus, Diogenes Laërtius, Cicero, Plutarch, Nicanor, Hippo, Epicurus and the Sadducees of ancient Judaism as virtuous atheists.[32] Among the moderns, though, Bayle is more careful to attribute the label of atheism. He reports the execution by fire of an atheist in Paris in 1573, but it is Vanini that is considered the best example of a modern atheist. What is more important in Vanini's case is that it validates Bayle's point that people do not act according to their principles. For Vanini preferred to die a horrible death than to retract his statements, even though they had no consequence for him in the afterlife, according to his own beliefs. Adding to Vanini's example, Bayle cites a certain Mahomet Efendi (sometimes spelled Effendi), executed 'recently' in Constantinople for similar disbelief in God.[33] Bayle's theorising on atheism can thus be summarised in four parts: atheism is a crime, but a lesser one than idolatry; atheists are those who either do not believe in God, or do not believe in Divine Providence; an atheist can be just as virtuous as anyone else, for we do not act morally based on our principles but based on our passions; and a society of atheists is just as possible as any other society. These four positions will be repeated, in various forms, in many of Bayle's later works but they were already formulated in his first writings in 1682.

Conceptually, Bayle introduces a positive notion of atheism for the first time in history. With the caveat that it is still considered a wrong opinion and a false belief, Bayle nevertheless introduces the possibility in the domain of ethics of the virtuous atheist to his readers. Not only are atheists just as capable of virtue, they actually have advantages over the idolatrous when it comes to virtue, for they have no belief in a cruel, vengeful and violent God to justify their vices. In the context of the religious controversies of the seventeenth century, it would have been clear to Bayle's readers what the implications of his argument are: it is better to be an atheist than a papist, better to deny the existence of God than to worship the Virgin Mary, better to lack belief in Divine Providence than to believe that God will reward one's religious persecution of others.[34] The atheist, who according to Bayle is more likely to have a calm, composed and studious nature than the zealot, is not a threat to society, whereas those who argue for violence based on religious belief are. Bayle may have been mistaken for a defender of atheism, and with good reasons: he is arguing that the philosophical position alone may be wrong, but that it is not a reason for persecution of those who hold it but otherwise act as peaceful members of society. On the other hand, those who use their beliefs to shake the foundations of the state are much more pernicious to society and deserve the full wrath of the law.

The Erring Conscience

One such act of devout persecution occurred in 1685 with the revocation of the edict of Nantes, prompting Bayle to write his *Philosophical Commentary* in 1686. Yet recent personal and political dramas were only the tip of the iceberg for Bayle, who had seen religious tensions and persecutions grow over the past decade of his life. Of particular relevance for his work is the practice of the *dragonnades*, or the quartering of troops in Protestant homes in France to force conversions before the edict of Nantes was repealed. These had started roughly at the time that Bayle left for the Netherlands, but the second-hand accounts of these practices left a vivid impression on the philosopher's mind. In his other work of 1686, *Wholly Catholic France*, Bayle shows how effective the troops were in their endeavours. It would have required an insurmountable amount of will and determination to escape the logic of conversion under such circumstances. If the invasion of one's home is not enough of a hardship, Bayle goes on to describe the various forms of torture imposed on the Huguenots by the dragoons. The soldiers 'tormented' their hosts by 'tickling them, making them dance, tossing them in the air, and mocking them'.[35] These methods may seem mild, but they are a sign of assured cruelty. These enhanced conversion techniques culminate in the art of sleep deprivation, the strongest of the torments inflicted on poor Protestants. For 'it is no small thing to deprive someone of sleep, the one thing in the world without which we cannot live, and those who are tormented by insomnia would pay their weight in gold for a bit of sleep'.[36] In addition to these novel techniques, the old techniques of 'Dungeoning' and 'Cloistering' are also blamed for the woes of Huguenots.[37] It was these that had cost his brother's life, making the theoretical angle of the book all the more concrete for Bayle and his fellow Protestants. If these are insufficient, 'Murder, Robbery, Banishment, Rapes' follow, and Bayle is amazed that there are not more freethinkers and deists in the world, given how organised religions have supported such practices.[38]

The Catholic Church is particularly to blame for these practices, Bayle argues. By inventing a neologism, the *Convertist*, he shows the mind-set that created space for these practices to emerge, with widespread support among the French population. Starting off as 'a Soul sincerely zealous in propagating the Truth, and undeceiving those in Error', the Convertist quickly becomes a sombre figure.[39] Using the poetic figure of the 'Monster, Half-Priest and Half-Dragoon',[40] Bayle paints the picture of the zealot who initially wished to promote truth, but ultimately turned his quest into one of bloodshed, persecution and torture. This slip, from an initial noble quest – to convince others of the veracity of one's beliefs – to the most brutal of quests, hinges on the interpretation of one passage of the New Testament, Luke's *Compel them to come in*, after which the commentary takes its title. If recent Gallican Catholic practices are the most recent incarnation of this Convertist spirit, Bayle is keen to point out that Protestants are not innocent in this respect. They too have used, and continue to use, Luke's passage to justify forced conversions. In a damning judgement on his fellow Protestants, Bayle exposes that the only difference between them and Catholics is the Truth they claim to profess. Protestants are just as ready to use force to enforce their truth as Catholics are. However, Bayle claims that no one

could, in good conscience, impose their own truth on others –
irrespective of how deeply they believe it.

The first half of the commentary is dedicated to one task
only: arguing against those who insist on a literal reading of the
Bible, especially in moral matters. In Bayle's terms: '*That all literal
Construction, which carries an Obligation of committing Iniquity, is
false.*'[41] Far from throwing these passages away, however, Bayle
argues that it is down to one's reason, down to one's conscience to
determine what is to be done when a literal reading of the Bible
would lead to unjust actions. The light of nature that illuminates
men, Bayle continues, must be God himself, and the act of reasoning is akin to taking part in the Divine.[42] God speaks to us directly
in our conscience, Bayle further explains, and though we may deviate from our course because of the influence of our passions, the
conscience is prior to other commands, including those of revelation.[43] It is thus a theological argument that Bayle is making here,
and one that appeals to Protestants' critiques of Catholics in particular – being grounded in one's own reading of the Bible, rather
than an acceptation of doctrine. Bayle is once again a sincere – if
unorthodox – Calvinist, providing a theologically based philosophical argument for the right to follow one's conscience.

One should be left free to follow the dictates of one's conscience, for Bayle – *even though it be erroneous*. Because following
one's conscience is the equivalent of following God's commands,
not following it would be to commit a sin knowingly.[44] It is better,
Bayle argues, to follow one's reason and do an action that is
otherwise considered evil (for one is following one's love of God
and abiding by His commands by following reason) than it would
be to do good by knowingly disobeying the dictates of conscience
and thus disobeying God's command.[45] This conclusion brings an
immediate problem for Bayle, one he will struggle with for the rest
of his life. What if the dictates of one's conscience demand that
one '*employ Fire and Sword for the establishing the Truth*'?[46] Clearly,
since the argument for the erring conscience had been an attempt
to limit bloodshed and violent practices, this is not a conclusion
that Bayle wishes to promote. He therefore puts together a two-
pronged argument against the persecuting erring conscience. In
the first instance, he does not deny that this may be a demand

of one's conscience, and thus a possibility as a moral law. On the other hand, he argues that in a plural world, where different religions coexist, one has to accept that the same principle will apply to all – those who have the truth as well as those who are in error.[47] Thus, fire and sword, once used *even by the one true faith*, will be used by all and plunge the world into violence: 'Crime becomes necessary, and a total Confusion ensues'.[48] God could not have meant for such chaos to ensue, and thus the only valid reason for persecution (that one is following one's conscience), is dismissed. If the erring conscience is better than the imposition of truth, Bayle, by his own account, has provided only a weak defence against the issue of persecution. His main argument rests in the fact of pluralism – that different religions will all be able to use persecution, and that total religious war would ensue. This would be insufficient to convince true zealots, of course, for they will always entertain the hope of winning, and thus of doing away with the fact of pluralism, as the proponents of a wholly Catholic France argued.

The possibility of an outright victory for the zealot was seriously considered by Bayle, as it would be a daunting outcome and directly contradict his argument that pluralism prevents persecution. In the context of a strengthening of the French state under the rule of Louis XIV, France had secured large territorial gains in the decades preceding the revocation. In the treatises of Westphalia (1648), the treaty of the Pyrenees (1659), the treaty of Aix-la-Chapelle (1668), and the treatises of Nijmegen (1678–9), as well as in its growing assertiveness in North America and the Caribbean, the French state had shown its military superiority over most of its neighbours, including Spain, the Empire and the Dutch Republics. Bayle directly links these territorial expansions to the woes of French Protestants. When at peace, these troops that had contributed to France's victories had to be put to some use, and the miseries of Protestants can be seen as a consequence of French expansion, particularly through the *dragonnades*. In the same way as Louis's armies had defeated enemies abroad, they have clearly defeated enemies at home. France, the text argues, is indeed wholly Catholic, but this has come at an unbearable price. The soldiers themselves are part of the picture, but the general depravation of public morality is the real victim here. From the highest noble to the lowest peasant, 'you have all been complicit in these crimes', exclaims the angry Protestant, one of the voices of the text.[49] Even the moderate Protestant, another voice in the text, appeals to the moderation of his correspondent, a Catholic abbot, to condemn the use of violence for conversions. Recognising that not all Frenchmen are responsible for the abuses of the soldiers and magistrates, he nonetheless condemns the apologists who have defended such practices in writing.[50] Widespread conversion, in other words, may be possible, but it comes at a price which even the moderates will have to pay. They will have to make a choice, according to their conscience, whether to condemn or condone the use of violence. Any quest for religious unity, in other words, will lead to a clash of consciences, where the moderate among Catholics and Protestants are left with unappealing alternatives: going against their conscience, or going against their country.

Toleration

Bayle's defence of the possibility of a virtuous atheist and of the erring conscience culminate in a call for toleration that was to prove a radical solution to the problems of his day. Immediately, Bayle has to face the issue of the prejudice against toleration, put forward and defended by some of his contemporaries such as Jurieu, who accused him of *tolérantisme*. The accusation can be twofold: that one is denying the true faith by tolerating heretical beliefs (in particular those of Roman Catholics); and that toleration is dangerous because it leads to a breakdown of social and political order as it takes away the rationale for punishment of crimes. The latter issue was addressed by Bayle in his *Philosopical Commentary* by showing that it was certainly not the case that toleration led to disorder, as illustrated by historical examples. The Romans, Bayle explains, accepted numerous practices and beliefs, often adopting others' gods as their own, while Athenians permitted all philosophical schools to espouse the beliefs they wanted about the gods. Despite this, there was no breakdown of social order, no wars of religion, and in the instances in which religious persecutions occurred, such as Nero's persecutions of Christians, they were done for political rather than religious reasons.[51] In his *News from the Republic of Letters*, Bayle argues that contemporary examples further exemplify the possibility of peaceful toleration. In Siam (modern-day Thailand), as well as China, toleration is widespread even against religions the local rulers deem dangerous, such as the Jesuit. Islam, Bayle continues, has been tolerating other religions under its rule for centuries, despite its reputation as a violent religion. It seems to Bayle that intolerance is in fact a Christian vice, and that other religions do not share it to the same extent.[52] Far from being a policy exclusive of Catholics, furthermore, Bayle insists that many Protestants fail to condemn all persecutions when they condemn those of the Catholic Church. Once in power, they will persecute just as well as their Catholic counterparts, if they haven't rejected compulsion as a principle.

To the first objection against toleration, that it allows for false religion and does not promote true faith, Bayle will oppose his freedom of the erring conscience and his general sceptical outlook. How is one to know that one's position is the true one, as opposed to merely having strong faith that it is? Forcing others to come in, converting them to one's faith through the action of secular powers – thus any form of organised state religion – will inevitably lead to turning religion into a public display rather than a genuine act of faith. Christianity, Bayle further argues, will lose its distinctive characteristics that differentiate it from previous pagan religions, which had obligations of public worship.[53] As Labrousse argues, this position of Bayle is not entirely surprising, as it largely coincides with important movements within Protestant churches. Calvinists, she notes, who were well aware of the plurality of Protestant movements, tended to perceive their church as the best, not the only one able to guide one to salvation.[54] Furthermore, although Bayle had argued against the case for forced conversions – compel them to come in – he did maintain the right of a religious community to exclude those who deviate too much from their faith: *compelle exire*, compel them to exit.[55] Religious tolerance is thus not without teeth: ecclesiastical communities are able to police themselves, but they cannot legitimately use state power for compulsion. This becomes possible only if toleration is turned into a political principle. Political toleration demands the guarantee of certain freedoms (of the erring conscience, or practice, of belief), but it does not regulate what religious communities can demand of their members.[56] After all, Bayle's toleration includes atheists, who have no ecclesiastical community to speak of, and thus allows for exit from all religious groups. Any particular church can then maintain its own beliefs and practices, and attempt to convince others that these are the means to salvation, but it cannot compel anyone to become a member. A church's most powerful tool, in other words, is excommunication – and that power is both necessary and sufficient for any religious community. This reflects a shift from a moral argument for toleration to a political argument: intolerance is rejected because of its negative consequences.[57]

The Republic of Letters

An often-overlooked contribution that Bayle made to scientific inquiry, the News from the Republic of Letters (News for short), an academic review journal he started in 1684 and that was continued by others when he gave up the enterprise in 1687, it is sometimes credited as the first review journal in history. More modest than this, Bayle explains, in the Preface to the first volume of the journal, that he had been motivated to undertake this enterprise by other works of a similar nature such as the Journal des Sçavants of Sallo.[58] An impressive enterprise in its own right, the News benefits from the tolerant laws of the Netherlands to quickly establish itself as a major intellectual force in Europe. Bayle worked on the first eleven issues of the journal, each containing dozens of reviews of books, from all fields of human knowledge that he could get his hands on. Meant for the erudite amateur, it explains in plain terms what are sometimes highly technical works and aims to provide a balance between the depth of reviews and their number. But Bayle does not shy away from making political points in this preface to the first edition, as well as in the body of the various volumes he worked on. He warns his reader that he will not attempt to find out what these authors' true religion was, or accuse them of heresy or atheism. Citing Virgil, he exclaims: 'Tros Rutulusve fuat, nullo discrimine habebo' ('Trojan or Rutulian, I will regard them both without distinction'), a citation Hume was to use on the title page of his *Essays, Moral and Political*.[59] The spirit of ancient toleration, which had inspired Bayle's call for contemporary toleration cited above, runs deep in his works. The celebrity of the authors whose works are studied in the *News* will come due to their science, not their orthodox or heterodox beliefs, and the journal clearly aims to be accessible to all denominations alike – despite being authored by a Calvinist. This culminates in a call for equality in the republic of letters:

> In this sense all scientists shall look upon one another as brothers, or from equally good houses. They shall say,
> *We are all equal*
> *We are all related*
> *As children of Apollo.*[60]

Bayle continues his enterprise for freedom of conscience which we have just discussed; he continues to advocate for toleration, and turns this quest into a call of equality and fraternity between scientists ('Sçavans'), irrespective of their religious beliefs. He promises that the monk will deserve as much praise from the Calvinist author of the journal as any other author: for he will be judged on his science and nothing else. Irrespective of your religious beliefs, in other words, your work will be judged in front of the tribunal of reason – whether it be atheistic, deistic, Catholic, Protestant, Jewish, Muslim or other, it is the quality of the argument that will be evaluated. There is thus some truth to Israel's assertion that Bayle is one of the founders of the radical Enlightenment, in that his republic of letters, exemplified in his *News* from this republic, is fundamentally egalitarian, open-minded and founded on reason.

This contrasts sharply with the oft-cited view that Bayle is a royalist and an absolutist. Certainly, there is some truth behind those labels being assigned to Bayle, for he defends the view that monarchs are exempt from general laws regarding religious practice that may otherwise affect public servants:

> I always except the Persons of Kings, because the Royal Dignity, and sacred Unction of their Character, dispenses with the most

general Laws in their favor; and therefore it may be lawful for them to turn Papists, if they please, Jews, Turks, Infidels, without the least danger of forfeiting what they have a Right to by their Birth.[61]

According to this maxim, Bayle supported two monarchs highly unpopular with fellow Protestants in the Netherlands: James II of England, the Catholic king deposed by William III of Orange, Stadtholder of the Netherlands (and then King of England under the same name); and Louis XIV of France, considered the greatest enemy of Protestants everywhere. According to Bayle, both had a right to rule their respective kingdoms, despite their Catholicism and their actions against Protestants. When it came to the right of William to overthrow James for the thrones of England and Scotland, as well as in the arguing for a neutral policy against France (at least until 1688 when war with France broke out), Bayle sided with the regents in the United Provinces rather than with the stadtholder,[62] that is, with the republicans rather than the royalists. In the political context of the 1680s and 1690s, this meant that Bayle was firmly siding with the republican *Staatsgezinde* faction against the Orangists.

Nothing illustrates Bayle's position on the use of force to depose of monarchs better than his controversy with Jurieu which rages in the *Dictionary*. When Bayle is speaking in favour of James II or Louis XIV, he is doing so on the basis that they are the rightful rulers, and possess legitimacy, not on the basis that all of their actions are ethical or moral. The question of Bayle's *absolutism* is really a question of whether there is a right to resist tyranny or unjust rule, including with political violence and rebellion. Bayle's politics here is clearly on the side of endurance: one needs to tolerate the evils being done to oneself, because this option is better than the alternative which necessitates war. Throughout the *Dictionary*, Bayle attacks Jurieu for defending the use of violence to achieve religious unity.[63] As Mara van der Lugt argues, the article on Mahomet provides one of the clearest instances of the vociferousness of Bayle's attacks on Jurieu, after the latter had managed to get Bayle's chair at the Ecole Illustre revoked. In this article, Bayle draws a distinction between the fanatic, who seeks to use any means for his cause to succeed, and the impostor, who only uses religion for self-aggrandisement.[64] True to his earlier statements about the erring conscience, Bayle does not exclude the possibility that the fanatic at least is true to the duties of his own morality – whereas the impostor is not since he is insincere. While Bayle leaves the two options open in his judgement of Jurieu, he certainly spills a lot of ink attempting to show that there are signs that Jurieu is not even sincere in his beliefs. This would imply that he is an impostor rather than a 'mere' fanatic, and that it is not his erring conscience pushing him to calls of violence and regicide, but personal calculations and interest. If this is the conclusion that Bayle is pushing us to make, then it would mean that Jurieu's position need not be tolerated, as it does not derive from the freedom to philosophise but from his politics. Combined with the insights of the Erasmus article, within which Bayle self-identifies with the philosopher of Rotterdam,[65] we see the contrast that he wanted to draw with Jurieu. Whereas Jurieu is compared to Muhammad, Bayle is put in parallel with Erasmus, in particular his peace-loving and anti-war writings. But what of the war against the oppressor, what of the war against Louis XIV, ultimately responsible for Bayle's brother's death, his exile, the *dragonnades*, sleep deprivation, murders, rapes and other atrocities? As van der Lugt argues, Bayle is a defender of the moderate party against the extremist party – but he may not even be the most representative of other moderates of his time. His continued opposition to deposing Louis XIV, even after war between France and the Netherlands broke out in 1688, put him at odds with other moderates. Bayle was thus an 'extremist in his moderation',[66] or, to put it in the terms of this book, a radical pacifist. His radicalism is to be seen in his refusal to make compromises to his love of peace, even if this means tolerating intolerance. War is not the way to achieve social change and peace, and to establish a tolerant society, and Bayle remained radically engaged in his attitude to foreign policy – even as other moderates were shifting their stance towards intervention. It might thus be better to say that Bayle was never a moderate, but rather was always a radical whose uncompromising position on peace and against war coincided with the position of moderates until war broke out, and then stood out as the radical position it always was.

Bayle's so-called absolutism is more akin to a legitimism than anything else: whoever has a legitimate claim to rule should be considered the rightful ruler, irrespective of their religious views. The philosophical justification for this legitimism lies on the shoulders of two thinkers Bayle greatly admired, but also critically engaged with and used in his work: Hobbes and Spinoza. From Hobbes, Bayle takes the fundamental importance of peace; and from Spinoza the theory of active toleration. Bayle's political thought has first accepted that Hobbes's claim that the first law of nature is peace. For Hobbes, we differentiate between natural rights, which in his state of nature give men a right to all things, and natural law, which binds and obligates men to certain principles which are more likely to bring about their self-preservation.[67] In other words, while we maintain the right to continue in a state of war, reason forces us to conclude that our own self-preservation is best served by peace, and thus that peace is the first law of nature. Because this law of nature cannot be enforced unless there is some form of authority, a commonwealth is instituted for all 'to live peaceable amongst themselves'.[68] Hobbes's theory of sovereignty had established peace as the prime reason for the establishment of political rule. Although Bayle does not follow Hobbes all the way, he accepted the English philosopher's claim to the primacy of peace. Bayle further agrees with Hobbes that a sovereign cannot rightfully be overthrown, that the sovereign has the right to pass laws to regulate the behaviour of subjects, including to repeal acts of toleration as Louis XIV had done – though Bayle thought such an exercise of the right was misguided. In his *Wholly Catholic France*, Bayle even goes so far as absolving the person of the king from having made the mistake of repealing the edict of Nantes. The king must have been duped by his advisers, and by the Church, for him to have made such a decision going against the peaceful coexistence of his subjects.[69]

In the event that peaceful coexistence is no longer possible, Bayle still insists that exile is preferable to open rebellion. This is justified on the grounds of endurance and tolerance – the latter term being expanded from the concept of toleration to include the ability to sustain displeasure and iniquities. Lars Tønder has proposed reading Spinoza's theory of toleration as one of active tolerance (as opposed to passive tolerance), driven by Spinoza's theory of affects, human finitude and worldly pluralism.[70] Certainly, Bayle had accepted that in this world, religious pluralism is here to stay, and that our capacity to know truth is limited due to our human finitude. Since affects are what make Spinoza's toleration *active*, as opposed to passive, it is important to look into what affects drive Bayle's theory of endurance and tolerance. In *Wholly Catholic France*, Bayle uses various voices to discuss the condition of France after the revocation.[71] The moderate Protestant, writing to his Catholic correspondent about a letter written to him by an angry Protestant, attempts to mediate between the two parties. Surely, the angry Protestant went too far when he exclaimed that there are no honest men in France for all are complicit in the tragedy of the revocation. The moderate Protestant argues, on the other hand, that only those who perpetrated the forced conversions, or those who pushed the king to take the decision in the first place are to blame. These are the men, citing Virgil, that Bayle says have '*hearts no human prayers can soften*',[72] bringing the debate to the realm of affects. He adds:

> For their sake I hope they are not acting against their consciences, nor according to human motives, but through zeal for the church they believe to be the one true one. But oh, if it is through zeal, I'll pray to God morning and night that I never have such zeal![73]

Staying true to his philosophy of the erring conscience, Bayle admits that even intolerance and persecution may be motivated by belief and zeal, making them at the very least philosophically tolerable under the principle of the erring conscience. His own affective strategy of toleration also becomes clear: one needs to fight against urges, passions and affects that push one towards zeal. Active toleration is first and foremost an anti-zealous strategy. The act of active toleration, whereby one is driven to bear and endure injustice, is one that is motivated by a desire to avoid the passionate, zealous temperament of those whose heart can no longer listen to the pleas of peace and justice.

By bringing together these two concepts, of active toleration and the erring conscience, I have shown that Bayle's contribution to political thought is critical to debates on foreign intervention and political resistance. At a time when no one else made this argument, Bayle put forward that there is more virtue to be gained by bearing the persecutions of intolerant despots than there is to be gained by active resistance, military intervention and civil strife. Tolerance, acting as an affective tool, can moderate our passions, which otherwise rule our actions much more than our principles do. While Bayle still accepts that the fanatic may be a principled person (thus acting in accordance with their morality), in practice he shows that those who advocate for fanatical positions, such as Jurieu, are not guided by their principles but rather by their self-interest and their passions. Toleration, which enables one to temperate one's passions, is a helpful tool for resisting fanaticism, without compromising one's erring conscience. Bayle is almost formulating a guidebook for avoiding fanatics, which nonetheless preserves the rights to one's conscience. Starting with his positive theory of atheism, that it is no stranger for an atheist to be virtuous than for anyone else to be virtuous, Bayle's call for toleration of atheists is extended to all 'fanatics'. It may be the final piece of the puzzle when it comes to Bayle's religious belief, that he is ready to call for toleration of his own enemies, at opposite ends of the spectrum: from the most devout Protestants calling for military intervention against Catholics, to Catholic monarchs who propose intolerant policies towards their subjects, not forgetting the atheists whose lack of belief in Providence creates a world without hope and faith. Where Gianluca Mori had insisted that the recourse to conscience provided an irrational argument in Bayle that he was keen to dismiss,[74] I have shown that the erring conscience, combined with an active toleration that insists on the fact of pluralism, makes it possible for Bayle to keep the central aspect of conscience at play, without giving way to the fanatic. The fanatic has to entertain the hope that everyone might come to see the world as they do; whereas this contradicts the fact of pluralism that diversity has always and will always exist.

Critique as Method, Critique as Theory

One more topic needs to be covered to unveil Bayle's radical potential. Bayle's project for a critical and historical dictionary was exposed in a letter which outlines the reasoning behind such an endeavour. In this letter, reprinted in the dictionary itself under the entry *dissertation*, Bayle explains his endeavour. As Yves Zarka notes, this project exposes a triple method in Bayle's *Dictionary*. It proposes an epistemology that is meant to answer the Pyrrhonist challenge, in line with the Protestant ethic that pushes one to 'protest against everything that is said and everything that is done'.[75] In the first instance, its method is to generalise the idea of critique, already found in biblical exegesis, such as that of Calvinist theologian Louis Cappel who had already spent time dispelling myths about religious beliefs. Critique steps out of its philological context with Bayle, and becomes an instrument of historical research, generalising the practice he had found in others. It also opens up critique to further epistemological domains, and, as we shall see, it has consequences for the fields of ethics and politics. In the second instance, critique becomes a place where truth is achieved. Extending the Cartesian method beyond its realm, Bayle argues that critique can provide us with a way to achieve truth in the historical domain. Transgressing the Cartesian distinction between reason and fact, Bayle argues that our knowledge of facts is only possible if we attempt to point out errors in past interpretations. Certainty is of different kinds in the two domains, in geometry and in history, but that is not say that truth cannot be attained at the level that is appropriate for the level of analysis. As Bayle notes of mathematicians: 'it is not as easy for them to arrive at the certainty they need, as it is easy for historians to arrive at the certainty that suffices them'.[76] Importantly for Bayle's argument, the truth that is established by history is more useful than that established by geometry, for more people will be able to use it. It is an argument for public critique that is being professed here, rather than an argument for elitist method à la Descartes. Third, critique is compared to a tribunal, or described as the '*Chamber of Insurances of the Republic of Letters*',[77] a space that has its own procedures and laws. Bayle argues that historical critique has created a public space – res publica, or republic. This republic is one of 'lettres', described by Bayle in Hobbesian terms as it resembles a state of nature. In this space, everyone is sovereign, and friends have to guard against friends and fathers against sons. The only powers that exist there are truth and reason, and everyone is as free as they can be. Of course, such a 'warre of all against all' is quite innocent when it comes to a war of ideas. We see that the 'rationalist Bayle' thesis, notably as it is put forward by Mori and Israel,[78] is not without its merits. There is considerable space for reason to play here, at least when it comes to historical exegesis and critique. Contra what Zarka concludes, however, this method is not without ethical and political consequences.

In addition to providing us with a triple method of critique, as a general method, a quest for truth, and a public space, Bayle's critique also takes the shape of an ethical and political challenge. In his attempt to answer the Pyrrhonist challenge, for example, Bayle makes a case for the public service that his Dictionary can provide. Who is not confused, he asks, when one reads a book which one agrees with, and then we agree equally with a critical review of the book? It would take a life of devotion to texts to be able to develop a strong critical sense for them. Without access to large libraries, such an endeavour is beyond the scope of most readers, and the Dictionary provides such a public service to its readers. Even finding errors in the books reviewed in the News or the subjects analysed in the Dictionary will not prejudice what are otherwise great works. For error is natural, and if someone's conscience is free to err, so are their works and books. The authors critiqued, in other words, have a 'zeal for the instruction of the public',[79] and, as with religious zeal, it is allowed under the freedom of the erring conscience. Unlike religious zeal, however, this educational zeal has many positive social and political consequences, beyond their narrow confessional confines. The acquisition of knowledge and the practice of the arts is a great good for human beings, who take pleasure in the quest for truth. Moreover, the act of critique provides a character lesson for human beings. Critique 'will teach man to know his weakness',[80] and make authors more careful of the claims they make, resulting in better arguments and better books. Fundamentally, critique has moral qualities that cannot be overshadowed by its mere usefulness as a method. Critique also provides a political space of equality, where those without access to vast libraries can become critics in their own right, and where all authors, great and small, ancient and modern, are scrutinised by a watchful public. It finally fulfils the promise of the erring conscience, as all are free to make mistakes as long as they agree to enter a public debate where these mistakes can be argued against rationally – rather than censured by the force of law.

This public face of critique is at the heart of the Baylian enterprise. Bayle himself went to great lengths to publish his works of critique, and paid a high price for the public nature of his oeuvre – both personal, in the harassment he faced from Jurieu and the persecution and death of his brother at the hands of the French authorities; and public, in his estrangement from fellow exiles in the Netherlands following his dismissal from *the Ecole Illustre*. What makes Bayle's critique *political*, however, remains to be seen. What better place to look for this meaning than Bayle's article on Machiavelli in the *Dictionary*? There, Bayle critiques the critics of Machiavelli, who is 'misinterpreted by many who would understand him better were they to cease reading him from so prejudiced a perspective'.[81] Bayle's critical method has direct consequences for understanding the art of politics, and he continues by saying that the perspective to be followed in this domain is 'from the perspective of a minister or the perspective of a prince'.[82] Note that Bayle is not quite arguing that only ministers and princes are able to grasp the *raison d'état*, but rather that scholars and historians have a duty to try to adopt the perspective of those who are making the decisions, and not pre-judge them from their own standpoint. This capacity to put yourself in the shoes of others is essential to Bayle's hermeneutic – even if it can never fully be achieved.

Nowhere are the virtues of the *politique*, the virtuous politician, clearer in the life and work of Michel de l'Hôpital, Chancellor of France, about whom Bayle dedicates an article of the *Dictionary*. Bayle does not hold back his praise for the *politique*, who was 'one of the greatest men of his time',[83] making him Bayle's equivalent to Machiavelli's Cesare Borgia, the two even sharing a lack of fortune.[84] After dismissing accusations of atheism against the

Chancellor and noting his attachment to the Calvinist faith, Bayle is adamant that de l'Hôpital's defence of Huguenots was not due to his or his family's faith, but rather due to 'his incorruptible attachment to the good of the state, to the preservation of its laws, and to the welfare of its peoples'.[85] Against the *parlements* who opposed peace with the Protestants, de l'Hôpital vehemently defended a vision of pluralism based on the ideal of toleration of difference. France, according to Bayle, was in such a dire state during this period that '[h]ad Charles V been reigning at that time, France would unquestionably have become a province of his dominions, or rather she would have been divided into a thousand parts'.[86] The genius of the Chancellor was to accept a model of plurality that also allowed for the maintaining of the territorial unity of the state. Motivated chiefly by a love of peace, both Bayle and de l'Hôpital share similar ideals. Unattached to religious denominations, they seek partners wherever they may find them that share their desire for peaceful coexistence. Whether these are Catholics or Protestants, atheists or Muslims, matters little to the virtuous *politique*. They seek to use the critical method to defend peace, and to discredit those who would use the means of war, civil or international, to achieve their ends. Therein lies the engaged power of critique: to expose the enemies of peace for what they are, to reveal that their arguments for unity are really justifications for conflict in what is essentially a pluralistic world.

Conclusion

Pierre Bayle remains a man of mystery. More than three centuries after his death, we can still debate about the essentials of his works, the meaning of his texts, and his underlying beliefs. Partly, it is his style that is responsible for such plurality of interpretations. He does not always write in his own voice, uses copious amounts of other texts, often verbatim, to make his case, and often exposes contradictory arguments to paint a picture of the varied reception of an author or problem. In his *Wholly Catholic France*, to take only one example, the three voices of the Catholic, the moderate Protestant and the angry Protestant oppose each other with no clear winner or preference from the author. Precisely because of this, the text can be read in a myriad of different ways. Applying Bayle's own method of critique, I have sought less to delve into the details of the particular texts than to paint an overall picture of the author, from his earlier to his last writings. From this analysis surfaces a consistent and persistent desire for peace, often at the detriment of other values. This applied, for Bayle, both to internal and external matters of the state, both domestic and international politics. Peace implies an often imperfect defence of the status quo, as Bayle's defence of Louis XIV testifies. However, for Bayle, this ideal of peace is worth pursuing even at great personal cost (and in fact, it always demands a great sacrifice, for peace is only made with one's enemies). He was himself ready to let go of his own brother's imprisonment, torture and death, and to let go of any hope of ever returning to his native land, in order to defend this ideal of peace. This is, in many ways, Bayle's profound radicalism. It is underscored by an acceptance of the fact of pluralism: that one is never going to convert the whole world to one's perspective, and that if one wants to minimise conflict and maximise peace, one has to promote toleration. Bayle praises those who sought this goal and attacked those who sought other ideals in contradiction with it. Bayle will, of course, be remembered for his defence of the virtuous atheist, another radical idea of his writings that remains consistent throughout his life. This would have, as we will see, a profound impact on those who claimed the label of atheism for themselves, notably Meslier and Holbach, who both admired the arguments of the philosopher of Rotterdam.

Notes

1. Jenkinson, 'Introduction', in Bayle, *Political Writings*, xix.
2. Labrousse, *Pierre Bayle*, vol. 1, 31.
3. Ibid. 66.
4. Ibid. 72.
5. Ibid. 86.
6. Ibid. 159.
7. Sandberg, 'Pierre Jurieu's Contribution to Bayle's *Dictionnaire*'.
8. Labrousse, *Pierre Bayle*, vol. 1, 226.
9. Ibid. 248.
10. Ibid. 269, my translation. The original reads: 'je meurs en Philosophe Chrétien, persuadé et pénétré des bontés et de la miséricorde de Dieu.'

11. See, in particular, the long exchange between Thomas Lennon and Gianluca Mori: Lennon, 'Did Bayle Read Saint-Evremond?'; Mori, 'Bayle, Saint-Evremond, and Fideism: A Reply to Thomas M. Lennon'; Mori, 'Introduction', in Bayle, *Avis aux réfugiés*; Hickson and Lennon, 'The Real Significance of Bayle's Authorship of the *Avis*'.
12. Heyd, 'A Disguised Atheist or a Sincere Christian?'; Mori, *Bayle philosophe*.
13. See also Stunkel, 'Montaigne, Bayle, and Hume'.
14. Israel, *Enlightenment Contested*, 264; McKenna, *Études sur Pierre Bayle*.
15. McKenna, *Études sur Pierre Bayle*, 53.
16. Bayle, *Political Writings*, Art. *Spinoza*, 288–338.
17. See Brykman, 'Bayle's Case for Spinoza'.
18. Cited in Sutcliffe, 'Spinoza, Bayle, and the Enlightenment Politics of Philosophical Certainty', 70.
19. Ibid.
20. Bayle, *Dictionnaire*, Art. *Pyrrhon*, remark C.
21. Hochman, 'The Other as Oneself: Mendelssohn, Diogenes, Bayle, and Spinoza'.
22. Popkin, 'The Skeptical Precursors of David Hume'; Mossner, *The Life of David Hume*.
23. Pascal, *Pensées*, section 233.
24. Bartless, 'On the Politics of Faith and Reason'.
25. Bayle, *Pensées sur la comète*, 154.
26. Bayle, *Pensées sur la comète*, vol. I, §103, 280.
27. Ibid. vol. I, §113, 301 to I §122, 320.
28. Ibid. vol. II, §133, 5.
29. Kow, 'Enlightenment Universalism? Bayle and Montesquieu on China'.
30. Bayle, *Pensées sur la comète*, vol. II, §135, 9–10.
31. Ibid. vol. II, §157, 102–3.
32. Ibid. vol. II, §174, 105–14.
33. Ibid. vol. II, §182, 135–8.
34. Rex, *Essays on Pierre Bayle and Religious Controversy*.
35. Bayle, *Wholly Catholic France*, in Laursen, 'Pierre Bayle's *The Condition of Wholly Catholic France Under the Reign of Louis the Great* (1686)'.
36. Bayle, *Wholly Catholic France*, in Laursen, *The Condition of Wholly Catholic France*, 343.
37. Bayle, A *Philosophical Commentary*, 40.
38. Ibid. 64.
39. Ibid. 36.
40. Ibid. 37.
41. Ibid. 66, emphasis in original.
42. Ibid. 68.
43. Ibid. 70.
44. Ibid. 220.

45. Ibid. 227.
46. Ibid. 227; see also Delvolvé, *Religion, critique et philosophie positive chez Pierre Bayle*, 145.
47. On the concept of generality in Bayle, see Riley, 'General and Particular Will in the Political Thought of Pierre Bayle'.
48. Bayle, *A Philosophical Commentary*, 232.
49. Bayle, *Wholly Catholic France*, 327.
50. Ibid. 354.
51. Bayle, *A Philosophical Commentary*, 56–8.
52. Labrousse, *Pierre Bayle*, vol. 2, 521–2.
53. Ibid. 530.
54. Ibid. 533–4.
55. Ibid. 537.
56. Ibid. 540.
57. Mori, *Bayle philosophe*, 50–9.
58. Bayle, *Nouvelles de la République des Lettres*.
59. Box, *The Suasive Art of David Hume*, 150.
60. Emphasis in original. The original French reads: 'En ce sens-là tous les Sçavans se doivent regarder comme freres, ou comme d'aussi bonne maison les uns que les autres. Ils doivent dire, *Nous sommes tous égaux Nous sommes tous parens Comme enfans d'Apollon.*' Bayle, *Nouvelles de la République des Lettres*, 9.
61. Bayle, *A Philosophical Commentary*, 48.
62. Israel, *The Dutch Republic*, 842.
63. Van der Lugt, *Bayle, Jurieu, and the Dictionnaire Historique et Critique*, 119. See also Sandberg, 'Pierre Jurieu's Contribution to Bayle's *Dictionnaire*', 64.
64. Van der Lugt, *Bayle, Jurieu, and the Dictionnaire Historique et Critique*, 130.
65. Ibid. 148.
66. Ibid. 156.
67. Hobbes, *Leviathan*, chapter XIV, 91.
68. Hobbes, *Leviathan*, chapter XVIII, 121.
69. Bayle, *Wholly Catholic France*, 328, 334.
70. Tønder, 'Spinoza and the Theory of Active Tolerance', 698.
71. On the style of this text and its link with Bayle's correspondence, see McKenna, 'La correspondence du jeune Bayle'.
72. Bayle, *Wholly Catholic France*, 353, emphasis in original.
73. Ibid. 353.
74. Mori, 'Pierre Bayle, the Rights of the Conscience, the "Remedy" of Toleration'.
75. Zarka, 'L'idée de critique chez Pierre Bayle'.
76. Bayle, *Dictionnaire*, Art. *Dissertation*, IV, 613, my translation.
77. Ibid. 608, my translation.
78. Mori, *Bayle philosophe*; Israel, *Enlightenment Contested*.

79. Bayle, *Dictionnaire*, Art. *Dissertation* IV, 613, my translation.
80. Ibid. 614, my translation.
81. Bayle, *Dictionnaire*, Art. *Machiavelli*, remark E, 168.
82. Ibid. 169.
83. Bayle, *Dictionnaire*, Art. *De l'hôpital*, 93.
84. Ibid. remark D, 99.
85. Ibid. remark H, 107.
86. Ibid. remark K, 112.

2

Meslier the First Atheist

Few outside the specialised literature have heard of Jean Meslier's contribution to political thought in the Enlightenment. Yet his pivotal role in the radical thought of the period cannot be over-looked, and his particular position as the first self-avowed atheist has dramatic implications for any theory of positive atheism. This chapter will show that Meslier is a radical figure in his own right, putting forward critical and philosophical versions of the radical-ism discussed in the introduction. We can read him, today, not merely as a figure of historical significance, which he no doubt was, but also as a radical philosopher who pushes the boundaries of knowledge and of political agency. The marriage between atheism and a form of radical politics becomes a concrete possibility with Meslier, who does not shy away from the organisational, institu-tional and economic consequences of his thought to put forward a radical theory of republicanism.

In the first instance, this chapter will discuss a brief biographi-cal and intellectual introduction to Meslier the man. This section will prove helpful for interpreting Meslier's works as calls for justice and equity and will provide a grounding for his materialist ontology. In the second instance, Meslier's anti-religious thought will be discussed and shown to be much more radical than it was read later in the eighteenth century, notably by Voltaire. In the third section, we will see that his radicalism evolves into a viru-lent form of atheism, which details the positive contribution that this turn can make. No analysis of Meslier would be complete without his engagement with some of the philosophically radical thinkers of his time – the Cartesians. But in the fourth section, I will show that his Cartesian engagement is tainted by his materialist ontology. Although he never manages to break free from the shackles of Descartes and his followers, Meslier is able to turn the argument on its head, and to provide good arguments for a materialist philosophy after Descartes. Once Meslier has defended his philosophical materialism, we will look at the consequences that this has for ethics more widely in the fifth section. Unsurprisingly, he builds on Bayle's argument in favour of the virtuous atheist but pushes it even further. Whilst many Christians have no doubt been virtuous people, Meslier argues, they have been so despite their religious beliefs. For the maxims of Christ, Meslier puts forward, have had detrimental effects on morality, and a consequentialist, utility-based argument for virtue is a much stronger basis on which to build a new ethics. In the sixth section, I will show that this radical ethical turn pushes Meslier to speculate on the way in which we treat animals. This important parenthesis will illustrate how a form of critical radicalism can push speculation well ahead of its time and begin a debate that we still face today. In the seventh section, I will discuss the political turn that Meslier takes, one where domination by earthly or divine sources creates a nefarious nexus of power. Meslier's critical philosophy will put forward a radical reconceptualisation of power as one that is not passive but active, not reactive but creative. Citizens are encouraged to resist in order to bring about a world with more justice and material equality, a world without God or master. This critical political turn has led many in the secondary literature to label Meslier a communist. In the eighth section of this chapter, I discuss the inadequacy of such a label, alongside the importance of Meslier's radical and positive contribution to political theory. In lieu of this label, I propose one that is much closer to Meslier's own self-understanding in the ninth and final section. There, I propose that we revisit the label of *republican*, understood as an aversion to domination in all its forms. Meslier is a perfect candidate for this new form of radical republicanism, one that is mindful of all forms of domination, whether social, political or economic. Meslier's materialist radical political theory will be rehabilitated and can serve as the basis for further discussions about what radical atheism has contributed to our thinking about political theory.

A Biographical and Intellectual Introduction

Jean Meslier was born in 1664 in the village of Mazerny in the vicinity of Rheims in the Champagne Ardennes. A talented young boy, he learned to read and write and studied Latin at an early age. Driven by his 'love of study', as one posthumous biographer notes,[1] he entered the seminary at Châlons-sur-Marne and eventually became the priest of the parishes of Étrépigny and Balaives, a few miles from his birthplace. He came from a modest family, his father being a merchant, and could just afford the patrimony necessary to enter the service of the Church. This important detail highlights the role that the priesthood played in the *ancien régime* in terms of social promotion. Meslier himself notes that he was led in his youth to the ecclesiastical state to please his parents who sought for him 'a state of life softer, more peaceful and more honourable in the world than that of the common man'.[2] These worldly concerns, as Desné notes,[3] are very far from a theological vocation. Meslier, in addition, prides himself on having fulfilled the *social* aspects of his function. His biographers note that he was considered a charitable man,[4] confirming Meslier's own statement that he had 'taken more pleasure in giving than in receiving [. . . and] had more regard for the poor than for the rich, following the maxim of the Christ'.[5] The scene is set for the radical clash of ideas that was going to take place. Exposed to Christian theology and the philosophy of the Cartesians during his studies, as well as the thought of libertines and freethinkers of the sixteenth and seventeenth centuries, this socially minded man driven into priesthood for worldly concerns mounted one of the most potent attacks on Christianity of the early eighteenth century. Most significantly, he was the first to *claim the label* of atheism and he radicalised anti-religious thought in the Enlightenment.

Very little could have foretold the radical destiny of Meslier. While he lived in a time of religious upheaval with the Jansenist movement challenging the Catholic Church from within, he never joined the movement. His relative proximity to the United

Provinces, and to Reformed territories such as Sedan where Bayle taught when Meslier was a young man, could also have exposed him to unorthodox theologies, but he did not seek conversion. He is not alone in this situation. And there is no evidence that Meslier accepted either the Jansenist or a Reformed critique of the Church. Meslier's critique, as we will see, is much more radical in its rejection of all religions and theologies. Nor is there any historical evidence of particular circumstances in Meslier's life that differ much from others in a similar situation.[6] Only two – rather small – biographical episodes show any deviation from the expectations of his hierarchy. In the first place, he is accused of employing an underage female servant (i.e. younger than fifty years old), although the case is by no means exceptional.[7] Some have speculated about this situation, arguing that it had an impact on Meslier's thought, either positively or negatively.[8] But it is inferring a lot from a couple of lines on an archbishop's report. Only a brief statement by Meslier points to the conclusion that he had tasted the pleasures of the flesh: 'But it is dumb also, in my opinion, to not dare, at least sometimes, because of bigotry or superstition, to taste what it is.'[9] A second episode of Meslier's encounter with the Church hierarchy is more important. It involves a conflict with the local lord, de Toully, with whom disagreements rapidly escalated in 1716. The dispute seems to be rooted in Meslier's criticism of the lord for his unfair treatment of the parishioners, as well as for claiming privileges that his ancestors had not enjoyed. In other words, it is a political contention, based on the gross inequalities of the *ancien régime*. After Meslier preaches against the lord during mass, de Toully complains to the archbishop, who reprimands Meslier. Meslier, instead of retreating, professes against the lord the following Sunday, in his presence:

> Here is the ordinary destiny of poor countryside *curés*. Archbishops, who are the grand lords, despise them and do not listen to them; they only have ears for the nobility. Let us then recommend the lord of this place. We shall pray God for Antoine de Toully so that He converts him and gives him the grace not to mistreat the poor and to dispossess the orphan.[10]

Meslier is punished for this insolence and has to spend a month at the seminary. Yet this episode should not be overestimated. The offence is relatively small, and the punishment fits the crime. After all, five years later Meslier will rescue one of de Toully's servants who was being assaulted outside the church.[11] Meslier did not discriminate in fighting what he perceived as injustice.

Meslier is most famous for his *Memoir* (often labelled his *Testament*), written between 1723 and 1729 and discovered after his death that year. Written on 366 octavo leaves, in Meslier's spare time, it was copied three times by its author, emphasising his attempt to distribute it widely.[12] The book takes the form of eight 'proofs', which can be summarised easily. *First*, every religion is an imposture. Then, the Christian religion is analysed and attacked, particularly its Catholic variant. Meslier attempts to discredit faith in miracles (*second* proof), revelation (*third* proof), prophecies (*fourth* proof) and Christian morals (*fifth* proof). In the *sixth* proof, Meslier turns to the roots of tyranny, and in the *seventh* discusses the existence of God. Finally, the *eighth* proof deals with the nature of the soul.[13] The whereabouts of these texts between Meslier's death in 1729 and 1752 are unknown, but some versions of the text had circulated in the clandestine book networks of Paris since the early 1730s. Voltaire mentions Meslier in his correspondence in 1735,[14] and he famously published an abstract of his works much later, in 1762 and again in 1768. Voltaire's abstract, however, drastically alters Meslier's message: he cuts out any atheist remarks, turning Meslier into a deist, and excludes the political thought, sticking to Meslier's first five proofs.[15] The most radical and original elements of Meslier's thought are removed. But enough copies of the unabridged text circulated in Paris – and the rest of Europe. La Mettrie, Diderot and Holbach clearly had read the text, and Frederick II had a copy of it in Potsdam.[16] In addition to the *Memoir*, Meslier wrote notes on the margins of Fénelon's *Démonstrations de l'existence de Dieu* – a text nicknamed the *Anti-Fénelon* by Desné. It is particularly useful for establishing the limits of Meslier's readings and influences. As Geneviève Moëne notes, Meslier's culture is inherited mostly from French sixteenth- and seventeenth-century authors. He had read Rabelais, Montaigne, Malebranche, Fénelon, Descartes, Richelieu, Naudé, Bayle, La

Bruyère, Marana and La Boétie.[17] He also references a plethora
of ancient authors, but most of these seem to be from secondary
sources – through Montaigne in particular. Despite his relative
isolation in the Champagne countryside, Meslier clearly partakes
in debates of his time – as his engagement with Cartesian philosophy testifies – and develops radical arguments found in Bayle in
particular to entirely new levels.

Meslier's inspiration was firmly grounded in the sixteenth and
seventeenth centuries. In particular, the inheritance of libertines
and freethinkers from that period is apparent in his work, and
the significance of those thinkers merits an introduction. Often
taken for a synonym of atheism, the term 'libertine' is often attributed to thinkers by their opponents or adversaries. Many thinkers
could fall within this historiographic category, including Thomas
Hobbes, La Mothe Le Vayer, Cyrano de Bergerac, Gassendi,
Naudé, or the anonymously published text *Theophrastus redivivus*.[18]
What characterises their works and their common description as
libertine texts, despite all their differences, is a critique of religion,
notably by using ancient pagan sources to launch barely veiled
attacks on Christianity. But *libertinage*, as a word, also denotes the
quest for pleasures in all areas of life, from gambling to food and
drink and, of course, erotic pursuits. Importantly, libertines are
typically described as those who do not seek to provide a critique
of Christianity in order to improve it, but dismiss debates about
the 'true' religion.[19] Vanini appears here as the most accomplished
of these libertine freethinkers – and one whom Meslier knew, at
least through Bayle's descriptions. The Italian doctor, born at
the end of the sixteenth century, was writing his *De admirandis
naturae arcanis* in 1616, before being burnt at the stake in 1619.
This piece of writing, quickly banned by the Church, proposed a
rationalist reading of natural phenomena, going so far as to suggest
that humans might derive from monkeys – perhaps the first formulation of the theory of evolution.[20] Finishing the book on historical considerations, Vanini concludes that religions have emerged
to formalise systems of domination, and supports Machiavelli's
theory of imposture: religion really only benefits the two dominant
social classes: princes and priests. Vanini had the genius to sum-
marise the past century of Italian irreligious thought for the wider

public, creating an earthquake in French intellectual circles that cost him his life. Meslier will, a century after Vanini, still have to draw consequences from the movement of libertines the latter so marvellously epitomised.

Anti-Religious Thought

Meslier's anti-religious thought was widely known in the eighteenth century. Voltaire, despite his drastic editorial judgements, did have the merit of popularising the first five proofs of the curé's work. Meslier's arguments against religion are diverse and varied but can be categorised easily. There are *hermeneutic* arguments based on a close reading of the Bible, and *logical* arguments based on inconsistency with the Bible or between the Bible and the subsequent Christian traditions. Broadly speaking, these arguments can be seen to aim at introducing doubt and scepticism in the reader's mind. If there are inconsistencies in the holy texts and in doctrine, its claims to perfection grow thinner, and Meslier's attempt at persuasion has to be put in his Catholic context. The arguments also aim to place Christianity on a par with other religions. If one is dismissive of most religious traditions practised in the world, what evidence is there to sustain such a dismissal? Or better still, why not reject *all* religions if none of them have sufficient proofs in their favour? Alongside these arguments is an attempt to *historicise* Christianity. The historical method, inherited from Bayle, contextualises Christianity, showing that it shares more than it admits with prior religions and is relatively insignificant given the vast differences in religious beliefs throughout the ages.[21] And the history of Christianity is not more accommodating of claims to divine inspiration, as Meslier notes the late decision on which constitute the holy texts (at the council of Carthage in 397 CE).[22] The selection of the holy texts being contingent on human decision helps to cast doubt on the claims of the Church. Taken together, these types of argument pose important questions for Meslier. Why do we still follow Christian teaching if they can no longer sustain a claim to universal truth? Why not get inspired by other traditions since Christianity is just as contingent? At the very least, Christianity and religious teaching in general are on a par with other attempts to understand the world, including non-religious philosophies. These arguments taken together thus constitute a call for a more radical form of pluralism in our inspirations, an openness to diverse traditions and philosophies, and a challenge to the universalist message of Christian churches.

Alongside these hermeneutic, logical and historical arguments in Meslier's proofs, there are a plethora of *political* arguments. These further radicalise the contextualisation of the previously mentioned arguments. Essentially, Meslier's claim is that religious belief, and Christian belief in particular, has a negative effect on politics. From the very beginning of his *Memoir* Meslier is adamant that religion and politics are intimately intertwined. How else could one explain the survival of false beliefs throughout the ages? It is in the alliance between the political rulers and the priests – who have a vested interest in maintaining their privileged positions – that Meslier perceives the origin and continuation of religion. Pagan religions as well as the monotheistic ones exhibit signs of these kleptocratic tendencies. There has been, and still is, for Meslier, a conspiracy of prince and priest. One of his most notorious sentences, which was taken up by Diderot much later in his poem *Les Eleuthéromanes*,[23] is worth quoting:

> I remember the wish of a man a while back who had no culture or education, but who, to all appearances, did not lack the common sense to pass sound judgments on all these detestable abuses and tyrannies. [. . .] His wish was that all the rulers of the earth and all the nobles be hanged and strangled with the guts of priests.[24]

This collusion of rulers and priests is blameworthy, but not exactly in the manner advocated by this man of no culture or education. For Meslier would prefer to 'have the arm, strength, courage, and body of Hercules to purge the world of all vices and iniquities'.[25] It is the gross inequalities that are being attacked here. Israel's thesis of the *Radical Enlightenment*, that it is essentially a political message that emanates from this current, fits Meslier's concerns very well here. A benign religion without negative political consequences, in other words, would not have attracted his wrath. It is even more troubling that religions, which should have offered relief from the abuses of political power and stood up for the people against tyrants, have so often collaborated with their abuses.

Meslier's strongest critique of religion is surely his *moral reversal* of Christianity. As we have seen, the critical issue at the turn of the seventeenth century was whether atheists could be trusted to be moral persons, or indeed whether they could be trusted at all. Bayle had already challenged this conception, by showing that belief (or lack thereof) in an afterlife had little to do with moral behaviour. Meslier accepts this argument, as he was keen to use Bayle's insight to his advantage. The unorthodox believer, or the atheist, is perfectly capable of moral behaviour founded in social utility. But Meslier does not stop there and pushes the argument much further than Bayle had. If it is true that the atheist is immune to arguments in favour of ethical behaviour founded in an afterlife, Meslier argues, it is also true that religion has provided many sectarian arguments in favour of persecution of unorthodox thinkers, heretics, believers of other religions, and atheists. Against the potential benefits for morals of believing in an afterlife, Meslier retorts that religious beliefs have provided many detrimental effects in the here and now. The question of the possibility of a virtuous atheist is thus turned on its head by Meslier: is it possible to have a virtuous believer? The answer, for Meslier, is clearly positive. Many believers have also been virtuous people, and there is little doubt that those who are immune to the most doctrinal and superstitious elements of religious belief are capable of promoting social virtue. But religious belief has the potential for danger, especially when education is monopolised by priests. The central reversal, from Bayle's thought to Meslier's, is on the role that *faith* plays. For Bayle, faith in the Scriptures had been a fallback position in the face of uncertainty raised by scepticism. For Meslier, however, faith is 'blind belief' and justifies moral discrimination from those of a different faith. In the first instance, it leads to ignorance through refusal to engage with facts that contradict one's faith; and in the second it leads to sectarian attitudes. Since Meslier rests his morals on social utility, faith has little to contribute. It keeps one in ignorance rather than enlightens, and it divides rather than unites. Reason is a much better guide, and is for Meslier the best guide for moral behaviour.[26] And what reason teaches us, Meslier further claims in order to put a final nail in the coffin of Christian morals, is that even if we were to return to the maxim of Christ, purified from the negative influence of his followers and the Church, we would not find a moral doctrine in line with social utility. Christianity in its purest form, which blesses the poor and the persecuted, idealises suffering whilst it denies the pleasures of this world. This goes against the utilitarian arguments that are underlying Meslier's ethical reasoning: pleasures should not be avoided when they create no subsequent pain. Christianity has a superstitious attitude towards the pleasures of the flesh, once again contradicting Meslier's underlying utilitarian thought. Lastly, even the maxim to love one's enemies, for Meslier, is against rational morals. Not resisting evil leads to passivity, idleness and uselessness. It leads to injustice, and no society would survive without some sense that justice is being rendered. These three critiques of the purest forms of Christianity, based on its cultivation of suffering, aversion for sexual pleasures, and inversion of justice, illustrate the radical critique of the Christian religion that Meslier had proposed. And many of these arguments, though certainly not all, were accepted by his readers throughout the eighteenth century, including many who were critical of his conclusion: that there is no God.

Self-Avowed Atheism

Meslier's atheism was so radical that Voltaire felt compelled to hide it when he published his *Extrait* of Meslier's works. Purged of the 'poison of atheism',[27] the curé's work could thus be used by Voltaire in his struggle against *l'infâme*. This injustice needs to be remedied and Meslier's anti-religious thought read in the light of a positive doctrine of atheism. The portrayal of atheism as a parasitic doctrine, as Michael Buckley's thesis goes,[28] is unconvincing as it does not take the arguments of self-avowed atheists seriously enough. One needs to read past the negation of belief in God in order to understand atheistic claims.

Meslier's negation of religious belief can best be summarised by his use of two neologisms: *christicoles* and *déicoles* – and their fusion into the word *déichristicoles*. The first term (*christicoles*) refers to the 'adorers of Christ', from the Latin – a term used by non-Christians to pejoratively refer to them. *Déicole*, on the other hand, is usually a positive term, and is a synonym of *theist*. It is not a term imposed by one's adversaries, but a term claimed by those who render a cult to God.[29] For Meslier, however, this use is turned around, no longer signifying the cult of the *correct* God, but every cult of a god or goddess, including pagan cults rejected by Christianity. The Christ-cultists and God-cultists, as Michael Shreve translates the terms,[30] are fused into the *déichristicoles*, the GodChrist-cultists,[31] those who adore Christ as their God. Meslier is already far from being a theist, but similar critiques could have been put forward by either a sceptic, a deist or a pantheist.

Meslier's subtitle for his *Memoir* is clear: he seeks to show 'Clear and Evident Proofs of the Vanity and Falsity of All the Divinities and of All the Religions of the World'.[32] He knows full well that he will be called an atheist but claims that 'it will not bother me in the least'.[33] This is significant given the seriousness of the accusation in his day, in particular what happened to Vanini, that 'famous atheist', as Meslier notes,[34] tortured and burnt at the stake in Toulouse – despite his repudiation of atheism and his embrace of a form of pantheism. Furthermore, Meslier rejects the accusation of impiety that he associates with bad morals, while he embraces the atheistic position. Meslier's seventh proof clearly and unambiguously states his atheism: 'there is no such being, i.e., *there is no God*'.[35] The statement is reiterated throughout the seventh, eighth and ninth proofs, as well as in the *Anti-Fénelon*. When it comes to other thinkers, Meslier's list of unorthodox religious believers is too vague to be of much help for defining atheism. He cites Socrates, Aristotle, Plato, Diagoras, Pythagoras, Vanini, Theodorus, Jozias, Aetius, Averroës, Pline, Tribonian, Lucian, Rabelais, Spinoza, the popes Julius III and Leo X, as well as Philippe, duke of Orleans and Regent of France until 1723. Meslier, in other words, is unaware of his own originality. He does not know that he is formulating, for the first time, a theory of self-avowed atheism that none of these thinkers had developed themselves.

One needs to piece together the allusions to atheists in Meslier and the differences between that position and other unorthodox religious beliefs. Both atheists and god-cultists agree, he says, that there is infinity. However, they disagree on what that infinity is. '[T]he god-cultists call it "God" and that atheists call it "Nature" or "material being" or simply "matter."'[36] Meslier's atheism is thus a materialist doctrine, where matter possesses movement within itself and no longer needs to receive it from an immaterial being. The debate, as I will show next, is about the possibility of moving, but also of *thinking* matter. His contrast with the theist position is clear, but so is a contrast with a deist position. Matter does not need a prime mover, an intelligent architect or designer. It moves itself and is capable, on its own, of producing thought.

So much for the materialist doctrine – it still remains to be seen what is *atheistic* about Meslier's thought. There are three categories of 'deniers' or 'doubters' of the existence of God, according to Meslier. There are (1) those who have never known divinities, (2) those who have called them into question, and (3) those who have denied them completely.[37] Simplifying, we could call them (1) primitive atheists, (2) sceptics (one is tempted to use the anachronism 'agnostics'), and (3) complete atheists (paraphrasing the accusation brought against Socrates at his trial – τό παράπαν άθεος). Meslier's categorisation is indeed an expression, *avant la lettre*, of a complex typology of religious unbelief.

Yet the above arguments are compatible with a pantheistic position à la Spinoza. One needs to go into the *Anti-Fénelon* to find the clearest contrast between Meslier and this position. Meslier's critique of Fénelon establishes that the pantheist position cannot be so easily dismissed. For if God exists without being anything in particular, as Fénelon claims, Meslier says that 'it must be either everything that is, or nothing at all'.[38] To rephrase this in terms that are not his: the God hypothesis can be answered in one of two ways – either the pantheist answer (everything is God) or the atheist answer (God is nothing). A few pages later, Meslier writes that atheism 'is certain'[39] and dismisses conceptions of infinity and substance that seek to define matter as perfect.[40] The pantheist alternative is dismissed. But it is done against a Cartesian philosopher's critique of Spinoza. Meslier, it seems, had never read the famous radical Dutch philosopher directly, and his defence of atheism contra Spinoza remains unconvincing because of this.

Meslier's reading of Cartesian philosophers has led some commentators to label him an 'extreme-left Malebranchist'.[41] In many ways, Meslier remains indebted to Cartesian philosophy. He lacks the conceptual tools to free himself from clear and distinct ideas, for example, or from speculation about how matter moves in 'whirlwind' motions. What is most relevant here is to look at the differences between Meslier and Cartesians. The main difference remains that Meslier is a materialist and an atheist – and his critiques of Descartes, Fénelon and Malebranche are focused on those two aspects.

As Deprun notes, Meslier remains indebted to the system of Descartes. It is, however, quite clear that although Meslier had had access to Descartes' work at the seminary, he no longer had the text with him when he was writing the Mémoire, and that his sources during that time were the works of Malebranche and Fénelon.[42] Despite his criticism of them, Cartesians remain 'the most sensible among déicole philosophers'[43] for Meslier and there are numerous areas where he accepts the Cartesian method and philosophy. But he never does so uncritically. He accepts the conclusion that one can demonstrate the existence of a being of which we have a clear and distinct idea but refuses that this applies to God.[44] He accepts that clear and distinct ideas can make us demonstrate a triple infinity – spatial, temporal and numerical infinities[45] – but he refuses to accept that infinity proves anything beyond infinite matter. Meslier turns Cartesianism against itself, refusing to accept its dualism in favour of a purely material explanation – a materialist ontology, unambiguously claimed and defended.

One passage best illustrates the indebtedness that Meslier can never free himself from when it comes to Cartesian philosophy. Clear and distinct ideas, Meslier concedes, are independent from material reality:

> We can even say that truth, generally speaking, is so independent of everything we can think or imagine that although there be no body or mind, no form or matter, no creator or creature,

even no thing in the world, there would still at least be a truth because in this case, it would be true that there was nothing.[46]

The ambiguity that this poses for the materialist philosopher is clear: he needs to concede that we have clear and distinct ideas of truth, even if that truth would be a lack of matter. Later materialist philosophers, building on a sensualist philosophy, will sidestep this issue, but Meslier, with strong links to Cartesian method, is unable to provide a thorough critique of this conception of truth.

What Meslier manages to do, in contradiction to Cartesian philosophy, is to argue convincingly (from within the bounds of his natural philosophy) that matter is not created, but that it has existed forever. Against Descartes' cogito, which seeks to explain existence from thought, Meslier formulates his own cogito. Our thoughts, he argues, are mere modifications of matter. They cannot prove the existence of the world around us, but various ways of being, on the other hand, show that matter *can* think.[47] Various modifications of matter, in particular animals, show that they have sensations, and most importantly feel pleasure and pain. Against 'gentlemen Cartesians' who speculate that animals have no soul and thus feel nothing, Meslier opposes the wisdom of peasants who understand that other material beings are just as capable of feeling. We no longer have the 'I think therefore I am' of Descartes, but the 'I am therefore I think' of Meslier – and animals are the key to understanding our relation to being in general. The Cartesian heritage is thinner already.

Meslier did not have access to Spinoza's work, but it is clear that he had read Bayle, whom he quotes numerous times. It is likely that he had read in Bayle the defence of the virtuous atheist. Certainly, Bayle meant something quite different when he spoke of atheism. As Jonathan Israel shows, Bayle 'defines "atheism" to mean denial of divine Providence and reward and punishment in the hereafter'.[48] We are far from the *complete atheism* of Meslier! But Bayle had argued that atheists can be virtuous, just as much as Christians can be vicious. Bayle argues that the field of moral worth is independent of that of belief, an argument that Meslier accepts and develops. Although he is happy to accept the label of the 'atheist', Meslier is not content be called 'impious' (*impie*).

The latter label, for him, signifies the iniquities and injustices inflicted by one person on another. Whereas atheism is based on a materialist concept of being which includes a natural moral duty to take into account the pleasure and pain of others (certainly an early utilitarian doctrine), the impious is the one that treats others unjustly. The divorce between these terms follows the distinction made by Bayle. The virtuous atheist is no longer a theoretical possibility, he is materialised in the figure of Jean Meslier himself, who sought to rid the world of some of the injustices he perceived.

A Proto-Utilitarian Ethic

Meslier's radical thought is dominated by an attack on the inequalities between the different États of the ancien régime. The alliance between nobles and priests reflects the domination of the populace by a powerful minority in his time. Meslier's thought is certainly grounded in an appeal to equality but phrased in terms of justice and utility. It is the injustice arising from the gross inequalities that anger the curé, and in particular when the least useful of society seem to benefit the most. References to utility are rampant throughout the Memoir, and best illustrated by two sections of the sixth proof. Sections 44 and 45 have unfortunately been lost somewhat in translation. Whilst the French text is clearly proto-utilitarian, using variations of utility thirteen times in three pages; the English translation's use of variations of the word 'useful' loses that theoretical edge.[49] In section 44, it is the rich and the privileged that attract Meslier's wrath. There are those who 'trample, pillage, and oppress the people', whether they are noble themselves or accomplices to the rule of the nobility, who live from their rents and annual incomes; and there are those who are of no utility (d'aucune utilité): 'they must necessarily be a public burden since they only live off the work of others' and must be 'severely punished'.[50] For one's utility to fellow citizens is clearly the criterion, for Meslier, of justice. Section 45 makes this abundantly clear. Bishops, priests and vicars are useless in their theological functions, but they have a clear utility when it comes to teaching the moral virtues. If only they were to give up their useless functions, they could focus on their role as moral educators. There is hope for the utility of the clergy, in Meslier's thought. There is a role for them in a just republic but their role will be significantly redefined. Since all must share equally in various types of work, and since there is utility in work of the body and mind (*utile travail du corp ou de l'esprit*), a certain *spiritual* dimension – albeit understood within Meslier's materialist framework – is not excluded.[51] Utility is central, but not yet understood in terms of a utilitarian calculus of various actions, as it includes the works of the body and *esprit* that are beneficial to the social. Whilst Meslier's utilitarian arguments remain relatively undeveloped, they do occupy a central place in his conception of justice, and his insistence on the utility of social work has been instrumental in his reception in the twentieth century by communist authors, as we will see.

What this proto-utilitarian grounding for ethics does is to continue in the line of argument that Meslier had found in Bayle. Morality is not based on one's beliefs, creed or lack thereof. Morality is based on tangible virtues in human beings. All human beings, whether they are Christians, Muslims, Jews or atheists, are thus capable of virtuous behaviour. Utility is a means to ground a conception of morality in a principle even more tangible, as it is at least observable through the medium of work. And the model is as radical as it gets in the *ancien régime*, a social structure still based on aristocratic principles of inheritance. While Meslier may fail to convince the reader that utility provides the sure foundation for morality he thought he had found, it does propose an egalitarian means of promoting social justice.

The Materiality of Animals

A parenthesis on Meslier's defence of animal rights further illustrates the radical nature of his thought. There is a material equality between men and animals, for Meslier, in that animals are composed of the same bodily organs as us, meaning that 'all animals are capable of knowledge and feeling like us'.[52] If equality between human beings is based on similar capacities and material needs, as we saw above, then there is no good reason to exclude animals from some form of basic equality. It is as a direct consequence of his materialist ontology that Meslier comes to this conclusion. Since matter is capable of moving itself and is capable of thought through particular modifications located in the brain, it is clear that animals with brains are capable of thought. The Cartesians, who deny animal knowledge, but also the capacity for sensation (pleasure and pain), 'are obviously ridiculous'[53] to Meslier. Animals are not the 'pure machines'[54] of Cartesians, since they are capable of sentiments and knowledge, and since they possess a language, are capable of sociability, love, hatred, happiness, fear, and so forth. Instead of our 'feelings of gentleness, kindness, compassion' towards animals, such philosophical speculation justifies the most vicious of behaviours against our animal companions.[55] Railing against the practice of cat-burning, still practised in his time, Meslier attacks these 'brutal, cruel, and detestable' pleasures.[56] Such cruelty against animals leads to vices in those that perform and witness the cruelty against living beings, and as such it enters Meslier's moral critique. Meslier phrases it in terms of injustice and is clear that his criteria for justice (natural equity, personal merit, and punishment of injustice) apply in this case. It is because of our equal capacity to feel pleasure and pain, and because animals are often useful to our life and work, that any injustice against them should be punished: 'cursed be the nations who treat them cruelly, who tyrannize them, who love to spill their blood and who are hungry for their flesh'.[57] Although not a vegetarian himself, Meslier clearly defends the position here. The only reason he gives for not being one himself is that he is not 'superstitious or inclined to the bigotry of religion', otherwise he 'would have surely joined the party of those who make it a religion to never kill innocent beasts and never eat their flesh'.[58] The deontological interdiction is too strong for the consequentialist thinker: surely there are times when eating animal flesh satisfies his criteria of justice. Nonetheless, he clarifies that he had 'never done anything with so much repugnance' as to have an animal killed for his food.[59]

Ni Dieu ni maître

In many ways, Meslier's political thought is an extension of his anti-religious, materialist and atheist philosophy. Meslier struggles to establish clear lines of difference between his critique of religion and politics, and he generalises tremendously. There is a little more subtlety when it comes to the role of the priesthood, as we have just seen, whose members may be salvaged because of their social utility. When it comes to political rulers, Meslier's anti-monarchical thought is (almost) unequivocal. The tyrants of the earth are his targets, accompanied by their legions of servants. Most importantly, it seems that Meslier has inherited La Boétie's critique. The latter's famous *Discourse of Voluntary Servitude* finds echoes in Meslier's work. La Boétie had argued that 'it is the people who enslave themselves, who cut their own throat. Having the choice between being a subject and being free, it leaves its freedom to accept the yoke'.[60] As for Meslier, he repeats this argument by saying that 'It is only from the people (whom they care so little about) that they get all their grandeur, riches, and power. In a word, they would be nothing but weak, little men like you if you did not support their grandeur.'[61] The kings, or rather the tyrants that rule over people, are the summit of this pyramid of injustice in Meslier's thought, providing little utility to their citizens. The injustice of this stratified social structure bears close resemblance to the model of a tyrannical, all-powerful God promoted by the alliance between priests and princes. Believing in an all-powerful God, for Meslier, is the first step towards accepting tyrannical rule. It is, for him, a logical consequence of his materialism and atheism that there should be a more equal set of social relations, since the current order is based on a false hypothesis of absolute rule – by God or the king. Meslier even goes so far as to promote tyrannicide. He particularly praises this practice of the ancients as an act of courage and devotion to the common good. Against the cowardice of his contemporaries, who merely suffer injustices rather than resist them, according to the maxim of Christ, he advocates for a return to more spirited acts of resistance. Meslier does not hesitate to place Ravaillac, murderer of Henri IV and perceived as a religious fanatic even in Meslier's time, among those who have freed peoples of the earth from tyrannical dominations. Meslier's preaching style is apparent here, as in so many other places in the *Memoir*, but the message is clear. The injustice of tyrants needs to be resisted, by whatever means possible. He is even willing to put aside religious differences to support those who act for social utility. And killing the tyrant does not suffice. It is widespread revolution that is being advocated by Meslier. Domination needs to be overthrown, by violent means if necessary. The *Memoir's* conclusion is crystal clear on this:

> Work to unite all of you, as many as you are, you and your fellow men, to completely shake off the yoke of the tyrannical domination of your kings and princes. Overthrow the thrones of injustice and impiety everywhere! Break all the crowned heads![62]

One does not get much more radical than that.

As such, fears by anti-atheist polemicists have come to materialise themselves. It turns out that challenging the existence of God does lead (at least in Meslier) to a threat to political authority – including the threat of death and revolution. Of course, this is not necessarily the case, as others will either develop apolitical consequences of their disbelief – such as La Mettrie – or have much milder political consequences in mind – such as Holbach. But for Meslier the complete and utter revolution of social structures is a direct consequence of his atheism. Once one has broken the Divine hierarchy, one breaks the Church's hierarchy and political domination to create a free and equal society based on shared work aimed at common utility.

It is of little wonder, thus, that Meslier has been co-opted by many communist authors; or that he was accused of communism by others. Maurice Dommanget is the clearest defender of this hypothesis. Himself a French syndicalist and author of many books on revolutionary figures, his interest in Meslier's radical political thought is no surprise. The subtitle of his book, 'athée, communiste et révolutionnaire sous Louis XIV', points out the radical nature of his thought.[63] Of course, one needs to be very careful of anachronism, and the label 'communist' is not easily applied to the curé. What does Dommanget point out about Meslier's atheism? Dommanget claims that Meslier's atheism is only secondary to his communism, as the social critique takes precedence over the theological and philosophical concerns.

Meslier, for Dommanget, is no less than a precursor to Marx and Engels' *Communist Manifesto*.[64] He has invented the theory of the general strike.[65] Meslier is 'an ancestor of revolutionary socialism and of communism',[66] his *Memoir* is a socialist and revolutionary programme,[67] Meslier formulates a communist theory with the village or the parish at its centre, and Meslier caries the flag of ideological communism.[68] Dommanget's own analysis, though, finds some contradictions between Meslier's political thought and Marx's. In particular, Meslier's socialism is not yet 'scientific' but no longer 'utopian',[69] Meslier – unlike Marx – is concerned with the agrarian class;[70] he defends a role for the priesthood;[71] and he nowhere addresses the problems of equality of women or of 'people of colour'.[72] Dommanget, in other words, is at pains to reconcile his own bias with the works of Meslier and cannot conceive of way of thinking about Meslier outside of his own political inclinations.

But the label of Meslier as a communist stuck, as it is used by most commentators since. Jean Deprun, Roland Desné and Albert Soboul, the three editors of Meslier's complete works, defend a similar thesis. A little more nuanced than Dommanget, they see Meslier's communism as 'cosubstantial with his atheism',[73] and thus no longer primary. But it is not less teleological in their analysis, as it 'the perspective is already open which, linking communism with materialism, will end up with Marx'.[74] Luciano Verona continues with this thesis, changing the terminology only slightly to call Meslier a 'revolutionary socialist'.[75] He had 'revolutionary clairvoyance', and many of the passages of the *Memoir* 'presage Karl Marx'.[76] More recently, Geneviève Moëne, Alain Sandrier, Michel Onfray, Miguel Benítez and Serge Deruette have taken up this label, with only minor qualifications. For Moëne it is a 'rural communism',[77] for Sandrier a 'violent communism',[78] for Deruette 'the first atheist communist',[79] for Benítez he is a communist who 'universalises work',[80] for Vaneigem he possessed a 'real attachment to the revolutionary origins of Christianity',[81] and for Onfray he is a 'political communalist'.[82] There are good reasons why this anachronism has survived in the literature.

I have already noted that it is Meslier's universalisation of work that has been instrumental in his reception in the twentieth century. The sixth proof, discussing the roots of tyranny, provides a

list of 'abuses' that the Christian religion tolerates. The first abuse
sets the ground for the uncompromising theory of equality that
Meslier purports:

> All men are equal by nature; they all hold equally the right to
> live and to walk upon the earth, the right to enjoy their nat-
> ural liberty and to share in the goods of the land, with every-
> one working usefully to have the things that are necessary and
> useful in life.[83]

Meslier qualifies this uncompromising equality – as I will later
show – but it nonetheless serves as a basis for the entire sixth
proof – if not the *Memoir* as a whole. The first abuse, then, is
that Christianity has allowed for a 'huge disproportion' between
persons – some born to be masters, some to be slaves. Meslier's
alternative is clear: natural equality and liberty are incompatible with the existing inequalities of the *ancien régime*, and with
any other kind of pronounced inegalitarian social structure. Once
again, it is the nobility and the clergy that bear the brunt of the
social critique. The hierarchical structure justified under aristocratic principles is critiqued for its vicious genealogy; 'a criminal
and fateful birth and source'.[84] And the Christian religion is not
only passively culpable, for Meslier, but actively promotes similar
principles among its own ranks. The monastic orders are pointed
out as the culmination of this ethic of uselessness (*inutilité*), as
highlighted above, which Meslier so forcefully disapproves of. The
hypocrisy of the monastic orders is all the more shocking, as they
collectively possess great wealth despite their individual vows of
poverty. Such practices, tolerated and actively promoted by the
Catholic Church, lead to great inequalities, which for Meslier are
so contrary to natural justice. A just society cannot emerge when
these social classes (the 'disproportion of the state and conditions
of men'[85]) persist. Justice can only be achieved when all work
together towards the common good, not when some are exempt
from this requirement by appeals to ancient or spiritual privileges.

It is in the third abuse of the sixth proof that one finds another
argument in favour of Meslier's early 'communism'. It is a thorough critique of the 'individual appropriation that men make of

the goods and riches of the land, instead of, as they should, possessing them in common'.[86] This critique of private ownership of land – the primary means of production in Meslier's time – clearly possesses radical potential. The organisation of such an economic system is even spelled out, if only in schematic terms. Men and women will unite, Meslier says, according to territorial units of proximity ('a city, town, village, or parish and community'[87]) where they will all regard one another as 'brothers and sisters' and conclude alliances with neighbouring communities. This, Meslier speculates, will allow them to have 'the same or similar food and being all equally well clothed, well housed, well bedded, and well heated, and applying themselves also equally to the labor, i.e., to the work or to some honest and useful job'.[88] This ideal of small, autonomous communities collaborating with one another where shared work forms the principle of the association and material well-being the ultimate goal is indeed not far removed from a form of early communism. The models Meslier has in mind are – ironically – the form of the early communities of Christians, or the organisation promoted in monastic orders.[89] Meslier interprets the 'communion of saints' to mean the common ownership of goods among these early Christians, but the model has been corrupted and largely destroyed. Even its monastic incarnation renders monks unhappy because of its attitude to the pleasures of the flesh. The Christian communities may point the way to the possibilities of common ownership, but they are not a model worth following. But the 'people', Meslier claims, could do better than the monks. They could build 'solid houses to live in comfortably with their flocks', 'construct pleasant, useful gardens and orchards', 'carefully cultivate the land', and 'obtain everywhere an abundance of all goods'.[90] The agrarian ideal of common ownership is the only one that Meslier can conceive of – unsurprisingly, given his particular context.

What this critique of private property and defence of common ownership point out, as many commentators show, is Meslier's materialist philosophy. Meslier's materialist conception of nature – with matter being capable of moving itself and of thought, has direct consequences for his political thought. It is, after all, the material conditions of the people that Meslier was worried about.

Feeding, housing, heating and working conditions are explicitly mentioned. It follows that if matter is capable of thought, it certainly needs particular material conditions to do so. Without access to these basic goods, human beings are not capable of personal development. Since the political conditions of the *ancien régime* tolerate and promote inequalities that prevent many people from having these basic goods, the regime no longer fulfils the conditions of the materialist philosophy of Meslier.

Given this unjust political order, resistance is justified. Tyrannicide is not excluded, as we have seen, but resistance is much wider than this single act of political violence. Deruette, following Dommanget, hypothesises that Meslier is the first to come up with a 'theory of the general strike as a revolutionary weapon'.[91] This is certainly an overstatement, as Meslier takes his cue from La Boétie here, but Meslier does theorise the link between the work of the people and the power of their masters. 'For, it is only from the fruit of your hard work that all these people live.'[92] Power is conceptualised much more subtly in this sixth proof than it had been earlier in the *Memoir*. The so-called power of the greatest princes is entirely dependent on the work of the people: 'they would not have more power or authority than you if you did not want to submit to their laws and will'.[93] Combined with the concluding thoughts of the *Memoir*, where Meslier shames those who 'cowardly submit themselves to unjust laws',[94] the revolutionary potential of his thought is complete. La Boétie's *Discourse of Voluntary Servitude* had made the argument that it is the people themselves who are responsible for their own misery, since they so easily submit to the will of their masters, and take for natural a condition that is only social.[95]

Meslier is a revolutionary thinker. He wants to change the world, not through a return to a golden age where social relations were just, but through a new mode of association. And this revolution will necessitate, for him, the replacing of private property with common ownership of land – the primary means of production. But there are internal problems to the secondary literature's reading of Meslier as a communist thinker. Besides being anachronistic, the label is not easily applied to some of Meslier's thought. Dommanget's, as we have seen, is at pains to reconcile his own bias with the works of Meslier. Onfray provides another challenge to the interpretation of Meslier as a communist by applying the label of 'anarchist' to him.[96] After all, the above description of Meslier's political thought can be equally valid under the two labels – if one is unafraid of applying one, why not the other? Once again, however, the new label reflects the prejudice of the author writing on Meslier (Onfray is a self-described anarchist), rather than Meslier's own.

Radical Republicanism

There is a way out of this anachronistic impasse, however. One can apply Meslier's praise for *republics* to his political thought and show him as a radical republican. This will imply a double movement, though. In the first instance, it is useful to resituate Meslier in the context of republicanism understood as freedom from domination. In the second instance, however, it is also help-ful to move past this debate, and illustrate how Meslier's concern for the common thing (the *res publica*) moves him further to the left of other republican ideals.

In the first instance, one must turn away from the notion of democracy advocated by Israel as a feature of the radical Enlightenment, to turn to the notion of republicanism, par-ticularly well articulated by Philip Pettit, Quentin Skinner and Michael Sandel. For Pettit, republican freedom is defined by its insistence on freedom as non-domination, with the modern form of republicanism having its roots in eighteenth-century France. Domination, Pettit specifies, is 'exemplified by the relationship of master to slave or master to servant', when 'the dominating party can interfere on an arbitrary basis with the choices of the domi-nated'.[97] This conception of freedom is opposed to the notion of freedom as non-interference, for interference can occur without any real loss of freedom for republicans, with the most practical example of this distinction being rule under good laws, where interference is common but freedom is preserved and enhanced. Skinner further characterises the neo-Roman theory of republi-canism as a worthy alternative to liberalism – a sadly forgotten alternative given its historical weight. What the republicans bring to the table, for Skinner, is the insistence that monarchical power, even in its benevolent forms, is detrimental to a good politics. This is because the mere fact of living under the will of another is akin to servitude, as it induces a situation of dependence.[98] Sandel, finally, adds an economic dimension to the republican critique of dependence.[99] Though his analysis remains largely focused on later debates about the dependence inherent in wage labour, the larger republican point about economic dependency applies.

Meslier's radical political thought does promote a certain conception of a just republic, over and above the arguments discussed above. If Meslier is highly critical of the wide inequalities of the *ancien régime*, he is not against all forms of interference. Just after having declared the fundamental equality of all men cited above, Meslier adds:

> But since they live in society and since a society or community of men cannot be ruled well or maintained in good order without some kind of dependence and subordination between them, it is absolutely necessary for the good of human society that there be some kind of dependence and subordination among them.[100]

This subordination, Meslier continues, 'should be just and well proportioned',[101] even though its precise terms are never fully discussed by him. In his conclusion, Meslier adds that his contemporaries will only be happy when delivered from tyranny and superstition, and 'governed only by good and wise magistrates'.[102] There are some who deserve to rule over others, as magistrates, based upon their personal merit and virtue. It is, Meslier further states, those with an even better knowledge of injustices than he has who should be entrusted with the ruling of such a republic.[103] Although Meslier rejects tyrannical forms of domination, he does not fully exclude social hierarchy, the need for rulers, or laws. While the institutional discussion of these changes is inexistent, the message is clear: political power has only one basis, and that is to contribute to the preservation of a sense of justice in the republic.

In the absence of Divine justice, Meslier attempted to find

grounds for earthly justice. His conception of justice can be broken down into three parts: natural equity, personal merit, and punishment of injustice. Of these three, the topic of natural equity has already been discussed above and is the basis of his critique of the social classes of his time, as well as his defence of the equal sharing of work by all. Meslier had vehemently protested against miracles in the second proof on the ground that it favours certain peoples over others. These 'exceptions of peoples' are rejected by Meslier on the ground that they would be fundamentally unjust, since they apply with complete disregard for personal merit, judging entire peoples simultaneously.[104] Any sense of justice needs to incorporate this sense of merit, in order to promote virtue and deter vice. It is the worldly concerns of a moral education that drive Meslier to this conclusion. The same reason that had led him to defend a role for the clergy in terms of moral and spiritual education of the populace leads him to formulate a general theory of justice. Since we cannot expect this justice to come on its own, it needs to be enacted by the judges and magistrates of the republic. These magistrates, 'who were established to suppress vices, to maintain justice and good order everywhere, and to severely punish the guilty and wicked, do not dare to do anything about the vices and injustices of kings'.[105] It is the ability to hold those in power accountable for their actions that makes a just republic. This implies that injustice is worthy of punishment. Not only is it just to discourage vicious behaviour, it is just to punish those who practise injustice. Against the Christian conception of forgiveness and turning the other cheek, Meslier defends the necessity of retributive justice. The very figure of Christ, the innocent who pays for the crime of the guilty, is against Meslier's conception of justice. Christianity has thus inverted natural justice, by permitting 'so many evils, vices, and wickedness for the greatest manifestation of [God's] glory, power, justice, and mercy'.[106] Human justice may be imperfect and flawed, it may require retribution, but it has better consequences than Divine justice.

It is ultimately a defence of a consequentialist approach to politics and morality that is defended by Meslier, both in his proto-utilitarian doctrine, and in his radical republican ideals. His 'three principal errors of Christian morality'[107] point in this direction.

Christianity's pursuit of pain and suffering, its condemnation of
the pleasures of the flesh, and its pursuit of non-resistance to evil,
are attacked for their negative consequences on human happiness.
'We cannot deny that pain and suffering, hunger and thirst, harm
and persecution are contrary to Nature', Meslier claims.[108] The
'greatest good and happiness of man' cannot rest in this principle.
But Meslier goes further. Even Christianity's morality attempts to
justify itself according to these consequentialist principles, when it
claims that rewards will be enjoyed in heaven. Meslier rejects the
reality of the rewards, not the consequentialist principle utilised.
As we have already seen, Meslier rejects Christianity's condemnation of the pleasures of the flesh. That is not to say, he further
claims, that they are always good:

> I am not, however, saying this to approve of or favour in any
> way the debauchery of men and women who would indiscreetly
> or excessively abandon themselves to this animal inclination,
> and I condemn this excess and disorder as well as all other kinds
> of excess and disorder.[109]

His critique of Christian non-resistance provides an additional
twist. For Meslier, 'it is obviously a natural right, natural reason,
natural equality and justice to preserve our life *and goods* against
those who want to take them from us unjustly'.[110] Despite his
attack on private property illustrated above, it is clear that Meslier
does not disapprove of private possessions. It is only just to have
what is ours, but it is the consequences of the wide disproportions
of goods that he is critical of. Great inequalities lead to the short-
age of primary material goods that make a happy life impossible.
That is not to say that resistance is always necessary. There are
times when the consequences of resistance are too harsh, and
prudence is warranted.[111] Meslier may be defending his own life
choices here, as he decided to resist through his *Memoir*, not
through more radical actions. The consequences for publishing
were radical enough, as the example made of Vanini testifies, and
Meslier was coherent in his moral outlook by refusing to suffer a
martyr's fate.

Despite Meslier's defence of tyrannicide, he did not advocate widespread regicide, because of this consequentialist ethic. It is not the presence of a king that is the role reason for a tyranny. Their claims to receive their authority from privileged – divine – sources play a role in this corruption, as does the randomness of birth coupled with a hereditary throne. Ultimately it is the kings' lack of interest in their subjects' happiness that is attacked vehemently. But there are such things as good princes. Or at least there have been, and Meslier cites Marcus Aurelius as the exemplar.[112] And ultimately it is a different concept of republic that Meslier is defending here. For the Roman emperor Antoninus is said to have ruled justly when he stopped paying those he found 'useless to the republic'.[113] The republic has to be understood as the *res publica*, the public thing, the polity – irrespective of its particular constitutional arrangements. An empire is a republic, just as much as the institutions of 'the brave Dutch [. . .] or the Swiss'.[114] Of course, there are no examples of virtuous princes in Meslier's work that are contemporary to his time. Only these brief mentions of the Dutch and Swiss republics, 'who were nobly delivered from tyranny', point towards a model of rule that Meslier approves of in his period.

Bearing in mind Sandel's discussion of the economic dimension of republican thought, it is also important to note that Meslier's contribution extends beyond the formal political structures of power. It is clear, as I have already shown, that Meslier's radicalism partly rests on an economic reaction against dependence. In lieu of an economic system where one is placed under the arbitrary will of a sovereign, a landlord or the church, he had advocated a self-organising economic model where the material interests of all citizens are taken into consideration. While the details of this model are never spelled out, they necessarily include a redistribution of land, a revocation of privileges by the two leading orders, and a potent role for the productive force in society. It is this last point that can be overshadowed by a more liberal interpretation of the radical Enlightenment. Meslier is nowhere defending a liberal constitutional regime with a separation of power as the solution to the problem of economic domination. While his solution is based on local participation in decision-making, the above discussion shows that he is not opposed to wider deliberations at a republican level. Perhaps Meslier would have in mind a confederate model of association, where local communities come together on an equal basis to make decisions about the wider polity. This would certainly follow his praise for the Dutch and Swiss republics, although he does not deal with the issues associated with this comparison, such as the mercantilist outlook of the Dutch states or the paralysis of the Swiss diet. But that is not to say that a novel form of republican association cannot emerge, and one that takes the materialist roots of Meslier's economic concerns to heart. Freedom from domination, it is now clear, also meant the freedom to decide on key economic policy and would have to safeguard itself from the interest of any class of citizens seeking to exert control over others.

Conclusion

Meslier's materialist and atheist position leads him to radical conclusions, in critical, philosophical and positive terms. Critically, he uses the tools he had found in Bayle and others, such as La Boétie, to both destroy the injustices of the *ancien régime* and provide a political alternative to it. This critical turn entails a thorough attack on religion, on belief, and on the institutional links between these two and politics. But Meslier is also a philosophical radical. He disputes with the Cartesians, to reverse their ontology and defend a materialist outlook. Matter, for him, cannot only move itself, but it is capable of thought, feelings and emotions. This philosophically radical argument is best illustrated by Meslier's defence of animals, who as material beings deserve to be treated as sentient beings. Finally, Meslier does not shy away from the positive and materialist aspects of his radicalism. His materialist philosophy becomes the basis of his ethical and political thought, and his defence of justice understood on utilitarian grounds. Finally, and perhaps the most important conclusion, it comes from Meslier's radical republicanism, for it encompasses all forms of radicalism discussed here. It is critical in that it rejects all forms of domination encountered; it is philosophical in that it applies a materialist ontology to all aspects of life, including political agency; and it is positive in that it allows for a sketch of a new form of political association, however roughly drawn in Meslier's works, where formal domination is as nefarious as informal forms of domination, particularly in economic terms.

Notes

1. Meslier, *Œuvres complètes*, vol. III, 395. The complete works include a series of critical essays by the editors in volume I, as well as Meslier's notes on Fénelon (henceforth *Anti-Fénelon*), and historical documents on Meslier in volume III. The English translation is: Jean Meslier, *Testament: Memoir of the Thoughts and Sentiments of Jean Meslier*, henceforth *Memoir*. This first complete translation of the *Memoir* in English is quite accurate, although it cannot act as a substitute for the critical edition in French. I have used Michael Shreve's translation for the *Memoir* where possible, and have translated relevant passages in the editors' commentaries or the *Anti-Fénelon* in the *Œuvres complètes* myself.
2. Meslier, *Memoir*, 39.
3. Desné, in Meslier, *Œuvres complètes*, vol. I, xviii.
4. Meslier, *Œuvres complètes*, vol. III, 390.
5. Meslier, *Memoir*, 40.
6. See in particular the case of another curé, Guillaume, whose works are lost but whose situation resembles that of Meslier to a significant degree – without an outright claim to atheism. Hémon-Fabre and Mothu, 'Un lecteur des curés Guillaume et Meslier'.
7. See Meslier, *Œuvres complètes*, vol. III, 415, citing a report by Le Tellier.
8. Lachèvre, for example, puts forward a Freudian analysis of Meslier's resentment as emanating from being deprived of his mistress by his superiors (Lachèvre cited in Morehouse, *Voltaire and Jean Meslier*, 17); and Onfray speculates that Meslier had sexual relations with the servants, putting into practice a free contractual union (Onfray, *Les ultras des Lumières*, 46).
9. Meslier, *Memoir*, 267.
10. *Abrégé*, in Meslier, *Œuvres complètes*, vol. III, 390–1.
11. Meslier, *Œuvres complètes*, vol. III, 429.
12. Ms Fonds Français, 19458, 19459 and 19460, Bibliotèque nationale de France, Paris.
13. For a full discussion of Meslier's *Memoir*, see Benítez, *Les yeux de la raison*.
14. Meslier, *Œuvres complètes*, vol. I, xlvii.
15. Pellerin, 'Diderot, Voltaire, et le curé Meslier: un sujet tabou'.
16. Meslier, *Œuvres complètes*, vol. I, lciii–lx; Moëne, 'Jean Meslier, prêtre athée et révolutionnaire'.
17. Meslier, *Memoir*, 120–1.

18. Schino, 'La critique libertine de la religion'.
19. Foucault, *Histoire du libertinage*, 9.
20. Ibid. 262.
21. Morehouse, *Voltaire and Jean Meslier*, 4.
22. Meslier, *Memoir*, 114.
23. See Pellerin, 'Diderot, Voltaire, et le curé Meslier: un sujet tabou'.
24. Meslier, *Memoir*, 37.
25. Ibid. 38.
26. Meslier, *Œuvres complètes*, vol. III, 141.
27. Ibid. 487.
28. Buckley, *At the Origins of Modern Atheism*. Alan Kors's detailed account of atheism in France before Meslier follows a similar line of argument. Kors, *Atheism in France*. See the Introduction above for a full discussion of these two authors' theses.
29. See the respective entries in Littré, *Dictionnaire de la langue française*.
30. See Meslier, *Memoir*, 349–51 in particular.
31. Meslier, *Memoir*, 221.
32. Ibid. 5.
33. Ibid. 43.
34. Ibid. 343.
35. Ibid. 341.
36. Ibid. 382.
37. Ibid. 343–4.
38. Meslier, *Anti-Fénelon*, vol. III, 318.
39. Ibid. 337.
40. Ibid. 325.
41. Deprun, in Meslier, *Œuvres complètes*, vol. I, lxxxviii.
42. Meslier, *Œuvres complètes*, vol. I, lxxxviii.
43. Ibid. lxxxviii.
44. Meslier, *Œuvres complètes*, vol. II, 191.
45. Deprun in Meslier, *Œuvres complètes*, vol. I, xciii; Buckley, *At the Origins of Modern Atheism*, 269.
46. Meslier, *Memoir*, 380.
47. Ibid. 538.
48. Israel, *Radical Enlightenment*, 9.
49. Variations in French include *utilité* (6 times), *inutilement* (twice), *utilement*, *utile(s)* (3 times) and *inutiles* (Meslier, *Œuvres complètes*, vol. II, 29–32). See also Meslier, *Memoir*, 281–3.
50. Meslier, *Memoir*, 281–2.
51. Meslier, *Œuvres complètes*, vol. II, 74; Meslier, *Memoir*, 303.
52. Meslier, *Memoir*, 553.
53. Ibid. 558.
54. Ibid. 559.
55. Ibid. 562.

56. Ibid. 563.
57. Ibid. 146.
58. Ibid. 146–7.
59. Ibid. 146.
60. La Boétie, *Discourse of Voluntary Servitude*, 402.
61. Meslier, *Memoir*, 304.
62. Ibid. 581.
63. Dommanget, *Le curé Meslier*.
64. Ibid. 298.
65. Ibid. 299.
66. Ibid. 7.
67. Ibid. 105.
68. Ibid. 346.
69. Ibid. 273.
70. Ibid. 281.
71. Ibid. 316.
72. Ibid. 350.
73. Soboul, in Meslier, *Œuvres complètes*, vol. I, ci.
74. Ibid. ci.
75. Verona, *Jean Meslier*.
76. Ibid. 19.
77. Moëne, 'Jean Meslier, prêtre athée et révolutionnaire,' 114.
78. Sandrier, *Le style philosophique du baron d'Holbach*, 64.
79. Deruette, *Lire Jean Meslier*, 30.
80. Benítez, *Les yeux de la raison*, 94.
81. Vaneigem, *The Revolution of Every Life*, 82.
82. Onfray, 'Jean Meslier and "The Gentle Inclination of Nature"', 5.
83. Meslier, *Memoir*, 273.
84. Ibid. 277.
85. Ibid. 273.
86. Ibid. 295.
87. Ibid. 295.
88. Ibid. 295.
89. Ibid. 309–11.
90. Ibid. 311.
91. Dommanget, *Le curé Meslier*, 299; Deruette, *Lire Jean Meslier*, 31.
92. Meslier, *Memoir*, 304.
93. Ibid. 304.
94. Ibid. 581.
95. La Boétie, *Discourse of Voluntary Servitude*, 60.
96. Onfray, 'Jean Meslier and "The Gentle Inclination of Nature"'; Onfray, *Les ultras des Lumières*, 85.
97. Pettit, *Republicanism*, 22.
98. Skinner, *Liberty Before Liberalism*, 69.

 99. Sandel, *Democracy's Discontent*, 250–73.
100. Meslier, *Memoir*, 273.
101. Ibid. 274.
102. Ibid. 582.
103. Ibid. 590.
104. Ibid. 116.
105. Ibid. 335.
106. Ibid. 530.
107. Ibid. 263.
108. Ibid. 264.
109. Ibid. 266.
110. Ibid. 267, emphasis added.
111. Ibid. 268.
112. Ibid. 331.
113. Ibid. 292.
114. Ibid. 584.

3

D'Holbach's Systematic
Materialist Ontology

Paul-Henri Thiry, baron d'Holbach was a key figure of the Enlightenment, and one of the 'radicals' who developed the clearest materialist ontology of the period. Of German origin, educated in the Netherlands, he held the most critically engaged of the salons in Paris for four decades, hosting European and American thinkers twice a week in an atmosphere of openness, debate and toleration. In the first section of this chapter, we will explore the setting of this salon, and the larger context of intellectual challenge it was situated in. We will also discuss Holbach's writings and show that they can be grouped in three general categories: the early polemical works, the systematic materialist ontology, and the ethical and political thought. The last portion has been particularly little discussed in the literature, with a few notable exceptions. But even the previous two periods led to many misinterpretations. The polemical works themselves have been portrayed as aggressive, dogmatic and intolerant. But in the context of the time, the ironic tone of many of the works is better read as an oratory tool to instil doubt against the dominant, Catholic discourse of the time. Nonetheless, the baron's early works provide a plethora of arguments to challenge the monopoly on truth claimed by various churches and religions. The second section will thus explore this early period and show the various rational, historical and psychological arguments put forward by the baron. His attack on faith is particularly potent, following from the critique that Meslier had already put forward. He also proposes even more radical polemical arguments than the *curé champenois* had – for example, by placing Paul as the founder of Christianity, rather than Jesus.

Holbach's middle period comes at the end of a decade of these polemical writings. Building on some of his previous critiques, he exposes a *positive* theory of atheism in a much more consistent way than anyone before him had done. He put forward a full theory of a materialist ontology, where nature is equated with all material beings, and importantly including the movement of matter as an essential part of the universe. In the third section, we will discuss this radical ontology, as it plays an essential and unavoidable part in the next two sections, since Holbach's materialist philosophy also includes a theory of the social. Human beings, after all, are part of the material world, and their social relations are no exception to this rule. Holbach's later ethical and political works cannot be divorced from this framework, as they constantly refer back to it. In the fourth section, Holbach's ethics is discussed, and shown to be original in that it proposes a unique blend of virtue ethics with utilitarian principles. Sharing the emphasis on utility with other Enlightenment thinkers, the focus in Holbach's works is much more on the material conditions of living rather than on the later utilitarianism of Bentham and others. This virtue utilitarian ethics is centred around three concepts: those of humanity, toleration and justice. Justice in particular, as the primary virtue of human beings living in society, has inherent political consequences. In the final section of this chapter, we will discuss Holbach's political thought, including the complex demands of liberty, property and safety – three key concepts that are interlinked in complex ways in the thought of the baron. What these three concepts show is an inherent concern for the well-being of others in society, and a progressive account of citizenship based on the expansion of the propertied class. Finally, Holbach's concept of *ethocracy* will be explored, where this mode of 'ethical rule' is conceptualised as a radical form of republicanism, rather than a defence of liberal democracy, as Holbach has sometimes been interpreted as espousing.

Holbach's Salon

Born on 8 December 1723 in the Palatinate, within the bounds of the Holy Roman Empire but in a region under heavy French influence, Holbach was predisposed to the international life he was to live. He was not born into nobility, however, and only inherited his title of baron alongside a considerable fortune at the age of thirty, bequeathed unto him by his uncle who had himself been ennobled after making a fortune on the Parisian stock market. Holbach studied in the Netherlands, at the University of Leyden, where he acquired his taste for geology and other natural sciences, and made a number of English friends, most notably John Wilkes,[1] to whom he was to remain close. In 1746 he also spent some time at his uncle's property in Heeze near Eindhoven in the Netherlands and witnessed first-hand the horrors of the war of Austrian succession as a young man.[2]

After his studies, Holbach moved to Paris, a city that attracted a great many European minds at the time. In 1749, he began to host his famous dinners at his house on the rue Royale and acquired the title of 'maître d'hôtel de la philosophie', as theists and atheists, clergymen and philosophers, diplomats and nobles joined him twice a week around the table. His salon was 'the most famous'[3] of the time and was ironically called the 'Synagogue d'Holbach',[4] the 'Philosophical Church',[5] and the 'coterie Holbachique'[6] or, more accurately, 'le café de l'Europe'.[7] The tone at his salon is considerably more defiant than in other salons of the time, a peculiarity often attributed to the lack of a hostess to prevent conversation on sensitive topics, notably religion and politics. But the atmosphere of the salon is less that of a coterie than of a debating club. Some of the most famous participants included Diderot, Grimm, Rousseau (until 1753), Marmontel, Boulanger, Chastellux, Helvétius, Naigeon, Galiani, Hume, Beccaria, Franklin, Priestley, d'Alembert[8] and later de Tracy.[9] But they also included clergymen, such as the abbés Galiani, Morellet and Bergier, the latter who became the official apologist hired by the Sorbonne to refute Holbach's *System of Nature*, and who shared drafts of his refutation with its (supposedly clandestine) author. Morellet did not hesitate to label Holbach a dogmatic and absolute atheist,[10] but also praised the tolerance of the salon and claimed that theists and atheists were all on good terms within his walls.[11] One episode, related by Diderot, best illustrates the atmosphere at these dinners. Whilst David Hume was visiting the baron, he made the unfortunate comment that he did not believe atheists really existed. 'The Baron said to him: "Count how many we are here. We are eighteen." The Baron added: "It isn't too bad a showing to be able to point out to you fifteen at once: the three others haven't made up their minds."'[12] While Holbach was certainly exaggerating the exact number of atheists present to make a point, it nevertheless illustrates the jovial nature of philosophical challenge within his walls.

In more ways than one, Holbach lived his ideal of sociability that he defended so ardently in his works. He financially backed his closest friend Diderot in his enterprise of the Encyclopaedia,[13] his friend Suard who was in financial difficulties,[14] the young literary man Lagrange,[15] and his friend Kohaut.[16] Kors comments that this liberality may even explain the initial success of the salon.[17] Even to strangers he offered advice and gifts, as his English friend Wilkes relates of a common visit they made to thermal baths while Holbach was visiting England. 'Mr the Baron d'Holbach became the doctor, the friend, the reliever of whoever came to the baths and he seems to me much less preoccupied with his illnesses than with those of others.'[18] Only Rousseau attracted the wrath of the baron, and 'was ungrateful enough to complain that Holbach's free-handed gifts insulted his poverty'.[19] Diderot similarly attacked the Genevan philosopher for his lack of gratitude,[20] and Hume experienced it first hand, despite Holbach's prior warnings. Holbach attempted to reassure his Scottish friend by telling him that 'you should not blush of having been a victim of your good heart'.[21] Rousseau, in other words, outright rejected the vision of friendship and sociability defended by so many *philosophes*, and his relationship with Holbach bore the brunt of this philosophical difference. As Niklas Luhmann notes, 'a new cult of sensitivity and friendship replaced religion'[22] in the eighteenth century, and Rousseau was very much swimming against the current.

While Holbach's salon provided him with a haven of free-thinking within which to develop his radical thought, the social context was not as tolerant. The threat faced by writers was very real if unevenly applied. Helvétius's example acted as a powerful reminder. Ignoring advice from his friends, Helvétius decided to publish his book *De l'esprit* under his own name in 1758. In a particularly tense political context, following the revival of the Unigenitus Bull dispute in 1754, an attempt on Louis XV's life in 1757, and French military defeats in the Seven Year's War, Helvétius's text came under enormous pressure. The book was attacked by Jesuits and Jansenists alike, by the Sorbonne, the Archbishop and the *parlement* of Paris and even by the Pope. Helvétius, who rejected the doctrine of free will and attempted to build a utilitarian basis for ethics – two critiques that Holbach was to make his own – had to publicly apologise for his work and retract some of its conclusions. This relatively mild punishment was a result of Helvétius's connections, notably Madame de Pompadour, the King's mistress, and Choiseul, the foreign minister who successfully lobbied for him at court.[23] There is little doubt that his unorthodoxy would have been punished more severely had he not had friends in high places. Others were not as fortunate. In 1765, the knight La Barre was arrested after having damaged a crucifix and said injurious and anti-Christian things. He was tortured and executed in Abbeville in 1766.[24] Diderot also relates the incident of a 'well-born' young man found guilty of buying Holbach's *Christianisme dévoilé* from a hawker. The young man, the hawker and his wife were attached to a pillory, whipped and marked. The young man was condemned to nine years of galleys, the hawker to five, and his wife sent to a hospital for life.[25] Diderot himself was famously sent to the prison in Vincennes for the much lesser offence of editing the Encyclopaedia. It is of little surprise, thus, that Holbach never signed any of his works during his life, and that he employed ingenious devices to get them published either in Britain or the Netherlands, notably with the help of the editor Marc-Michel Rey.[26] This ensured a widespread distribution of his works, the most famous of which were to be found around the world by the end of the century: in Frederick II's Prussia, in Russia thanks to Diderot's visit to Catherine the Great, in Hungary where it influenced the thought of Ignác Martinovics,[27] and in the United States where Thomas Jefferson even had a personal copy of the *System of Nature* in his library; and Benjamin Franklin attended the salon when he lived in Paris.

Holbach was a tremendously prolific writer. He published more than a dozen monographs, and wrote over four hundred articles for the Encyclopaedia, mostly on the natural sciences.[28] He was also a busy translator, including of numerous English deistic texts, and a translation of Hobbes's *De Homine*, and his translations have recently been the subject of a detailed study that shows his contribution to key debates of the time through his engagement with English, German and Swedish authors.[29] His original works can be grouped in three broad categories. In the first instance, the polemical works, then his systematic materialist and atheistic works culminating in the *System of Nature*, and finally the ethical, social and political works. These three periods of his writing will help us trace the argumentation from one of reaction to the abuses of religion, to the development of a materialist ontology, and finally to the social and political consequences of this ontology. Holbach had already acquired writing experience translating English deistic writings, and as Naigeon notes about his translation of Thomas Gordon's *The Independent Whig*, the baron 'atheised it as much as possible'.[30] It was only a matter of time until Holbach could no longer depend on translating other authors to make his own atheistic contribution, given that at best the English had embraced deistic positions and not his outright atheism. His first book, *Le Christianisme dévoilé*, started in 1761, was an immediate success and several editions were printed in its first year, despite being relegated to the underground market. The text was followed by many others in the coming years. The *Théologie portative* (1767), *Contagion sacrée* (1768), *Lettres à Eugénie*, supposedly written in 1764 but not published until 1768, *Histoire critique de Jésus Christ* (1770) and *Tableau de saints* (1770) all follow the polemical critique started in 1761, thus comprising the bulk of Holbach's early writings. The *Essai sur les préjugés* (1770) also follows this polemical line, although it already introduces political themes that will be developed later. The *Système de la nature*, published in 1770, marks the culmination of the new ontology developed by the baron. It is the best known of his works, and was republished in Spain, Germany, England and the United States.[31]

It was an immediate success, and similarly attracted the wrath of the authorities, and was torn apart and burnt by the public executioner. It was nonetheless influential, both negatively in terms of its thirteen refutations (the ones by Bergier and Frederick II being the most famous), and positively by the support it received from numerous *philosophes* (Helvétius and Payrard both defended it).[32] Even Voltaire, who supported Frederick II's refutation and rejected its atheism, had to admit that it was 'more eloquent than Spinoza'.[33] Such praise from the patriarch of Ferney was rare, as his opposition to atheism was virulent, as we saw when discussing his editing of Meslier's memoirs. Joseph Priestley also felt compelled to reject this *'bible for atheism'*,[34] as did many later German thinkers, such as Goethe and Hegel[35] – while Marx had clearly read his works.[36]

Yet the reception of Holbach's later period, that of the ethical and political works, is much sparser. Many commentators noted Holbach's contribution to social and political thought, but did not go into in-depth analyses of his works of the 1770s. Mark Hulliung, for example, notes that Holbach is more known for his atheism than for his republicanism, and Pearson Cushing laments that so many works are ignored by commentators.[37] Yet these constitute some of the most original elements of Holbach's works, and they have attracted considerable attention as part of wider studies, notably in Israel's *Democratic Enlightenment*.[38] In these works, Holbach builds on his materialist ontology to justify a new form of eudemonist ethics, based on utility but without embracing the (later) Benthamite system of utilitarianism. This ethics is then expanded upon to inform a political theory, where Holbach shows himself to be a subtle social contract theorist, where he offers his thoughts on international relations between states, and where he puts forward the clearest and staunchest defence of a system of toleration for all. These works comprise the *Politique naturelle* (1773), *Système social* (1773), *Ethocratie* (1776), *Morale universelle* (1776) and *Catéchisme de la nature* posthumously published in 1790.[39] Even Diderot's criticisms of the style of the two early works of this period disappear when it comes to the later writings, and during his visit to Russia he will ensure that all libraries be equipped with the *Morale universelle*.[40]

The Polemical Period

A few years before Holbach started writing his books, Helvétius's *De l'esprit* was officially accused of 'atheism, Pyrrhonism and tolerantism'.[41] It would be a mistake to perceive the Catholic Church as a tolerant institution at that period, as it still portrayed 'tolerantism' as a vice and an attack on the Church's monopoly of truth. The perception of tolerance as a positive virtue for social institutions was far from the public agenda, and Bayle's call for toleration will have to wait until 1787 when the *Edit de tolérance* comes into effect in France. It is in this climate of intolerance for any position that might challenge the authority of the Church that Holbach starts writing in the 1760s. While we do not read many of the counter-Enlightenment ideas today, that is not because they did not exist. In 1770 alone, ninety books were published in France defending Christianity;[42] the polemics was not a one-way street and Holbach was very much going against the current. Yet his arguments also follow the guidance of previous thinkers, notably Bayle's critical historical project that allowed Holbach to make claims that even Meslier shied away from, such as the idea that Christianity as a religion was created by Paul, not Jesus.

While the bulk of Holbach's works were aimed at Christianity, and Catholicism in particular, his arguments are wider in that they apply to all forms of religion. Following Bayle's lead, Holbach developed a technique of critical examination that aims to shake the foundations of uncritical belief and acceptance of Church dogma. Religion, in the works of the baron, is treated as a social institution, where priests play a dominant role. The very structure of many religious institutions, for Holbach, is detrimental to human happiness in the long run because they stifle critical thought by demanding obedience to the Book, the priest, or, by extension, to secular authorities. Using the myth of Pandora's box, with an irony that surely could not escape the notice of his readers, Holbach writes that religion is the place from which evils emerged.[43] The very title of the book within which this comparison occurs, the *sacred contagion*, proposes another metaphor to understand the religious phenomenon. Religion is perceived as an illness, and a very dangerous one since it has spread everywhere in the world. Of course, not all aspects of religious practice or belief are treated on the same level, and Holbach revives the old Lucretian theme against superstition as one of the worst aspects of religion. The critique is a straightforward Enlightenment one, denouncing the worst excesses of religion, while reviving an ancient tradition as a source of inspiration.[44] Many Christians themselves could accept these critiques, and Protestants had been keen on using them against Catholics since the beginning of the Reformation.

Yet Holbach took this critique one step further. What superstitious practices highlight is a more general trend in religious thought: a hostility towards reason. Holbach later claimed that there is a direct relation between lack of reason and religious growth in history,[45] exemplified in his early works by blaming the Middle Ages for the Church's hold on society.[46] Dogmatic practices such as circumcision, ritual cleansing, dietary requirements or baptism are similarly singled out as irrational.[47] It is the social role of religion that is here singled out as detrimental, while theological speculations are merely secondary. In the ironic *Théologie portative*, one finds the clearest definition of religion by Holbach, where true religion is defined as 'that of our fathers, who were too sensible to let themselves be fooled [. . .] that which we believe is true, to which we are accustomed, or that against which it would be dangerous to disagree'.[48] Religion is thus a set of social institutions and practices that are largely inherited, based on belief and custom, and defended by the use of force and fear.

No specific religion escapes the critical gaze of Holbach. Whether it is the pagan religions of the ancients, Judaism, Islam, or the various Christian denominations, Holbach is critical of all of them. The very plurality of religious beliefs and practices is used against each religion's universalist claims. But the details of the baron's arguments are less interesting for us today than the overall structure of his critique. Holbach puts forward a *materialist* critique of religion. While being adamant that human beings are the ones who have invented their own deities,[49] he also acknowledges that they are personifications of nature and natural forces. They change according to circumstances and take the flavour of the land in which they are born. Holbach proposes a *physiological* conception of religions. They are born, and eventually die, in particular material settings. Their diversity can be explained according to the climate, social setting, relations between classes of citizens, and interaction with other religions. The prime example of this physiological analysis is the beliefs that came out of the harsh climate of Egypt, a land that Holbach claims to be prone to various myths and superstitions. To turn the metaphor of divine creation on its head, Holbach claims that it is not gods who have created the earth, but rather the earth that has created different gods. If the ancient Egyptians were particularly prone to cruel and vengeful gods, it is no surprise for Holbach that Judaism developed and grew these practices, as the ancient Hebrews must have been influenced by their captors' beliefs. Two features of Judaism had particularly negative consequences for later religions. In the first instance, the rule of the priests, or theocratic government of the ancient Hebrews, and in the second place the almost exclusive preference for Israelites over all other nations.[50] As with his criticism of Islam, Holbach often plays on common prejudices against these religions to make not-so-hidden attacks on Christianity. His critique of Islam's rise to dominance by means of steel and fire is one such example, as Christians have also been keen to use violence to spread their faith.[51] Zoroastrianism is also ridiculed for its belief in resurrection, as well as preaching for the unity of God, the latter of which was clearly also embraced by Christianity and other monotheistic faiths.[52] For Holbach, the various religions and beliefs have roots in the material conditions around them, and change with time to fit the circumstances. Holbach's critique is thus characterised as a *radical* critique in that it seeks to find the roots of our beliefs and practices, and to expose them for their material origins.

Because of this materialist outlook, belief in itself is not Holbach's target, but a particular type of belief. Following Meslier here, Holbach criticised faith as *blind* belief, calling it a blind submission,[53] a blind belief,[54] a blind trust in priests,[55] a blind commitment and support,[56] a deep blindness that enslaves people to priests[57] and turns believers into instruments of their passions.[58] Ironically turning around his own commitment to utility as a principle of virtue, Holbach will admit that faith is useful, albeit for theologians.[59] Faith is never considered in its private nature, as a relation between a believer and God, but rather it is always already put in its social and political context. It has drastic consequences when it comes to epistemological questions, as it encourages credulity, but it is the consequences for ethics (the disproportion of faith's utility in favour of the clergy), and for politics (the enshrining of particular structures of power) that form the brunt of Holbach's critique.

The religion that has elevated faith to a virtue and attracts the strongest critiques from Holbach is, of course, Christianity. His arguments against Christianity are numerous and varied, but they range from genealogical arguments, critiquing the origins of the faith, to theological, political, economic and social arguments. Looking for the material causes of the Christian faith, Holbach sees a religion for the poor, the uneducated, the innocent victims and the unhappy.[60] Even in its early communities, where goods were shared in common (an ideal that Meslier had looked at with noticeable nostalgia), Holbach saw an idealised conception of equality and a failure to use property to interest citizens in the common good. But the religion of Christianity, for him, is not based on the thought of Jesus – however flawed it is – but rather on the Platonic and Pauline interpretations of Jesus' teachings. Plato, in particular, is isolated as the lens through which the ancients read Christian texts. The Bible is described by Holbach as a Platonic novel,[61] and the method of reading through mystical and allegorical hermeneutics are said to be inherited from Platonic philosophers, notably Plotinus.[62] For the early Christians, the second coming of Christ was eagerly awaited, but its failure to materialise led to questions of interpretation among subsequent generations. The sacking of Jerusalem in 70 CE also encouraged such readings, for any literal interpretation was thrown out of the picture when the promised land was definitely conquered and subdued by its pagan overlords. The ultimate victory of Christianity over paganism in the Empire, exemplified by Constantine's conversion, is further singled out for its political causes, rather than being a consequence of sound theological debate.[63]

Notwithstanding Holbach's disagreements with the philosophy of Jesus, Christianity is portrayed as having deviated from the teachings of the Messiah to follow the interpretations of Paul. Portrayed as an 'enthusiast' – we would say a fanatic – Paul can rightly be identified as the founder of Christianity as a religion.[64] Opting for the conversion of the idolatrous Greek, Holbach continues, Paul abolished the observance of Jewish law, creating a schism with the apostles that he ultimately won.[65] Holbach describes his writings as fanatical, rabbinical, cabalistic and Platonic, irrespective of whether these adjectives are compatible with one another.[66] His attacks on Paul, often ad hominem, rest on three distinct points of contention: the breaking away from Judaic law, the Hellenisation of Christianity to open it up to the Gentiles, and the proselytisation efforts of the thirteenth, self-proclaimed apostle. In the controversy against Christian belief, these arguments were aimed at instilling doubt in the mind of his readers, particularly when it comes to the Church's authority to interpret the word of Christ. To that end, historical material is used in a critical fashion, following the tradition founded by Bayle.

Following on from these historical critiques, Holbach further attempts to understand Christianity in psychological terms. One of the features of this religion, for Holbach, which brings it in direct opposition to preceding pagan cults, is 'its ability to tyrannise thought and to torment consciences'.[67] While ancient religions may have been superstitious, used sacrifices and conducted widespread acts of violence, they had not sought to rule over the psyche of their subjects. Christianity adopted new modes of disciplining, and although Holbach does not develop his psychological analysis, it is clearly singled out for its importance. Directly related to this desire to rule over the thoughts of its disciples is the proselytising zeal of Christianity. The desire for psychological domination is not sufficient for believers but must be universalised. Bayle, as we have seen, had already attempted to combat this desire to rule over consciences, and Holbach adds it to his arsenal against Christianity.

The sharpest weapon in Christianity's psychological arsenal is the doctrine of free will. This theological construct, Holbach claims, aims at rendering human beings responsible while absolving God of the existence of evil.[68] Following Helvétius's lead,[69] Holbach does not tiptoe around the notion free will as Locke had,[70] but categorically denies its existence. Unlike Meslier, who had accepted that free will is necessary for moral judgements to be made, Holbach adopts a purely materialist perspective on the topic. All movement is caused by antecedent causes, and these also affect our intellectual faculties and our moral judgement. The *Théologie portative*'s entry on *fatalism* best illustrates, with a large dose of sarcasm, what Holbach intends to convey here: 'Hideous system which subdues everything to necessity [. . .] If everything was necessary, good-bye man's free will, of which priests have such a great need to be able to damn him.'[71] Diderot will later make his the fatalist challenge, with the figure of Jacques taking prominence in his anti-novel. Without free will, there is no ultimate responsibility, as our moral judgements are themselves determined, and this has dramatic political consequences for the baron. While Holbach will not reject punishment of crime altogether, any punishment will have to have a clear causal relation to the easing of suffering and the establishment of justice. Punishing the guilty simply because they made a choice to perform evil acts is not justification enough if one rejects free will.

These psychological arguments are supplemented by moral arguments against Christianity. We will come back to Holbach's positive ethical beliefs, but in the early works it is primarily a negative drive against Christian morals that is being articulated. Holbach's message could hardly be more radical here and was a source of disagreement between himself and Diderot: for Holbach, belief in God itself is detrimental to morals, even if this belief is a belief in a benevolent deity.[72] Although both thinkers agreed that Christianity had been detrimental to morality, Holbach was quick to generalise, while Diderot erred on the side of caution. Holbach defended his view by arguing that religious morality had reversed natural morality.[73] Instead of an earthly, materialist basis of morals, religions had sought to base them on supernatural doctrines, which Holbach equates with this reversal of natural morals. Instead of a morality that perceives material benefits as goods, religion had emphasised other virtues and practices. Holbach cites, amongst others, idleness, contemplation, prayer, flagellation, torments, misanthropy, bile, fanaticism, obstinacy,[74] intolerance,[75] but also the three theological virtues: faith, hope and charity,[76] a revulsion for life and happiness on earth,[77] a humility turned into self-contempt,[78] a suffocation of feelings of humanity,[79] non-resistance to evil,[80] a fight against human passions and a submission to God – which in practice becomes a submission to its priests.[81] The attack is on multiple fronts. Religious practices are singled out when they are particularly detrimental to the public good, understood as the quest for material happiness, but social and political virtues such as intolerance, charity and obedience are also portrayed as inherently religious and detrimental to human happiness. Against those, Holbach will defend self-love and conservation, the quest for happiness, to take pleasure and give pleasure to others, moderation of the passions, enlightenment, quest for truth, education, sociability, nobility, citizenship and family virtues.[82] It is the ideal of sociability where human beings can interest each other in their mutual needs that Holbach is defending here, and it is seen as incommensurable with the inner-facing practices of Christianity, and its passivity in the face of material necessities.

This dichotomy between sociability and passivity is best illustrated by Holbach's critique of idleness (*oisiveté*) as a source of vice.[83] It is the clergy in particular who are isolated as the worst offenders. Priests are portrayed as inactive and idle,[84] theologians are preoccupied with childish subtleties,[85] and all this at the expense of wider society.[86] Monks are the worst offenders here, as their abbeys provide refuge for 'very useful [*utiles*] citizens that devote themselves to singing, eating, sleeping in order for their fellow-citizens to work successfully'.[87] Against Meslier's nostalgia for the early Christian communities, Holbach will attack this vision as a glorification of idle, useless and asocial beings.[88] It is difficult not to sympathise with Holbach's critique here when one looks at the economics of the Church in pre-revolutionary France. It owned up to ten per cent of land, and some of the best yielding; had the right to tithe on the rest of the land, consisting up to one seventh its total revenue; maintained a lavish lifestyle for the upper clergy, up to eight thousand bishops, abbots and cathedral canons with an income over ten thousand *livres*; and enjoyed fiscal exemptions, although it donated to the crown every five years.[89] As Meslier had done before him, Holbach points out that this uselessness was not always the case. The clergy had initially been useful, as the Greek word *pestis* refers to old men of experience.[90] Historically, priests were often involved in medical, legislative, scientific and political endeavours,[91] but their rise to power was coupled with a domination over the populace.[92] In line with his materialist ontology, Holbach argues that instead of contributing to the general interest, the clergy developed its own particular interest and used every event of life, from birth to death, to further its own material well-being.[93]

Finally, there is theological critique to be found in the polemical period. Man, for Holbach, created God in his image,[94], making his deities bloody,[95] unjust executioners,[96] perverts,[97] dreadful, treacherous, cruel, jealous,[98] choleric,[99] destroyers[100] and even unfortunate.[101] These human attributes show the anthropomorphic origins of gods, but so do the various contradictions between divine attributes. Miracles contradict divine immutability,[102] prayers suppose a capricious God,[103] divine perfection is challenged by the flaws of creation,[104] a revelation in time supposes that God is not immutable,[105] human suffering contradicts God's permanent goodness,[106] a changing God makes for shaky morals,[107] miracles are contrary to God's wisdom,[108] and so on.[109] As Buckley pointed out, theology was particularly poorly equipped to deal with these challenges as it had itself accepted the premises of analytical enquiry when it could have challenged them by insisting that Christianity was more about living a life in Christ than building a philosophical system.[110] Yet these attacks, by Holbach and others, must have been convincing to their contemporaries, at least to the extent that they challenged theologians' apologies for Catholic doctrine. The image of God built by Holbach is one full of human flaws and contradictions. It begs him to ask the question: 'Can we believe in the existence of a being about which we cannot affirm anything, that is nothing but a heap of negations and deprivations of everything we know?'[111] The answer to this question will be a resounding 'no', and Holbach will build his system to explain how we could live without this belief in God.

Systematic Atheism and Materialism

Speaking about outright atheism, Diderot wrote: 'I know only one modern author who has spoken clearly and without detour; but he is still unknown.'[112] This unknown author was Holbach whose *System of Nature* and *Bon sens* are both mentioned just before this observation. There is no doubt that Holbach put forward, in 1770, the clearest defence of atheism as a system of thought, and that he expanded upon his religious polemical works of the 1760s to propose a positive materialist philosophy.

Even before the publication of the *System of Nature*, Holbach had defended atheists in his twelfth and final letter in his *Lettres à Eugénie*. 'What will we think of those who ignore this god, negate his existence'?[113] 'What about those who see matter as eternal, acting of its own accord according to immutable laws? These are the people we call atheists, because they call nature what others call divinity, necessity what others call divine decree, fatality what others call God.'[114] While Holbach never claims his own atheism in this letter, and while the author of these letters is always referring to atheists in the third person, the seeds were already sown in this text for what was to come next. In the derisive tone of the *Théologie portative*, Holbach writes that atheists are those who do not believe in the clergy.[115] Holbach is forced to conclude that there are no real atheists – as Hume had famously suggested at his dinner table – because one cannot negate the existence of the clergy.[116] The power-plays between apologists and *philosophes* are never far behind the text.

In the *Essai sur les préjugés* of 1770, Holbach makes an important epistemological claim that applies to the atheistic position. There, he writes that 'to not have discovered anything is often a very useful [*utile*] discovery; it is to have learned a lot to disabuse oneself'.[117] Clearly, to have no clear conception of God in the first place is the first step to affirming the atheistic position, and the polemical works of the preceding decade had set the scene for the radical argument to come. Holbach's case rests on a genealogical approach. Since men created gods in their image, how did this process come about at first, and what are the *roots* of this belief? The first part of Holbach's answer is that it was ignorance of natural causes that pushed men to invent gods that would explain natural phenomena.[118] But this forms only part of the picture, because Holbach is well aware that this early state of affairs does not apply to his more enlightened contemporaries who nonetheless maintained a belief in God. The most striking example of this continued belief in spite of scientific knowledge was Isaac Newton himself, who maintained a strong belief in God.[119] Holbach here blames 'childhood prejudices' and inheritance from our fathers for this lack of atheism among great minds. His answer remains problematic, for it falls too easily into the discourse of courageous adulthood of the godless versus the childish comforts of believers which Charles Taylor has rightly identified as part of the conception of agency of the Enlightenment.[120]

But Holbach does not stop here. He is well aware that his staunchest adversaries are not the straw men of superstitious Christianity, but the deists and theists who have embraced many of the same critiques that he had against Christianity, without embracing his atheism. These two positions, Holbach explains, resemble his own, but retain a notion of divinity that possesses intelligence, wisdom, power and goodness.[121] The theistic position, that which still believes in a personal God, is dismissed rather fast. This is because many of the arguments from the preceding decade still apply to theists. How can they explain the problem of evil, or even know what our obligations to a deity would be? The God of the deists, however, is more difficult to dismiss. While Holbach still argues that there may be a slippery slope between the deistic position, that of a prime mover of the universe, and superstitious beliefs, his primary argument against the deists is that their god is *useless*. If a deity created the universe but subsequently left it to its devises, what use do we have of any type of religious activity?

Both deists and theists propose a deity of which we can say little before contradicting ourselves. The argument of creation, still important for both theists and deists, is stretched to what Holbach sees as its logical consequences. 'If creation is *bringing forth from nothingness*, does one not need to conclude that the god that has brought it from its own depths brought it from nothingness, and is himself this nothingness?'[122] The argument that atheists must believe in nothing, since they deny the existence of God, is here turned on its head by Holbach. Essentially, Holbach is making the claim that belief in God is itself nihilistic, since it ultimately rests on a belief that things, such as material reality, can come from nothing. Against this nihilism, Holbach opposes his own materialism that we will come back to.

How does Holbach define the atheist? An atheist

> is a man that destroys the chimeras which are harmful to humankind, in order to bring men back to nature, experience and reason. It is a thinker who, having meditated matter, its energy, properties and actions, has no need to invent ideal powers, imaginary intellects and beings of reason in order to explain phenomena of the universe and operations of nature.[123]

There is no doubt that Holbach is here proposing a self-portrait as the figure of the atheist. A scientist and defender of reason, the atheist is opposed to those who have recourse to superstition and metaphysical notions. Yet one cannot stop at this definition entirely, and Holbach attempts to build a form of spiritual atheism, understood an *athéisme de l'esprit*. Hence, while the *System of Nature* ends on a rather out-of-tone prayer to nature, it fits within the larger context of this spiritual atheism. If the theistic and deistic positions were rejected by Holbach on the slippery slope argument, why then include such an odd spiritual dimension at the end of the system? The clue to answering this question will only come much later, in Holbach's *Morale universelle*. There, Holbach writes that that 'very pious men believed that those who followed wisdom or reason could be regarded as very religious, *even when they were atheists*'.[124] The atheist can be perceived as spiritual or even religious if they have particular wisdom and follow the dictates of reason and experience. This spirituality will become clearer when we look at Holbach's social and political thought, where fluidity, prudence and temperament (in sum, a cult of sociability) mean more than religious allegiance or belief. This is because, ultimately, Holbach is well aware that atheism itself is a form of belief, albeit one that he believes to be more rational than its alternatives. If his materialism is a question of scientific knowledge, his atheism remains speculative, and

Diderot will be able to expand on this ambiguity better than Holbach ever could.

Holbach's materialist ontology is clearly put together in the first half of his *System of Nature*. In the first chapter, he defines nature as 'the great whole which results of the assemblage of different matters, of their different combinations, and of different movements'.[125] Nature, in other words, is a shorthand term for the *entirety of physical and material phenomena* in the universe. It is matter in the sense of the atoms which comprise larger material bodies, but also in the sense of the relation of forces between these. Holbach will take the example of the materiality of fire to emphasise this point. Matter is not uniquely the assemblage of atoms, but also comprises movement, which in the case of fire produces effects on our bodies, such as heat or light.[126] This illustrates the second sense that Holbach gives to nature, that is, the *particular* nature of individual beings. Often also called their organisation, he says, this nature is the set of properties that can be used describe these beings. It is a very Newtonian conception of matter that Holbach thus puts forward. And, in the late eighteenth century, it was still a controversial one, at least in the sense in which matter has an inherent quality of movement. This was already the case in Newton's theory – and a point of controversy with Locke – and was still used as an argument by deists for the necessity to have a prime mover of the universe. This question of the movement of matter forms the next challenge for Holbach's ontology. Movement is essential, for Holbach, because it is what underlies cause and effect, what explains interactions between bodies and changes within them. From movement we can observe and learn from bodies (*êtres*). Holbach distinguishes between two sorts of movements: external and internal. External movement is observable directly – when we see a stone fall to the ground, for example. But internal movements are not immediately observable, and only become known to us when their effects become perceptible. It is these hidden movements, for example, that allow flour to ferment and turn into bread.[127] Either of these movements, external or internal, can be acquired when inherited from another body, or spontaneously developed when they come from the body itself. These spontaneous movements are surely some of the most controversial, as Holbach points out that these are always themselves results of antecedent causes. The actions of men, taken to be spontaneous and possible because of free will, are themselves only spontaneous in appearance, for they derive from previous causes, including internal workings of the body and external stimuli. From these observations on movement comes a general claim: 'All is movement in the universe. The essence of nature is to act.'[128] In other words, there is no need for an external cause of movement, as it is itself a necessary feature of being, and the universe can be conceived as a perpetual moving whole.

This ontology culminates in the 'Nisus', a perpetual drive or effort between various material beings.[129] The Nisus, or vital force, is a principle of eternal movement, of combinations and destructions, which engender all natural phenomena, including life. Speculating based on observations by Needham, Holbach applies this Nisus to the movements of matter that ultimately create life itself. By a process of fermentation, Needham had claimed to have observed the emergence of life from flour and water, and Holbach takes this observation as an example of the potential for inanimate matter to become life itself.[130] The Nisus applies not only to inanimate matter, but also equally to the transition to life itself, characterised by this effort or struggle to keep its particular being united, and later applies also to social and political relations between human beings. Irrespective of the inaccuracy of Needham's experiment, whose living creatures were just movement resulting from fermentation, Holbach draws ontological, and later social and political conclusions from the natural movement of the universe. If life can emerge out of this movement, there is no need for a creator, and thus the deistic challenge is dismissed.

This, however, raises epistemological issues for Holbach. If nature is best understood as a whole where movement is eternal, and if human beings are part of this natural order, how can they get to understand it in the first place? The answer is always that understanding is partial and subject to change. We cannot observe the play of forces at hand in the Nisus, for example; we can only observe the effects it has on various bodies (êtres). Through careful observation, study of intermediate causes, and a principle of humility in the face of difficulties, ignorance can slowly give way to knowledge (*connaissances*). And the surest of these *connaissances* is that in nature there is only necessity. Newton was the ablest to show it in the physical world, through his law of inertia, but it applies beyond strictly physical phenomena. Holbach already draws us to the consequences for human societies, by making a direct link between the laws of inertia and the law of self-preservation, a quest for happiness and pleasure in life in human beings. This force, which he calls a self-gravitation, borrowing heavily from advances in the physical sciences, is as much a necessity in the nature of human beings than falling in a vacuum is a necessity for stone beings.[131] The Nisus is more than a regulatory concept for the physical world and applies to the moral world in equal measure.

If necessity applies equally to material bodies and human bodies, this has drastic consequences for notions of moral responsibility and free will. We will come back to Holbach's ethical theory later in this chapter, but his denial of free will is directly linked to, and indeed immediately follows, his treatment of the notion of necessity in the physical world. It is a mistake to make individual human beings responsible for their temperament, their passions or their will (*volontés*). There is no such freedom in nature, there are no miracles that are independent of the eternal cycle of movement of matter, and this equally applies to human beings. Their choices depend on causes outside of them, such as the climate they live in, as well as causes inside of them, such as the food they ingest, invisible movements in their own bodies, and so forth. In short, human beings are as much instruments of necessity as another being.[132] This will, however, create exciting opportunities for Holbach's thought. If our choices in life are influenced by various causes, then certainly some of them can be improved on, made easier or favour ethical outcomes.

Furthermore, if human beings are created by nature, this raises interesting questions regarding the history of the species as a whole. Has it always existed in its current form? Will it ever change? Holbach lacks the tools to answer this question and admits that any answer is mere speculation. Yet he ventures into saying that all living creatures surely are products of the earth on which they live, and that had they appeared on a different body in space, they would have been very different. Holbach is thus a believer in evolution *avant la lettre*, and even comes close to speculating about natural selection when he says that were our circumstances to change, we would be forced as a species either to change or to disappear.[133]

From the anti-religiosity of the early works, there is a clear evolution in the thought of the baron. By 1770, he is ready to affirm his own atheism loud and clear, and to ground this atheism in a positive philosophical system, which he calls the system of nature, but which is really an ontological theory about the nature of being in general, and beings in particular in the universe. This materialist ontology can be summarised as such: nature is everything that exists, including matter, movement and other physical forces. There is nothing outside of this whole, and we, as human beings, take part in it. This surely makes understanding it difficult, but it is the task of reason to find ways to navigate this complexity. Human beings have themselves been created by nature and have to be studied with equal care as other natural phenomena. The baron will spend the rest of his literary life addressing this question of the study of social patterns and attempting to reconcile humanity with its material being.

Virtue Utilitarian Ethics

Holbach had done his best to attack as forcefully as possible the notion of moral man and free will that so many of his contemporaries used to justify moral behaviour. It was thus a real challenge to reconstruct a notion of human beings as capable of ethical behaviour, if they were indeed unconstrained by supernatural forces, rewards or punishments in the afterlife, and were devoid of free will. This is a task that Holbach attempts in the *System of Nature*, but it is fair to say that it had preoccupied him for some time, and that his fullest exposition of the materialist and atheist ethics will come in his later works. Holbach's ethical theory can best be summarised as that of a virtue utilitarian. These terms rarely come together in ethical theory, yet it is this assemblage or composition of ancient and modern concepts, together with the baron's ontological positions, that make such an ethical system

come to life. We will see that Holbach first expands on his ontology to build a eudemonist basis for his ethics. This eudemonism
will make him reconceptualise what interests are and allow him to
embrace utility as the central criterion for ethical behaviour. But
this principle will only come to life when put in the context not of
individual actions, as others such as Bentham later did, but when
combined with character habituation, or the virtues. By showing
how utility shapes and forms the virtues of humanity, toleration
and justice, we will reconceptualise Holbach's contribution to
eighteenth-century ethical thought.

Holbach's two ancient models for ethics were Epicurus and
Aristotle. Following his ontological theory, the concept of
self-gravitation had already included the quest for pleasures and
aversion to pains that form the backbone to Epicurean thought.
Holbach defends the ancient thinker as the one who came
the closest to an ethics in line with human nature – by which
he means the nature of material man expressed in his *System
of Nature*. It was a balance between pleasures and pains, erring
on the side of caution and with a particular aversion for acts
of debauchery which inevitably create large pain, that attracted
the baron to Epicurus' thought.[134] The materialist ontology thus
necessarily implies, for Holbach, that ethics is about a balance
in the immanence of life, and that this balance is best served by
avoiding pains and seeking pleasures that themselves do not bring
about further pains. This Epicurean basis serves a double purpose
for Holbach. In the first place, it allows for combining his physical theory with his ethical theory. He perceives a particular 'fit'
between necessity in the physical universe, the rules of attraction
and gravitation, and necessity in the human sense, as a quest for
happiness. But it also allows him to answer the critics who say that
atheists are incapable of morals. It gives a particular purpose to
actions by atheists. One will act ethically in order to further one's
own quest for happiness. Given that unethical acts will result in
social punishment, one will avoid performing them to avoid the
pain of being shunned – or worse – by one's fellow human beings.
Against the moralities of Pythagoras and Socrates, Holbach prefers Epicurus for whom 'morality invited man to virtue, introduced
under the terms *pleasure, well-being, voluptuousness*. It is true and

has nothing to fear from the imputations of its enemies, and only sins by having not sufficiently explained itself.'[135] And this will be the task that Holbach will set for himself: to explain Epicurean ethics to his contemporaries, and build on its foundations to create new possibilities for virtue.

This immediately creates a number of problems, notably around what one means by pleasure, well-being and happiness. It also raises questions about whether what particular human beings consider as their self-interest is really compatible with what others consider as theirs. But Holbach does not shy away from these challenges. His eudemonism will lead him to embrace a theory of the *immanence of interest*. By this I mean that, for the baron, every human action can be explained as one that seeks what that particular person believes to be in their interest. As such, the religious and non-religious, the Christian and the atheist, the virtuous and vicious, the hedonist and the ascetic, all share in this immanence of interest. The diversity of their particular moral codes, and of their actions, are still driven by the same force: the belief that they are doing what is in their interest. Holbach, as a materialist, will then do his best to convince his readers that material interests are the real interests, and that spiritual or supernatural interests should be discarded altogether. But this does not change his theory of the immanence of interest, namely, that all of us act in what we believe to be in our interest.

This diversity of opinions about what constitutes one's true self-interests is not considered as a fatal challenge to Holbach's theory but is built in to its very foundation. Diversity is turned into a strength for human society considered not merely as an aggregate of individuals, but as a site where individuals can flourish and constitute their own interests altogether. Diversity, which Holbach also equates with inequality, is as much a feature of human being as it is feature of different grains of sand.[136] But far from being a negative trait, as Catholic critics of *tolerantism* would have it, diversity can also be a strength, inasmuch as it will contribute to mutual aid between persons. By making humans necessary to each other for their own happiness, diversity makes them into sociable and political animals. One human being will believe that acquiring knowledge is the best possible way to live one's life, another will acquire exceptional physical attributes, another will want to educate others. Individually they would not be able to lead the eudemonist lives while pursuing their goals, but together they create a social pact that makes their mutual goals possible. Holbach is well aware that such harmony is not necessary, and that different interests all too often result in strife and enmity rather than concord. It will then become the task of his political theory to create the best conditions for this concord to occur in the first place. By promoting diversity of opinions, passions and beliefs, Holbach is challenging the universalist moral code of Christianity, and proposing an alternative ethics, based on the careful study and juxtaposition of varied interests in society.

'Setting foot on French soil, one finds utilitarian arguments, utilitarianism nowhere.'[137] This is perhaps the most forgotten lesson of the history of utilitarianism. Before Bentham developed his theory of utilitarianism, there were utilitarian movements everywhere in Europe, including Scotland, Italy, Germany and France. Karl Marx noted the peculiarity of Bentham's thought as 'a purely English phenomenon', and Bentham as a man who merely 'reproduced in his dull way what Helvétius and other Frenchmen had said with esprit in the 18th century'.[138] Holbach was one of these authors whom Marx had read and had put forward, with *esprit*, a utilitarian ethics that refuses some of the pitfalls of later doctrines. Based on the immanence of interest described above, Holbach elaborates on the principle that he claims to be closer to human nature while also adding an element of purpose into our lives: the idea of utility. As Hubert has eloquently put it,

> against all of the borders that enclose the will to power that they [the *philosophes*] feel seep out around them, they are the apologists of the passions, they glorify their creative energy as they aspire to the enjoyments they procure, they negate the ascetism that subordinates them to the will, and even all of the virtues that contain them in necessary limits.[139]

One does not have to negate the passions, one can build on top of them in order to construct a stable ethical edifice. Against the interpretation of a naive Enlightenment, where a belief in the self-harmony of interests dominates, as Charles Taylor has argued,[140] one sees a much more complex picture emerge where the lack of harmony becomes a political problem. In other words, how can we interest all human beings in contributing to general utility, given that they so often oppose their personal interests to those of the collective? Holbach's *Morale universelle*, published the same year as Adam Smith's *Wealth of Nations*, contains a refutation of this theory of the harmony of interests.[141] Perhaps the two had discussed the topic when they met at Holbach's salon during Smith's visit to continental Europe in 1764–6, but there is no evidence for what constituted their conversations. Holbach was nonetheless familiar with Smith's earlier work, the *Theory of Moral Sentiments*, whose translation into French he had supervised.[142] It was not in Smith's work, however, but in Mandeville's *Fable of the Bees* that Holbach had found the argument for the harmony of interests which he reacted against. The debate was not to be settled, as indeed it still forms part of contemporary debates, but Holbach did his best to argue for a subtler, far richer understanding of how interests can come together in society.

In his early works, Holbach's references to utility had been largely negative – that is, in reference to a critique of the uselessness or *inutilité* of the clergy.[143] It is in the *Contagion sacrée*, published in 1768, that one finds the first positive formulation of utility; it merits citations. 'Right reason and a sane politics prove that it is utility that should be the sole and constant measure of the attachment, gratitude, prerogatives and rewards that each society must give to its members.'[144] As a positive concept, utility is first and foremost a political concept. It is the task of politics to guide utility and make all contribute to the public good. The 'greatest number' formula appears in the *Essai sur les préjugés* in 1770 and is repeated throughout all the later works. It first appears when the question of the utility of truth comes to the fore. Holbach wants to affirm that truth is always useful generally, but that in particular cases, lies may be useful to some in particular. In this context, Holbach claims that true opinions do not conform only to experience and reason, but also if they are 'really and constantly advantageous for the greatest number'.[145] This is quite an epistemic jump that Holbach makes, as he subordinates truth to general utility. Supposedly, then, a truth that does not conform to general utility would no longer be true. But one can read this the other way around. An uncomfortable truth, if brought to the general public, will never be against their utility. It is always useful to know truths, no matter how distressing and problematic they appear at first. In the context of the arguments between the *philosophes*, as to whether it would be useful to teach the general public about the existence or inexistence of God, Holbach was always firmly on the side that it was in the interest of general utility to disabuse oneself of all falsehoods.

According to Hruschka, it is in the thought of Leibniz that this greatest number theory first appears.[146] The famous 'magic formula' of utilitarian thought is also found in the thought of Francis Hutcheson.[147] Even Bentham, the most notorious figure of eighteenth-century utilitarians, attributes the idea of the greatest happiness for the greatest number to either Beccaria or Priestley, both of whom attended Holbach's salon.[148] Chastellux and Helvétius are sometimes regarded as the main French representatives of the movement.[149] Helvétius wrote the magic formula in *De l'esprit* in 1758, while Chastellux took it up in his work entitled *De la félicité publique* in 1772.[150] It goes without saying, as well, that both Chastellux and Helvétius also attended the baron's salon.[151] And there were rather important differences between the various conceptions of utility across the English Channel. As Scarre rightly notes – although he is unaware that this applies to Holbach – 'French utilitarianism was not so much careless of the individual, as careful of the mass of people whose interests were invariably subordinated to those of rich and powerful minorities.'[152] In other words, the French were using utility in a much more political manner than their English contemporaries.

Holbach's utilitarian thought not only contributes to this utilitarian literature but is also noteworthy because it combines a virtue ethics with the principle of utility. Instead of applying utility to individual actions, or even to rules, it is the virtuousness of the person that will be the most important safeguard for utility to flourish. Virtue itself is understood in utilitarian terms. It is a habitual disposition to contribute to the happiness and well-being of those with whom we live in society and applies to concern for the entire human species.[153] While there is a distinction between what we owe to parents, friends, fellow citizens and strangers, based on how essential they are to our own well-being, duties to the latter are an important part of Holbach's ethical theory. The first of the three essential virtues for human beings to have is therefore the virtue of humanity.[154] It is the virtue of humans by essence, that is, what we owe to other human beings qua human beings.[155] The content of such a virtue is vague but is elaborated upon when it comes to the second social virtue: toleration.[156]

Holbach had combated intolerance in his polemical period. Religious intolerance is particularly singled out in this respect, as a doctrine which demands punishment against those who do not share our beliefs. A corollary of this is that toleration demands that one allows other cults, beliefs and practices that one considers to be offensive to one's God. It was thus often portrayed as a weakness, as surrendering in the face of those who oppose one's most deeply held beliefs.[157] Atheism, in this respect, has an inherent advantage over religions – there is no God to offend, simply opinions and beliefs to be questioned. As Holbach puts it, it has no desire to rule over men's conscience, and does not promote hatred based upon opinions.[158] Since toleration is a virtue which does not seek to enforce metaphysical beliefs, it is obvious, for Holbach, that those with weak metaphysical beliefs will have an easier time adhering to it than others. Whereas Holbach had called for toleration of atheists in his early works, echoing Bayle's call almost a century earlier, his works of the 1770s adopt and promote a theory of universal toleration. 'If you need chimeras, you should at least allow your fellow men to have theirs.'[159] In the *Politique naturelle*, Holbach will bring this call for tolerance to its ultimate formulation, for if tyranny steals the citizen's possessions, 'it is a much more striking cruelty to steal his opinions about a god that is often much more important than his possessions or his own preservation.'[160] The worst tyranny is thus to attempt to regulate people's conscience, and this applies to atheists as well as to theists – echoing Bayle's call for the erring conscience. Those who attempt to restrict and regulate when other people think and believe, what they hold dear and are passionate about, will always commit the worst of crimes. Holbach unambiguously calls for a toleration of all religious views, extending what other philosophers had previously restricted in one way or another.[161]

The only limit that Holbach accepts to toleration is tolerance of intolerance. Toleration is a virtue, but it is also a *social* and *political* virtue. One can be tolerant of others, but if that tolerance is not reciprocated, the very system of toleration falls apart altogether. It was on that basis, Holbach claims, that the Chinese had banned European settlers from preaching their religion, as they required complete independence from political powers.[162] Involvement in society, as citizens, is essential to partake in toleration. Claiming special status and exemptions is not. Whether this is too stringent a condition remains to be seen, but it fits within Holbach's political model and demands of citizenship which we will discuss in the next section.

If humanity was a virtue of human beings qua humans, justice is a virtue of human beings living in society. This distinction itself needs to be understood within Holbach's social contract theory (which we will come back to in the next section), which denied a state of nature where human beings exist prior to social relations. Justice is not secondary to humanity but is coexistent with it and applies to others who live in the same society as ours where humanity applied to all human beings without distinction. For Holbach, justice is a habituated quality that pushes human beings to give other human beings their due. Almost paraphrasing Aristotle's definition, Holbach claims that 'a human being is just when he has a permanent will to give his fellow human beings what they are due and to treat them according to their merit'.[163] Justice further guarantees basic rights for human beings: property, liberty and safety (*sûreté*).[164] We will expand on these in the next section, as they are more overtly political, and explain how justice justifies social inequalities, and what this means for the materialist thought of the baron. One further aspect of justice, however, is more ethical than others, and merits greater attention here. It is Holbach's belief in natural justice, in the natural reward of virtue and punishment of vice.[165] This is particularly important since it seems at odds with the materialist ontology of the baron. But this is apparent only if one skims the surface, and a deeper reflection reveals a basic coherence to Holbach's belief in natural justice; albeit not a very convincing one.

We recall that Holbach had given nature two aspects: one related to natural phenomena, and one to social phenomena. Nature in general is the great whole which comprises all of the physical universal, including human beings and their relations to one another. As such, natural justice is also linked to social justice. As Crocker has rightly noted, the importance ascribed to natural justice does not in any way prejudice the need for praise and blame in society.[166] This is because praise and blame are not unnatural; they are in fact part of the order of nature conceived as general being. Yet this raises more questions for Holbach. Does he mean that virtues and vices will always see their reward and punishment in society, if not in nature? In several passages in his work he makes precisely this suggestion, that ultimately vices are punished, and virtues rewarded, a view that came under attack by commentators. In the words of Isaiah Berlin, '[t]he benevolent Dame Nature of Hume, Holbach and Helvétius is an absurd figment',[167] a criticism that Holbach faced in his own lifetime. In the *Morale universelle*, Holbach answers these critiques directly. He insists 'that there is no disorder that does not find punishment, even in this life, that there is no virtue that does not find some consolation or reward'.[168] The claim here is thinner already, for Holbach does not claim that full justice will be served. He clarifies his previous statements by showing that some form of reward, some form of punishment, will inevitably follow virtue and vice respectively. That is not to say that human beings will get what they are due – they may only reap minor benefits from virtue and suffer minor ills from vice. Although this thin belief in natural justice is a form of answer to those who denied that nature serves justice, it still remains at odds with Holbach's materialist ontology, where he had insisted that order and disorder do not have their place in nature as a whole, but only relate to the particular organisation of beings. Holbach here concedes too little, or claims too much in the first place, and his belief in natural justice had failed to convince his contemporaries – either theists or otherwise – for whom nature is not a sufficient counterweight to vice.

If Holbach's strong belief in natural justice is at odds with his materialist ontology, his strongest belief, indeed very much akin to an act of faith, is in the sociability of human beings. Against the perception that the Enlightenment is best described as a cult of Reason,[169] it is the notion of sociability that merits more attention than it has received. Holbach is explicit about this, claiming that 'social life is a religious act'.[170] There is thus a form of cult that is prescribed by nature, and more specifically by the nature of human beings, and that is why they must live in society, provide mutual assistance to one another, and act in accordance with the demands of virtue. In Holbach's words, 'this religion, in accordance with the nature of man [. . .] Every virtuous man is its priest, errors and vices are its victims, the universe is its temple and virtue is its divinity.'[171] This religion even has its prophets: the philosophers, who think for the future and are not of their own century.[172] This attention to the needs of posterity, of humanity conceived as not only the living, but the yet-unborn, clearly has religious overtones and may further explain Holbach's belief in natural justice. Although he had claimed that virtues would be rewarded in this life, his belief regarding his own work is that it will help others in posterity. The religion also has its saints: those who put their personal interests aside and deserve immortality through the gratitude of future generations.[173] It has its disciples (Holbach considers himself as one of them), its prayers, and even its priests: the legislators who will bring about greater utility.[174] The concluding chapter of the *System of Nature* provides this odd prayer to nature, where Holbach writes not so much about reason (the word appears only once in the passage), but rather about virtue and the natural punishment of vices.[175] As Niklas Luhmann put it: '[i]n the eighteenth century [. . .] a new cult of sensitivity and friendship replaced religion; self-love expanded to include concern for others'.[176] It is a religion of sociability that Holbach is advocating for,[177] one where the utility of the virtuous is rewarded by the homage of their fellow citizens[178] – or of future generations. While this cult, this religion of nature, may seem odd coming from the most notorious atheist of the period, it is consistent with his materialist ontology. The rewards of future generations, in fact, are more consistent with his other belief in natural justice. If virtue and vice will not be punished in this life, in other words, they might well be punished in the materialist afterlife, in the form of praise and blame by human beings yet unborn. This will have no effect on the dead, but it might just be enough to sway the living, for even atheists are concerned about how posterity will perceive them.[179] To finish on a poetic note, Holbach writes that

> [l]ife can be compared to a river whose waters push each other and follow one another, flowing without interruption. Forced to roll on an unequal bed, they intermittently meet obstacles that prevent their stagnation. They never cease to spurt, to bounce and to flow until they are returned to the ocean of nature.[180]

A Materialist Political Philosophy

As we have seen in the introduction chapter, Jonathan Israel's thesis is limited by some of the labels ascribed to radicals of the Enlightenment. Out of the values of democracy, equality and universalism, only the last really applies straightforwardly to Holbach and even then the baron shows particular care to take into account differences in his political thought. These differences, as we shall see, are the basis for some of his arguments against democracy and equality. But that is not to say that one needs to throw out the baby with the bathwater, that one needs to jettison Holbach as a thinker of the moderate Enlightenment, or even more fundamentally reject the thesis of the radical Enlightenment altogether. On the contrary, the nuances of Holbach's political theory will show that the radicalism of his thought does not come from his support for liberal democratic values, but rather from his materialist challenge to this liberal philosophy. If Israel proposed to reread the radicals of the Enlightenment on the left of the moderate, I thus propose to place Holbach firmly in a materialist tradition whose radicalism lies in a concern for the material well-being of all members of society. While Holbach's thought is much more prudential and less revolutionary than Israel suggests, its potential is also more far-reaching. It proposes, following on from his materialist ontology, to apply the principles he found in his claims about nature and ethics to the political realm, with consequences that still strike us as radical not only by the standards of the eighteenth century, but also by our own standards.

Perhaps the most important contrast with Israel's thesis on Holbach is the latter's critique of the notion of equality. Already in his *Système de la nature*, Holbach had disputed the notion of equality from an ontological perspective. The natural movement of matter, for Holbach, creates a diversity within the natural world, and this diversity is replicated in the social sphere. This inequality among human beings cannot be remedied, as it is part of a much larger ontological order, and it further makes us unable to work towards our own well-being. Holbach is making a claim that human beings are social animals by nature, inasmuch as they seek to fulfil their own happiness, and other human beings are useful (*utiles*) to achieve this end.[181] It would be a mistake to start with the individual and justify a social or political order from its particular self-interest. Ontologically speaking, Holbach is making a much more radical claim. That claim is that human beings, as material creatures that obey the same principles as other material beings in the universe, take part in natural diversity. This natural diversity in turn asks of them that they involve themselves in society, without which they could not make themselves happy – another natural tendency in their being akin to the physical rules of the universe. In short: human beings can never be in isolation from the political; they are by nature political animals, and the best way for them to fulfil this nature is to seek to interest others in their own well-being.

This ontology of diversity is directly opposed to that of one of Holbach's philosophical rivals, and challenger of the Enlightenment cult of sociability: Jean-Jacques Rousseau. Particularly in his *Discourse on the Origins of Inequality*, Rousseau had proposed an anti-social conception of human beings that put him on a radically equal footing. Going much further than Hobbes, who had already claimed a certain form of equality among human beings in that they can all kill and be killed,[182] Rousseau proposes that in their natural state, human beings share far more in common than anyone else had previously suggested.[183] This notably included human beings' lack of rational faculties, even lack of linguistic capabilities, which in turn make sociability a consequence of the institution of inequality after the creation of private property. As Mark Hulliung has suggested in his *Autocritique of Enlightenment*, this ideal of natural unsociability profoundly shocked the *philosophes*. But if they were ready to engage with it following the publication of the *Discourse*, they were not as ready for Rousseau's personal rejection of their company and their ideal of sociability when he left Paris for Geneva and reconverted to Calvinism.[184] At the heart of Rousseau's challenge to Holbach and others was the political question of whether human beings can fulfil their destiny in society, of whether they are political animals at all. While Rousseau will express different views in his *Social Contract* in 1762, the eight years that separate his second discourse from this later work did much to antagonise him to Parisian society. Holbach did his best in his work to answer Rousseau's anti-political challenge, and his defence of humans as political animals also has to be read in that context.[185] This was essential considering the popularity of Rousseau's works, not only at the time of their publication, but in the decades that followed.

In addition to justifying the political nature of human beings, inequality further justifies hierarchy and political power for Holbach. Some are just more able to lead than others or have acquired particular talents that warrant their position of authority over others. Inequality justifies unequal treatment in society,[186] as it is considered an important part of justice 'that the one that is capable of making others enjoy great things be preferred to the one that is good for nothing'.[187] It is thus, in a combination between his utilitarian ethics and his belief in an ontology of diversity which justified inequality, that Holbach builds his entire political philosophy. But this also means that if inequality is natural and justified, it places additional demands on those who are in positions of power over those who are in positions of inferiority. In other words, inequality does not equal inequity. Equity, for Holbach, becomes the means to combat the abuses of unequal positions of power within a political order. Equity is itself defined as a synonym of justice, and demands that human beings are given their due according to their contribution to social utility. It is just, or, to put it in different words, it is line with the principle of equity, that ranks and honours be conferred on those who are best equipped to contribute to the utility of their fellow citizens. Equally important, however, is the concern for the material well-being of the weakest in society. If those in positions of power do not do their best to contribute to the well-being of those who need their help the most, they forfeit their entire legitimacy for political rule, which merely rests on their ability to contribute to the social body as a whole. The concern for the material well-being of the poorest and weakest is never far away.[188]

If inequality is justified on ontological grounds, there are also ethical arguments which creep into Holbach's political thought. Against those who profess the division of ethics and politics, Holbach defends the need for the former in the latter. In a rare moment of praise for the revolutionary spirit, Holbach will go so far as to claim that it is a nation's duty to call back their leaders to morality, using force if necessary.[189] But what is the proper way to conceive of politics and ethics when they are juxtaposed to one another – or, to put it in more precise terms, what are the virtues most appropriate to the practice of politics? Holbach will claim that justice is the cardinal virtue which guides politics, and this is hardly surprising since he had described it as the virtue of human beings living in society. But justice takes on particular forms in the political realm, and Holbach further divides it into three other virtues: liberty, safety and property.[190]

The first political demand of justice is freedom. Notwithstanding Holbach's critique of free will under his materialist ontology, freedom remains the first virtue of political institutions. If freedom is not absolute in the sense that we are unrelated to others in society, if freedom as a social and political virtue must take into account the freedom of others, it is quite different from the negative conception of freedom proposed by Hobbes in Leviathan. Freedom is, first and foremost, 'the faculty to use all means that one judges to be likely to lead to one's happiness without harm to the happiness of others'.[191] It is subordinate to the value of utility, and thus also subordinate to some of the demands of justice, including giving others their due. As will become clear when looking at his social contract theory, Holbach proposes that being a fully fledged member of society entails an abandonment of unrestricted freedom.[192] Freedom is sacrificed for other advantages, and thus it is also a positive conception of freedom that Holbach proposes. Freedom comes with promoting human flourishing and is not merely conceptualised as the preservation of a sphere of non-interference, which is not a concern for Holbach who was well aware of what excesses of freedom entailed, particularly for powerful individuals. These abuses of freedom Holbach calls *license*.[193] Licence is a form of liberty that does not respect the rules of justice, that violates the liberty of others, or prevents them from attaining their particular mode of human flourishing. Unjust freedom, or licence, can also be a feature of democratic modes of government, Holbach warns.[194] Holbach's ideal is other than democratic, as we will see later. It is that of a mode of government that respects the rules of justice, and thereby limits the excesses of liberty. It is a republican ideal, and one that takes ethics at its core.

There are freedoms that one cannot do without in any well-ordered republic. Freedom of thought, freedom of expression, are at the forefront of these.[195] They include the right to express one's deepest beliefs and opinions, as Holbach's ideal of toleration had made clear, and this includes the right to criticise religion, political power and others' ideas generally.[196] Freedom of conscience, in other words, is not a mere personal freedom, it is a political freedom in that it demands that one's beliefs be communicable to others. It is an agonistic conception of freedom that is promoted here. All must equally be free to hold on to their deepest beliefs. But all must equally be free to address, examine and critique the beliefs of others. There is nothing that is too sacred to escape the critical gaze of the philosopher, and no public authority can dictate what one is to think or say. Freedom of expression also has positive effects for society, Holbach claims. Without it, population, agriculture, trade and trust are impossible.[197] 'Liberty ennobles man, elevates his soul, inspires in him the true feeling of honour, makes him capable of generosity, of love for the public good, of enthusiasm for his country, of nobility and of virtue.'[198] Holbach had, up until his visit to England when he changed his mind, praised English freedoms as ones that were much closer to his ideal constitution. His visit, however, disillusioned him altogether. Where he had believed that freedom reigned, he saw nothing but the corruption of parliamentarians to the crown, a feeling of superiority towards other nations leading to injustice in foreign policy, and the nefarious effects of the mercantile economic system and its quest for profits.[199] English freedoms, in other words, were mere licence for the rich and powerful to take advantage of others – whether their own citizens or those other countries.

The second political demand of justice is the preservation of the right to property. While Holbach's theory of property is, on the surface, quite close to that of Locke, in that he accepts that the fruit of one's labour should be considered one's property, there are important nuances when it comes to his theory of citizenship, and the two concepts cannot be divorced from one another. In the first instance, Holbach proposes to look at property as 'the faculty to enjoy the advantages that work and industry have procured to each member of society'.[200] Holbach does not, however, share Locke's theological basis for property to be acquired. The world is not given by God to the children of men, as it is in Locke.[201] Holbach's ontology had placed human beings as creatures that belong to the natural realm, and thus property is not taken as an external relation to something one can bend to one's will. Instead, as with his theory of freedom, Holbach's theory of property is inherently relational and political. Property is perceived as a form of relation between human beings living in society. While all must be able to gain the fruit of their own labour, this also entails a loss at the political level. Indeed, *private* property is seen as property that *deprives* others of access to the object which becomes one's property. As such, property is a relation between persons as well as a relation of one person to a thing. It says: you cannot use this object, since I have a claim to use it exclusively. One has a right, in other words, to deprive others of the use of things which one has made by the fruit of one's own labour. While this may still be hopelessly bourgeois, as Marx no doubt thought, it is also surprisingly close to Adam Smith's labour theory of value.

This type of property is not the main type of property which Holbach discusses in his work. While the fruit of one's labour is considered to be a fundamental right, even if it deprives others of access, the same cannot be said for landed property – the main means of production in Holbach's time and the focus of his economic thought. It is this type of property – that is, land – which forms the backbone of Holbach's theory of citizenship. Citizens are, by definition, property (land) owners.[202] Through land ownership, one gains access to representation at the level of the state, and gains responsibilities when it comes to contributing to public finance and the public good. The bulk of the population, then, as well as liberal professions such as artisans, merchants and others, are not citizens in the strict sense. While Holbach undeniably idealises the model of citizenship he proposes, and while it is an archaic agrarian ideal of the gentleman-producer who looks after his estate that is being proposed here, his model is not entirely without merit. It values the utility of the land above other demands (such as speculation and hoarding), gives particular duties to landowners to make good use of their property, and even introduces a special demand for financial contribution from those who benefit most from the economic system – that is, a form of progressive taxation.[203]

Most importantly, though, Holbach wants to enlarge the body of citizens. While he had accepted the Greco-Roman conception of citizenship, as his references to Cicero point out, he also wanted land reform – the dread of the powerful landowners of all times. Holbach actively calls for a body of citizens that is ever-increasing – an economic system where all are given opportunities to own their own piece of land and produce from it.[204] Economic prosperity for all, for Holbach, is a radical demand as the economics of oppression tends to create wider social inequalities, notably in terms of personal esteem.[205] In the eighteenth-century context in which he writes, this has clear and drastic consequences: large estates, which do not contribute to overall utility since they do not allow members of society to acquire their own piece of land and become citizens, need to be broken down and distributed to those who actually work the land and produce value from it. Whilst Holbach's physiocratic tendencies put him at odds with the mercantilist system, he insists that other professions have their role to play in society. The agricultural worker, the artisan, the merchant, the man of letters, the scholar all have their role to play. They may not be citizens, but they contribute to public utility, and are thus essential to society as a whole.[206] The citizen must be laborious, industrious and virtuous, have vigour, dignity and virility.[207] This does not, however, exclude women from citizenship. There are *citoyennes* who also contribute to society as a whole.

While Holbach will likely be read as rather paternalistic in his attitude to women, as he still ascribes to them highly gendered roles, his defence of women's rights is not that dissimilar from Wollstonecraft's a quarter of a century later.[208] As Elissa Guralnick notes of Wollstonecraft's politics, it is characterised more by a form of radicalism than by specific appeals to feminism.[209] Wollstonecraft had defended a vision of women's education and ultimate equality with men in her work, but her reflections go far beyond this particular contribution to the history of ideas. As Holbach had built a radical critique of society by linking religion with the lack of reason and with despotism, Wollstonecraft develops a theory of emasculation that shows that despotism in the army and for the rich come from their misogynistic sympathies and the degradation of female virtues. By neglecting to take their part in humanity, Wollstonecraft insists, the rich are unable to acquire the proper duties of their station and end up sharing in the effeminate degradation that women have been victims of by being denied a proper education. Holbach had already concluded that women can leave behind their supposed effeminate weakness and become full citizens of a republic where public education and virtue are a concern for all. Wollstonecraft follows this particular argument and constructs her own radical politics through radical equality between rational beings.

Holbach's third demand of political justice is safety. It acts as a bridge between liberty and property, in that it is 'the certitude that each member [of society] must have that he can enjoy his person and his goods under the protection of Laws, as long as he will loyally observe his engagements with society'.[210] While this is rather undertheorised in Holbach, the difference between security and safety, between *sécurité* and *sûreté*, is essential to the thought of the baron. Security is certainly important in all well-ordered societies, but safety demands more than mere security. Safety arguably includes the demands of liberty as well as those of property. It demands that one be able to make oneself happy while enjoying the fruit of one's labour. This is important, because safety has an economic dimension as well as a security dimension. In other words, it is not merely about being protected from interference by others, but also has a positive dimension in that it claims that one must be able to have access to the means (material or otherwise) to live a fulfilling life.[211] This will also have drastic consequences for his international thought.

Holbach is very little known as a social contract theorist, yet he participated in the debates at the time about what the ideal terms of such a contract should be. The differences with other major thinkers of the social contract tradition[212] can be summarised in five key critiques that Holbach puts forward. The first critique is a *historical* one. In the spirit of Bayle's historical criticism, Holbach attacks previous social contract theorists for having taken the state of nature as a historical feature. Hobbes had supposed that his war 'of every man against every man' exists among 'the savage people in many places of America', and between 'Kings, and Persons of Soveraigne authority'.[213] Locke similarly dismisses attacks on the historicity of the state of nature, arguing that 'because we hear not much of them in such a state, we may as well suppose the armies of Salmanasser or Xerxes were never children, because we hear little of them till they were men and embodied in armies'.[214] Rousseau is more subtle than Holbach allows, yet note J of the second discourse hints heavily that the Genevan believed in the historicity of the state of nature.[215] Holbach, however, is unequivocal. The state of nature never existed and, further, it is harmful to think that it did. The social contract should not be conceived as an initial contract to be respected, but rather is a constant test of the legitimacy of political power and authority. As such, the social contract constantly demands that those in powerful positions contribute to general utility, and deviations from these duties shake the foundations of power altogether.

Holbach's second critique is on the notion of *sociability*. Here the attack is aimed at Rousseau, as we have already seen. It is the orangutan as the model for human beings in the state of nature, in a pre-social state, that best illustrates Rousseau's thesis. As Robert Wokler argues, men in the state of nature 'are actually fallen apes' in a moral sense.[216] Rousseau had famously converted to Catholicism from Calvinism (before he converted back), at least partly because of the doctrine of the depravity of human beings in Calvin's theology. The Catholic model of the Fall, therefore, was a better fit for Rousseau, whose state of nature illustrates the theological concept well. Holbach did not share this theological *Weltanschauung*. Where Rousseau struggled to explain how infants would grow in a state of nature where human beings lived as solitary beings, Holbach explained that it was precisely this vulnerability which created a sense of sociability within us.[217]

Holbach's third critique of social contract theorists is explicitly linked to his *atheism*. Here, Holbach points out that religion has had a very large role to play in the corruption of the political model in place in his day: by turning monarchs into deities.[218] Against Hobbes (and Bodin), whose model of the sovereign was too close to a theological model,[219] Holbach turns the question around. The question is no longer: how can we best justify absolute power, but rather: how can an atheology fight the theological roots of absolute power? This atheistic challenge can also be seen in Holbach's critique of natural law. While he pays lip service to the concept, he undermines not only its theological foundations, but also its rationalist ones. In a passage on natural laws in the *Politique naturelle*, Holbach argues that these come from human beings' 'tribunal of [. . .] conscience' and that they consist in observing the 'duties of a social being'.[220] It is one's desires, coupled with caring for the interests and desires of others, that drive natural law in Holbach – not God or Reason. The old cliché that the *philosophes* worshipped reason thus has its limits, although the cult they practised was one of sociability.[221] Holbach's atheist critique also challenges the theological basis for Locke's theory of property. It is an important contrast to those of other social contract theorists, in that Holbach spends time elaborating a theory of the citizen which puts a much larger onus on those who benefit most from the contract, as we have already seen.

Holbach's fourth critique rests on a reconceptualisation of the *general will*. Against Rousseau's uniformising notion of the general will, which rests on heavily transcendental features Rousseau had inherited from Plato,[222] Holbach proposes a pluralist theory of general wills.[223] Holbach's utilitarian ethics may seem to point to a general utility which is at least potentially identifiable, but his notion of the general wills complicates this picture. First and foremost, it understands very well that many values are incompatible with one another. As we have already seen, there will be a tension between liberty and justice, and one's right to have property and the ability of the weak to pursue a fulfilling life. As such, the general wills oppose each other, and it is down to each society to make executive decisions on which values to prioritise and to which degree one value should trump another. In other words, Holbach is much more agonistic and pluralistic that Rousseau ever could be.

Holbach's fifth critique is against the belief in *equality* in previous social contract theorists. Whilst primarily aimed at Rousseau, again, it is Holbach's defence of natural inequality, from an ontological perspective, which is all-important here. Altogether, Holbach proposes a social contract which is different enough from those of other social contract theorists that he merits a place in the history books. But his social contract also has two further implications: it presupposes an international society of nations, for isolated nations cannot exist and have never existed historically; and it lays the groundwork for Holbach's republican ideal: that of *ethocracy*.

At the international level, therefore, Holbach also puts forward a social contract theory. In the same way that Holbach argued that a surrender of (part of our) liberty was necessary to live in society according to the rules of justice, the same applies at the international level. A surrender of sovereignty for a state is the equivalent to the surrender of liberty of individual human beings. Since this surrender of sovereignty is demanded, it must (as was the case in the social contract), be compensated by another value. The value of justice is here preferred to the balance of power doctrine, as Holbach remarks that monarchs only pay lip service to the balance of power, and always look for ways to tip it in their favour.[224] Instead, Holbach proposes another way to achieve justice at the international level. He calls it a 'grand society' of nations united against those who threaten collective security. This international society will be comprised of a special tribunal, responsible for settling disputes. This 'confederation against injustice' may lack depth, but it does predate Kant's *Perpetual Peace* and Bentham's similar advocacy of an international tribunal and provides as much detail on the topic as these authors do.[225]

It remains to be shown how Holbach's social and political thought culminates in a materialist form of radical politics, quite different from the one that Meslier had advocated before him. Holbach cannot quite be read as a democrat or a theorist of equality – for he critiqued both concepts in his works, as we have just seen. Yet the republicanism he proposes is no less radical in that it foregrounds the material needs of all inhabitants of the state – and indeed of humanity as a whole.

What makes Holbach's works radical is thus his materialist ontology, which is taken to have direct consequences for political thought. If human beings naturally depend on one another, sociability is equally a natural feature of their existence, and one cannot consider oneself as an isolated atom or individual. Even one's fundamental rights, such as those of liberty and property, are always subordinate to the interests of the greatest number – and in particular the weakest members of society. The type of polity that Holbach defends is what he calls an *ethocracy*, or a government that leads by ethics. It is the title of one of his books, and an integral part of his political thought. The ethocracy encompasses all of the demands of justice, the social contract, and political virtues discussed above. But it also proposes concrete political solutions to the problem of rule, and ones that further challenge some of the preconceptions of Enlightenment thought as unnecessarily uniform and inattentive to difference and diversity.

If Holbach is not a democrat per se, it is because he is all too aware of the shortfalls of democracies – along with other types of governments. Holbach follows the Aristotelian typology closely in his work: there are monarchies, aristocracies and democracies – as well as various mixed constitutions.[226] Each, however (and this includes mixed constitutions), 'carry within themselves the principle of their destruction'.[227] There is no point dogmatically defending any particular form, since none will perfectly fit all circumstances. Holbach is not alone in criticising democracy as a form of rule. The aversion for *le vulgaire*, the belief that anarchy is the logical result of democratic rule, is common among the most progressive of the *philosophes*.[228] Predating Tocqueville's infamous 'tyranny of the majority' thesis, Holbach had claimed that 'under a democracy, the people often turn themselves into an unreasonable tyrant'.[229] Democracies have an idol, equality, and Holbach has a particular aversion for this concept, for ontological reasons above all. If monarchies equally suffer from defects, notably the randomness of birth to determine who is to rule, and aristocracies often degenerate into the rule of the rich over the poor, mixed constitutions often carry the defects of all three modes of rule. In addition, mixed constitutions suffer a particular attachment to rules and institutions, even when they no long fit the circumstances of society.[230] The English constitution – which mixed the three elements and was praised by so many political thinkers – is no exception to this rule.

If there is a mixed constitution with a parliament and a monarch, corruption can be trampled by separating representatives from those employed by the crown.[231] This means they must collect a salary from the public purse, in order to avoid corruption. All public spending should be accountable, with no discretionary budget, or use of loans to finance costly and risky expeditions.[232] Once again, it is Holbach's concern for the material well-being of citizens that shows itself dominant here. Inasmuch as a government undermines public utility – understood as this provision of material well-being which gives the tools for many to achieve a fulfilling life, either through corruption, lack of foresight, or by putting the interests of a minority over those of the mass of the population – this government cannot claim to be a just, ethocratic republic.

One of the features of this ethocracy will be a new form of aristocracy. Very different from the aristocracy of the past (of which Holbach himself was a member, by inheritance rather than birth), it will reward utility and those who have the necessary political virtues to contribute to the well-being of others. A form of honours, where human beings are rewarded for their actions that have large benefits to others, is what Holbach has in mind here. This will entice many to do good, enable some to pursue their endeavours, and promote a social order where virtue is rewarded. It is a concrete application of the form of natural justice that Holbach had defended and which is discussed above. Instead of waiting for future generations to recognise the deeds of great individuals, an ethocracy will reward them in their lifetime, and further encourage their noble actions. We are far indeed from a traditional praise of aristocracy, and Holbach asks us to challenge our own preconceptions to return to a model where the aristocratic element can be understood as the rule of the best, here understood in ethical, eudemonist and utilitarian terms.

Holbach's ethocratic thought is also much less revolutionary than some have claimed.[233] Revolutions are perceived as symptoms of a disease, rather than praised.[234] Holbach thus has a more nuanced position than merely calling for or rejecting the revolutionary spirit. When a revolution occurs, it is a symptom of a much larger problem, and in a sense it shows that it is already too late to be dealt with in other ways. Far from encouraging revolutions, we should attempt to reform and get rid of the underlying causes of the problem. Rather than a revolution, which will use violence to change a regime, and thus replace one tyrannical regime with another, Holbach calls for active resistance against injustice, and attempts to remedy those injustices before they escalate. Although he died in January 1789, there is little doubt that he would have seen the French Revolution along these terms and been sceptical of its potential for peaceful change and constructive reform. What was needed was a revolution of ideas that can be supported by lovers of peace.[235] Although Holbach had risked his personal safety to publish his ideas, he advises others to only resist when they can do safely, for truth penetrates only slowly and any attempt to rush it would end with more negative consequences than positive ones. Following his materialist ontology, he compares the ills of society to those of the body. Violent remedies are always dangerous, and though they might be necessary as reactions to violent acts of tyranny, they are always a last resort.[236]

Finally, it is in his economic thought that Holbach defends a materialist ethocracy. Holbach criticises the heavy system of taxation that targets labourers and the poorest members of society particularly harshly, and emphasises the duty of landowners to take care of their land.[237] This contrast illustrates an important point in Holbach's economic thought: the citizen (i.e. the one who owns the means of production) is responsible for the bulk of the public purse, while non-citizens (those without ownership of land) should be encouraged to work, produce and ultimately acquire their own means of production. This ideal is no doubt the one that Marx had in mind when he labelled Holbach as hopelessly bourgeois. 'Holbach's theory is the historically justified philosophical illusion about the bourgeoisie just then developing in France, whose thirst for exploitation could still be described as a thirst for the full development of individuals in conditions of intercourse freed from the old feudal fetters.'[238] There is no doubt that Holbach was here developing an economic ideal at least partly as a reaction to the old feudal regime with its broad inequalities, privileges for the powerful, and support for the Church. But the belief in freedom in economic terms cannot be read anachronistically as a defence of the free market. Rather the opposite, the onus of public safety – understood as the provision of material needs for the well-being of a community – is placed on those who own the means of production, not on workers or artisans who do not. The political and legal structure of a society has to reflect this, Holbach claims, and certainly public funds are not meant to encourage 'bourgeois vanity'.[239] Treading the fine line between an agrarian ideal and the virtues of the man of the Enlightenment, Holbach criticises luxury in favour of a rather paternalistic and aristocratic defence of the country gentleman who guides his family, and families working for his estate, to more virtuous lives. This ideal may seem hopelessly antiquated to us, but the principles on which it rests, such as a concern for access to material goods for all members of society, an aversion to great wealth and abuses of power, and an affective concern for the well-being of fellow citizens, are not as foreign as they might appear.

Conclusion

This chapter has shown that a positive version of atheism is possible. Holbach had put forward a full ontological theory which places human beings as part of nature, not as apart from it or ruling over it. This new ontology largely informs his ethical and political thought, as these realms of human activity are also seen as taking part in the larger ontology. This immanent philosophy, which proposes a concern for the material well-being of others, includes one's fellow citizens, but also humanity at large. Nations that constantly ignore the material well-being of other nations – as mercantilist economies were seen as doing – are just as arbitrary and illegitimate in their actions as tyrants who ignore the well-being of their subjects. Holbach's radical republican thought here is essentially different not only from the moderates of his time, who were much happier with compromises with the powers that be, but also quite different from the later liberal philosophers who were more concerned with the rights of the individual than with collective development, well-being and material wealth. To put it in a different way, Holbach has strict limits on certain rights, such as those of liberty and property, that would be seen as interference by most liberal thinkers. For Holbach, however, the ideal is closer to one of non-domination, in the republican sense discussed by Philip Pettit and others we discussed in the last chapter. The emphasis is on the ability to live a life worth living, rather than on the abstract defence of particular rights. Where individual liberty comes at a social price, where the majority of people suffer from excessive licence by the wealthy and the powerful, then it is not a right worth defending. Holbach's atheism has also been shown to be radical in a number of ways. Negatively, he criticised Christianity for basing itself on the teachings of Paul rather than those of Jesus, while positively he saw atheism as a way to defend the ideals of humanity – where human beings are treated as members of the same species, not as members of separate religious communities; toleration – where all have an equal right to follow their conscience, without having the right to claim special protection from criticism by others; and justice – where humans' social nature is foregrounded as the most important feature of our material being. Holbach's political and ethical thought is thus much subtler than often perceived. It is surprisingly open to diversity and difference, for a thinker so well known for his universalistic thought. It is tolerant not just in a negative way, as a least worst scenario, but in a positive sense – in the way in which toleration can be an active virtue (à la Spinoza). It is also surprisingly spiritual, in the sense that *esprit* is a key component of the baron's works. Diderot will build on, but also disagree with, some of these aspects of his close friends' philosophy. With the genius for which he is known, he will put forward a much more ambiguous set of positions, and use his particular prose and literary style to constantly portray his religious, ontological and philosophical positions as part of a dialogue – or even a dialectic. What Diderot owed to the baron is unclear, but we do know that Holbach owed much to his friend, who shared his thoughts, his time, and who read the baron's work with great care.

Notes

1. Naville, *D'Holbach et la philosophie scientifique au XVIIIe siècle*, 28.
2. Holbach to Wilkes, letter dated 9 August 1746. Cited in Pearson Cushing, *Baron D'Holbach*, 9.
3. Artz, *The Enlightenment of France*, 45.
4. White, *The Anti-Philosophers*, 136.
5. Pearson Cushing, *Baron D'Holbach*, 13, my translation.
6. Buckley, *At the Origins of Modern Atheism*, 257.
7. Galiani cited in Hulliung, *The Autocritique of Enlightenment*, 7. For a thorough study of Holbach's salon, see Kors, *D'Holbach's Coterie*.
8. Hubert, *D'Holbach et ses amis*, 56–60.
9. Pearson Cushing, *Baron D'Holbach*, 15.
10. Wickwar, *Baron d'Holbach*, 24.
11. Hubert, *D'Holbach et ses amis*, 63–4.
12. Diderot cited in Mossner, *The Life of David Hume*, 483.
13. Pearson Cushing, *Baron D'Holbach*, 13–14.
14. Wickwar, *Baron d'Holbach*, 29.
15. Pearson Cushing, *Baron D'Holbach*, 18.
16. Letter from Diderot to Sophie Volland, 24 September 1767, in Diderot, *Correspondance*, 767.
17. Kors, *D'Holbach's Coterie*, 13.
18. Wilkes cited in Pearson Cushing, *Baron D'Holbach*, 18.
19. Pearson Cushing, *Baron D'Holbach*, 18.
20. Letter from Diderot to Rousseau, 22 or 23 March 1757, in Diderot, *Correspondance*, 65.
21. Holbach to Hume, 7 July 1776, in Greig, *The Letters of David Hume*, vol. II, 410.
22. Luhmann, *Essays on Self-Reference*, 110.
23. Smith, *Helvétius*, 2.
24. Onfray, *Les ultras des Lumières*, 114.
25. Letter from Diderot to Sophie Volland, 8 October 1768, in Diderot, *Correspondance*, 895.

26. McKenna, 'Les manuscrits clandestins dans les papiers de Marc-Michel Rey'.
27. Balàzs, 'Le matérialisme athée d'un "Jacobin" Hongrois'.
28. Lough, *The Encyclopédie in Eighteenth-Century England and Other Studies*, 128.
29. Kozul, *Les Lumières imaginaires*.
30. Cited in Pearson Cushing, *Baron D'Holbach*, 24.
31. Pearson Cushing, *Baron D'Holbach*, 38.
32. Ibid. 38–41.
33. Voltaire, quoted in Pearson Cushing, *Baron D'Holbach*, 39.
34. Priestley, *Letters to a Philosophical Unbeliever*, 160.
35. Naville, *D'Holbach et la philosophie scientifique au XVIIIe siècle*, 23.
36. Marx and Engels, *The German Ideology*, 110–12.
37. Hulliung, *The Autocritique of Enlightenment*, xiii; Pearson Cushing, *Baron D'Holbach*, 36.
38. Israel, *Democratic Enlightenment*.
39. Holbach, *Morale universelle*.
40. Hubert, *D'Holbach et ses amis*, 82.
41. Smith, *Helvétius*, 75.
42. Hampson, *The Enlightenment*, 131.
43. Holbach, *Contagion sacrée*, 123.
44. Martha Nussbaum, in Taylor, *A Secular Age*, 626.
45. Holbach, *Système social*, 135.
46. Holbach, *Essai sur les préjugés*, 132.
47. Holbach, *Contagion sacrée*, 247.
48. Holbach, *Théologie portative*, 589.
49. Holbach, *Contagion sacrée*, 145.
50. Holbach, *Tableau des saints*, 53.
51. Ibid. 53.
52. Holbach, *L'esprit du Judaïsme*, 153.
53. Holbach, *Histoire critique de Jésus-Christ*, 652.
54. Ibid. 653.
55. Holbach, *Lettres à Eugénie*, 399.
56. Ibid. 400.
57. Ibid. 401.
58. Ibid. 404.
59. Holbach, *Théologie portative*, 540.
60. Holbach, *Christianisme dévoilé*, 23–4.
61. Holbach, *Histoire critique de Jésus-Christ*, 790.
62. Ibid. 799.
63. Holbach, *Lettres à Eugénie*, 419; Holbach, *Histoire critique de Jésus-Christ*, 806.
64. Holbach, *Christianisme dévoilé*, 23; Holbach, *Théologie portative*, 515; Holbach, *Tableau des saints*, 71.

65. Holbach, *Histoire critique de Jésus-Christ*, 660, 731, 796.
66. Holbach, *Tableau des Saints*, 75.
67. Holbach, *Christianisme dévoilé*, 107.
68. Holbach, *Contagion sacrée*, 181; Holbach, *Lettres à Eugénie*, 356.
69. Smith, *Helvétius*, 13.
70. Locke, *Second Treatise of Government*, 152, II.xxi.xiv.
71. Holbach, *Théologie portative*, 538.
72. Letter from Diderot to Damialville, end of May 1765, in Diderot, *Correspondance*, 49.
73. Holbach, *Contagion sacrée*, 263.
74. Ibid. 263.
75. Holbach, *Lettres à Eugénie*, 411.
76. Holbach, *Théologie portative*, 610.
77. Holbach, *Lettres à Eugénie*, 399.
78. Ibid. 412.
79. Holbach, *Théologie portative*, 545.
80. Holbach, *Le bon sens*, 298.
81. Holbach, *Système de la nature*, 556–7.
82. See in particular Holbach, *Système de la nature*, 556–7 for a list of differences between what nature orders, and what religion prescribes.
83. Holbach, *Système social*, 231.
84. Holbach, *Christianisme dévoilé*, 133; Holbach, *Contagion sacrée*, 171; Holbach, *Essai sur les préjugés*, 17.
85. Holbach, *Christianisme dévoilé*, 108.
86. Holbach, *Système de la nature*, 541; Holbach, *L'esprit du Judaïsme*, 176.
87. Holbach, *Théologie portative*, 497.
88. Holbach, *Tableau des saints*, 188.
89. Callahan and Higgs, *Church and Society in Catholic Europe of the Eighteenth Century*, 15.
90. Holbach, *Système de la nature*, 397.
91. Holbach, *Contagion sacrée*, 161; Holbach, *Morale universelle*, 591.
92. Holbach, *Contagion sacrée*, 165.
93. Holbach, *Christianisme dévoilé*, 89–92; Holbach, *Tableau des saints*, 96, 131.
94. Holbach, *Contagion sacrée*, 193, 231.
95. Holbach, *Christianisme dévoilé*, 4.
96. Ibid. 28.
97. Holbach, *Contagion sacrée*, 132.
98. Ibid. 212.
99. Ibid. 231.
100. Holbach, *Lettres à Eugénie*, 354.
101. Holbach, *Christianisme dévoilé*, 23.
102. Ibid. 38.

103. Ibid. 87.
104. Holbach, *Contagion sacrée*, 138–9.
105. Ibid. 141.
106. Ibid. 210.
107. Ibid. 264.
108. Holbach, *Lettres à Eugénie*, 327.
109. See in particular Holbach, *Lettres à Eugénie*, 467.
110. Buckley, *At the Origins of Modern Atheism*, 33.
111. Holbach, *Système de la nature*, 512.
112. Diderot, *Oeuvres*, vol. I, 770.
113. Holbach, *Lettres à Eugénie*, 470.
114. Ibid. 470–1.
115. Holbach, *Théologie portative*, 495.
116. Ibid. 527.
117. Holbach, *Essai sur les préjugés*, 107.
118. Holbach, *Système de la nature*, 170.
119. Ibid. 476.
120. Taylor, *A Secular Age*, 565.
121. Holbach, *Système de la nature*, 522.
122. Ibid. 494.
123. Ibid. 587.
124. Holbach, *Morale universelle*, 590.
125. Holbach, *Système de la nature*, 172.
126. Ibid. 185.
127. Ibid. 175.
128. Ibid. 176.
129. Ibid. 184.
130. Ibid. 180.
131. Ibid. 194–5.
132. Ibid. 210.
133. Ibid. 216.
134. Holbach, *Système social*, 54.
135. Holbach, *Morale universelle*, 318.
136. Holbach, *Système de la nature*, 238.
137. Hulliung, *The Autocritique of Enlightenment*, 19.
138. Marx, *Capital*, vol. I, 571.
139. Hubert, *D'Holbach et ses amis*, 91–2.
140. Taylor, *A Secular Age*, 641.
141. Holbach, *Morale universelle*, 325.
142. Ross, *Life of Adam Smith*, 196.
143. Holbach, *Christianisme dévoilé*, 72.
144. Holbach, *Contagion sacrée*, 179.
145. Holbach, *Essai sur les préjugés*, 9.
146. Hruschka, 'The Greatest Happiness Principle'.

147. Hutcheson, *An Inquiry into the Original*, 106 and 177 (I.VIII.iii and II.III.viii respectively).
148. Stephen, *The English Utilitarians*, 178–9.
149. Scarre, *Utilitarianism*, 50.
150. Lough, *The Philosophes and Post-revolutionary France*, 71.
151. Hubert, *D'Holbach et ses amis*, 56.
152. Scarre, *Utilitarianism*, 52–3.
153. Holbach, *Lettres à Eugénie*, 398.
154. Holbach, *Politique naturelle*, 367.
155. Holbach, *Morale universelle*, 388.
156. Holbach, *Le bon sens*, 306.
157. Holbach, *Contagion sacrée*, 213.
158. Holbach, *Lettres à Eugénie*, 441.
159. Holbach, *Système de la nature*, 585.
160. Holbach, *Politique naturelle*, 491.
161. Locke and Rousseau are two examples of those who would not have extended toleration to atheists. See O'Connor, *John Locke*, 213–14, and Zurbuchen, 'Religion and Society', 801.
162. Holbach, *Politique naturelle*, 491.
163. Holbach, *Contagion sacrée*, 235.
164. Holbach, *Système de la nature*, 252.
165. Holbach, *Lettres à Eugénie*, 456; Holbach, *Essai sur les préjugés*, 82; Holbach, *Morale universelle*, 423.
166. Crocker, *An Age of Crisis*, 69.
167. Berlin, *Against the Current*, 21.
168. Holbach, *Morale universelle*, 781.
169. Frankel, *The Faith of Reason*, 70.
170. Holbach, *Morale universelle*, 500.
171. Holbach, *Contagion sacrée*, 280.
172. Holbach, *Essai sur les préjugés*, 159.
173. Holbach, *Système de la nature*, 344.
174. Ibid. 344.
175. Ibid. 636–40.
176. Luhmann, *Essays on Self-Reference*, 110.
177. Holbach, *Éthocratie ou le gouvernement*, 639.
178. Holbach, *Système social*, 171.
179. Holbach, *Morale universelle*, 637.
180. Holbach, *Système de la nature*, 378.
181. Ibid. 238–9.
182. Hobbes, *Leviathan*, 86 [§60].
183. Rousseau, *Discours sur l'origine de l'inégalité*, 39.
184. Hulliung, *The Autocritique of Enlightenment*, 214.
185. Whether a personal rivalry between Holbach and Rousseau had anything to do with the former's attack on the notion of equality is

unknown. In any case, as we have just seen, Holbach's defence of inequality is embedded in his materialist and atheist ontology, and therefore is not inconsistent with the rest of his thought.

186. Holbach, *Politique naturelle*, 426.
187. Holbach, *Morale universelle*, 382.
188. Scarre, *Utilitarianism*, 52–3.
189. Holbach, *Système social*, 197.
190. Holbach, *Contagion sacrée*, 158.
191. Holbach, *Politique naturelle*, 363.
192. Holbach, *Système de la nature*, 251–2.
193. Holbach, *L Morale universelle*, 380.
194. Holbach, *Politique naturelle*, 570.
195. Holbach, *Théologie portative*, 560; Holbach, *Essai sur les préjugés*, 14.
196. Holbach, *Essai sur les préjugés*, 38.
197. Holbach, *Politique naturelle*, 500.
198. Holbach, *Système social*, 158.
199. Diderot, *Correspondance*, 535.
200. Holbach, *Système de la nature*, 252.
201. Locke, *Two Treatises of Government*, 39.
202. Holbach, *Politique naturelle*, 409.
203. Holbach, *Essai sur les préjugés*, 47.
204. Holbach, *Morale universelle*, 610.
205. Blank, 'D'Holbach on Self-Esteem'.
206. Holbach, *Morale universelle*, 559.
207. Holbach, *Essai sur les préjugés*, 146.
208. Wollstonecraft, *A Vindication of the Rights of Women*.
209. Guralnick, 'Radical Politics in Mary Wollstonecraft's *A Vindication of the Rights of Woman*'.
210. Holbach, *Système de la nature*, 252.
211. Holbach, *Politique naturelle*, 488.
212. Here I compare him to Hobbes, Locke and Rousseau, because he makes explicit references to all three thinkers in this context. A more thorough comparison with others of the social contract tradition could prove further enlightening.
213. Hobbes, *Leviathan*, 88 [§62–63].
214. Locke, *Two Treatises on Civil Government*, 243 [§101].
215. Plattner, *An Interpretation of the Discourse on Inequality*, 17; Rousseau, *Discours sur l'origine de l'inégalité*, 106–12.
216. Wokler, 'Perfectible Apes in Decadent Cultures', 117, 124.
217. Rousseau, *Discours sur l'origine de l'inégalité*, 85 Foreword; Holbach, *Politique naturelle*, 347.
218. Holbach, *Politique naturelle*, 395.
219. Hamilton, 'Hobbes the Royalist, Hobbes the Republican', 420; Burgess, 'The Divine Right of Kings Reconsidered'.

220. For the theological basis of natural law, see Haakonssen, *Natural Law and Moral Philosophy*, 6; Holbach, *Politique naturelle*, 352.
221. Frankel, *The Faith of Reason*, 71.
222. Williams, 'Justice and the General Will: Affirming Rousseau's Ancient Orientation', 407.
223. Holbach, *Essai sur les préjugés*, 35.
224. Holbach, *Politique naturelle*, 559.
225. Hoogensen, *International Relations, Security and Jeremy Bentham*, 86.
226. Holbach, *Politique naturelle*, 373–5.
227. Ibid. 381.
228. Lough, *The Philosophes and Post-revolutionary France*, 17.
229. Holbach, *Politique naturelle*, 456.
230. Ibid. 379.
231. Holbach, *Ethocratie*, 602.
232. Holbach, *Politique naturelle*, 472.
233. Israel, *Radical Enlightenment*.
234. Holbach, *Système social*, 141.
235. Holbach, *Christianisme dévoilé*, 5.
236. Holbach, *Politique naturelle*, 399.
237. Holbach, *Ethocratie*, 617.
238. Marx and Engels, *The German Ideology*, 111.
239. Holbach, *Ethocratie*, 645.

4

Diderot the Metatheist

Today, Denis Diderot is by far the most well known of the authors studied in this book. There are excellent biographies of his life and studies of his works that have covered many of the angles of his thought. The purpose of this chapter is thus not to repeat much of what can be found elsewhere, but to provide an account of Diderot's thought that portrays him as a post-atheist thinker (or to use a neologism: a *metatheist*), and to show the extent of his radical political thought. In the first section, a short biographical introduction to Diderot's life will be provided, shedding some light on the major events that shaped his life, such as his theological studies, his imprisonment of 1749, his friendships with Rousseau and Holbach, and his visit to Catherine II's court in Saint Petersburg. I then turn to Diderot's 'atheism' per se and give an alternative reading to the dominant understanding that Diderot slowly made his way from religious belief to atheism via deism, and that this process was complete by 1749. I show that there is enough textual evidence to challenge this interpretation and to show that, if Diderot did embrace atheism, he did so with reservations that he kept for the rest of his life. He was too sceptical not to apply his scepticism to his own lack of belief, and it may be better to think of him as a post-atheist, or metatheist, thinker than as an atheist. What is unwavering in his philosophy, however, is a strong attachment to materialism. This materialism is complex and at the forefront of technological and scientific developments of his time. Notably, his biological materialism allowed him to speculate on the origins of species, almost a century before Darwin came up with his theory of evolution. Once these philosophical bases have been made clear, I detail Diderot's most important contributions to political thought, show that they largely derive from his religious thought and materialism, and that they provide innovative radical positions for his time. I also show that Diderot should be thought of as a contributor to the social contract tradition, and that he builds on Holbach's work and in some ways exceeds it by his subtle and often complicated analysis of the state of nature. Finally, I discuss how Diderot's materialism turned him away from the physiocratic school of economics, and towards a labour theory of value – with all the radical conclusions such an economic theory can engender.

Biography

Denis Diderot was born on 5 October 1713 in a small bourgeois family of modest means in the city of Langres in Burgundy. He had three siblings that survived childhood: Denise, just a year younger than him; Angélique, born in 1720; and Didier-Pierre, born in 1722, with whom Denis had many disagreements during his life. His father was hard working and a small spender – excepting the education of his sons – and when he died in 1759 he left a considerable inheritance in the form of vineyards and lands, which were to be a source of dispute between his two sons. Probably around the age of fifteen, Denis Diderot was convinced by the Jesuits to leave his home and go to Paris to pursue theological studies. Betrayed by a cousin, Denis was caught by his father on his way out of the house and persuaded to stay.[1] But his destiny was to bring him to Paris, where he moved, probably in 1730 at the age of sixteen. He finished his first two years of philosophy (logic and physics) in 1732, although which college he attended is not clear. By 1735, he had finished an additional three years of studies in theology, but by the end of that year he renounced his theological vocation and began a brief attempt to enter the legal profession. By all accounts, he was more interested in reading about mathematics, working on his Latin and ancient Greek (two languages he mastered), or working on his Italian and English rather than spending hours reading about law.[2] Furious at the news of his son's lack of commitment, Denis's father cut him off and Diderot lived for the next few years with small means, but with plenty of time to devote to his passions. These included reading, but also theatre and the company of women. A tall and seductive man, he was known for his laughter and *gourmandise*. In 1741, he met Antoinette, who was to become his wife and the mother of his four children (though three died in childhood). His precarious financial position resulted in delays in their marriage, which occurred in 1743. They lived in relative poverty, and Diderot's financial troubles were to continue for the next twenty years of his life – always seeking financial resources for his library, his wife, his daughter's dowry or other important transactions.

In 1745, Diderot began his literary career with a translation of Shaftesbury's *Inquiry Concerning Virtue and Merit*. An acquaintance of Bayle (and one of his avid readers), Shaftesbury had accepted the Baylian conclusion that atheists can be virtuous as morality is divorced from religious belief – a notion that Diderot picked up with interest. As with other eighteenth-century translations, Diderot's interpretation of Shaftesbury departed considerably from the original. Diderot pushed the Englishman's arguments further than he had, notably on his religious views.[3] These early years are also those of the friendship with Rousseau, who was less than a year older than Diderot. The two were to remain friends until the famous breakdown of relations between Rousseau and the coterie Holbachique in 1754. As we will see, Diderot will differ in important ways from the theories of Rousseau and acquired the label of a social contract theorist in his own right. But in their thirties, both authors were friends and it is conceivable that their relationship impacted on each other's work – though hard proof is difficult to come by. André Morellet, an abbot and author that attended Holbach's salon, relates the incident that broke the relations between Diderot and Rousseau. On 3 February 1754, Diderot had invited a Norman abbot to present his work at Holbach's house. The play he presented was so long and absurd that Holbach's guests made fun of the clergyman. Rousseau, irate at the situation, burst out and explained to the abbot: 'Your play is worthless, your discourse is extravagant, all of these gentlemen are laughing at you.'[4] The abbot left, furious, quickly followed by

Rousseau. Holbach, Diderot, Grimm, Morellet and their friends thought that Rousseau's rage would pass, but it never did. As Trousson explains succinctly: 'When friends cannot laugh at the same jokes, they are close to rupture.'[5]

Diderot had, however, benefited from Rousseau's friend-ship, not least during his short but formative stay in the prison at Vincennes. Diderot's literary career had then just started in 1747. Diderot and d'Alembert had been appointed editors of the Encyclopédie, bringing them notoriety but also a non-negligible income. Simultaneously, Diderot was also pursuing a number of his own projects, and secretly authored his Pensées philosophiques (1746), La promenade du sceptique (1747) and Les bijoux indiscrets (1748). But it was the Lettre sur les aveugles in 1749 that was to spell his doom. Way too atheistic for the authorities (as we shall see), the letter on the blind overstepped the mark and put Diderot under the gaze of the police. On 24 July 1749, at 7.30 in the morning, they knocked on his door. At his home, they found a manuscript of the Letter on the Blind – Diderot was caught.[6] He spent three and a half months at the prison in Vincennes, a short distance from Paris. But Diderot did not know how long his incar-ceration would last and admitted to being the author of the books cited above, demanding the pardon of the authorities. This time in prison at the age of thirty-five left a long-lasting impression on Diderot. During that time, he would still receive visits from his friends, almost daily from Rousseau, and from his wife. For the rest of his life Diderot was a lot more careful about what he would pub-lish, which explains, to a large extent, why so many of his works, including the most iconic ones we know today such as Jacques le fataliste, were unknown to his contemporaries.

In 1751, after a few years of hard work, Diderot published the first volume of the Encyclopédie. Initially planned as a ten-volume oeuvre, it grew out of proportion, finished by Diderot in 1772 and comprising twenty-eight volumes. Diderot himself contrib-uted more than five thousand articles to the work, which com-prised more than seventy thousand in total. It was a collective work, with over two hundred collaborations, but without Diderot it would have never seen the light of day. Even d'Alembert, his co-editor, cannot claim equal credit, as he abandoned the project

in 1758 when the authorities cracked down on it. Its initial success was overwhelming. Universally acclaimed as a major contribution to human knowledge, it gave Diderot and d'Alembert
international notoriety – as illustrated by their invitation to the
Royal Academy of Berlin in 1751. Diderot was largely inspired, in
many articles, by Bayle's work, Chambers' *Cyclopaedia*, Bourreau-
Deslandes, Brucker and Stanley[7] – though the Encyclopedia
moves well beyond the scope of all of these works. It is around
this time that Diderot made the acquaintance of Holbach, when
they became friends. Holbach contributed some four hundred articles to the *Encyclopédie*, from the second volume onwards. Not
all contributors to the project were radicals, or atheists for that
matter. It was a project of the republic of letters, where all were
universally welcome to contribute, so long as they were willing to
subject their work to critique.[8] Diderot, careful of not attracting
the attention of the French authorities after his imprisonment,
opted for a cautious editorial line – though many radical ideas
slipped past the watchful eye of the censor. Although it kept
Diderot busy until the early 1770s, the enormous project did not
stop him from continuing his own literary pursuits, as well as
providing editorial support to his friends, including Holbach. The
number of his works is staggering, and the breadth of his writings,
covering novels (though he disliked the label), short stories, plays,
philosophical essays, political treatises, dialogues, travel accounts
and works on science, makes for a well-rounded author passionate
about varying epistemologies.

It was the Helvétius affair that nearly crushed Diderot's ency-
clopaedic project and threatened his livelihood in 1758. By then
the first seven volumes of the project had already been published,
and although the Jesuits had attempted to get the project banned
altogether, they had not managed to significantly hinder its progress. But the publication of Helvétius's *De l'esprit* in 1758, which
followed an attempt on the King's life in 1757, changed the attitude of the authorities regarding what they considered dangerous
publications. Alongside Helvétius's work, Diderot's *Pensées philosophiques* was condemned, and on 8 March 1759 the *Encyclopédie*
lost its royal privilege.[9] The editorial team, along with Holbach
and a few others, proposed continuing the work clandestinely.

D'Alembert was enraged by this suggestion, thinking the plan a folly, and withdrew from the project.[10] But the work continued, often at Holbach's country house at Granval, where Diderot would work all morning before socialising in the afternoon. The following volumes were published, allegedly in Switzerland, without royal privilege in France, saving the publishers from bankruptcy and providing continued work for Diderot. From 1762, after the expulsion of the Jesuits, the climate for the publication of the *Encyclopédie* became a little more relaxed, and there were more radical works being published at the time, such as those of Holbach, to occupy the royal censors. In an irony of history, Le Breton, the publisher of the *Encyclopédie*, had bought printing presses confiscated from the Jesuits, and used them for the publication of the work.[11]

Following the completion of the *Encyclopédie* in 1772, Diderot suddenly found himself with a lot of time on his hands, and finally accepted an invitation from Catherine the Great to visit Russia. Catherine had been courting Diderot for some time, buying his library in 1765 when Diderot needed money, and generously offering him a salary as the curator of his own books (whose use he maintained until his death). She subsequently paid him his salary for life in advance, providing him with enough money for an investment returning a stable income, and a substantial dowry for his daughter. Diderot's financial stability had thus been guaranteed by the largesse of Catherine II, and it is perhaps with a feeling of a debt owed that he travelled to Saint Petersburg in 1773–4. This first international journey for Diderot, who had never left France and only travelled between Paris and Langres, was to take him through the Netherlands, where he spent considerable time both before and after his visit to Russia, and where he got acquainted with the republican and mercantile spirit of its inhabitants and met Dutchmen who had travelled the world. While in Saint Petersburg, he was given privileged access to the sovereign, who spent hours at a time with him. This attracted the wrath of the nobles, suspicious of this foreigner and his reformist ideas, but also the attention of the French ambassador, keen to exploit the situation to foment an alliance between the two countries. Although in the end Catherine followed few (if any) of Diderot's suggestions, Diderot maintained an imperishable memory of his sixteen-month journey.[12]

The next decade will see his work flourish into the anti-colonialism that we will detail later in this chapter, and a subtle exposition of his materialism. In 1784, at the age of seventy, Diderot suffered from chest pains and could feel his end nearing. Following a visit by Holbach on 31 July of that year, he passed away after lunch, making this the ultimate encounter between Denis and the baron. His body, donated to medicine, was autopsied the next day. Although he had refused the last sacrament, he was buried in his local Parisian church of Saint-Roch. Despite his notoriety in France today, there is no mention of him in the Church, no plaque or commemoration, though there are to other famous Frenchmen buried there.

Diderot's 'Atheism'

Diderot's thought often eludes simple classifications, as the philosopher's meanderings and dialogical style of writing make it difficult to identify voices within the text, or even to understand which argument comes out on top in any particular work. One can find all sorts of claims about Diderot's religious thought in the literature, from the claim that he was an atheist,[13] to the claims that he did not want to convert to atheism[14] and that he built a new, positive religion.[15] Diderot's religious thought changes throughout the years, and this means that he was at times an unbeliever, and at times wrote sermons.[16] David Adams has provided a survey of the oscillations in Diderot's religious thought,[17] ranging from him receiving the tonsure in 1726 and receiving his degree in theology from the Sorbonne in 1735, to the 'atheistic, tone of the Letter on the Blind'. Despite these various positions on Diderot's religious thought, there is widespread recognition that Diderot changed from a deistic position to an atheistic one, which become evident in the Letter on the Blind of 1749. After this, it is often assumed by commentators that Diderot's thought is more or less openly atheistic, depending on whether he is writing in private or writing for an audience with necessary precautions following his imprisonment of 1749. It is certainly the view advanced by Aram

Vartanian,[18] and many others have reproduced it. In this chapter, I will show that this view is unnecessarily reductive of Diderot's complex thought on God's existence. There are, I will argue, good reasons to accept part of the thesis – at least that Diderot's position was radicalised between 1746 and 1749, and that he came much closer to atheism than he was before – but there are also good reasons to reject this as a final destination for Diderot's thought. I will show that Diderot remains sceptical of both theistic and athe-istic positions throughout his life, and that while he often leans towards atheism, he never quite dismisses some theories about the existence of God. In particular, I will show that one definition of God – as a big animal which comprises the entire universe – is seriously maintained by Diderot until his final works.

There is little doubt that Diderot's early philosophical writings are much more moderate than later ones, and that he identi-fied quite closely with a deistic position that was not completely incompatible with Christianity. In his *Pensées philosophiques*, in 1746, he describes the logical consequence of painting God as a vengeful and cruel deity. Where this is the case, even the most 'rightful soul would like Him not to exist'.[19] Atheism is here seen as parasitic on bad theology – only because we have a portrait of a God without justice do we fall into the trap of believing there is no God. And Diderot will straight away defend the atheist: they are more just, more consistent and less dangerous than the super-stitious, following Plutarch (and Bayle). But the atheist can still be combated, as Diderot claims that the deist has unique tools to face him. Against those who deny God, knowledge of nature and experimental physics provide enough proof of the existence of a creator.[20] In particular, it is an argument against the spontaneous generation of life that Diderot puts forward against the atheist. It seems to him, in 1746, that life necessitates a divine creator, with-out which matter would never have turned into even the simplest of organisms. It is thus only the deist that can face the challenge of the atheist, for the deist is best equipped to understand the world as it is.

But who are the atheists that Diderot is attacking here, and how do we understand their thought? Diderot himself provides us with a helpful classification of three different types of atheists.

There are the *true* atheists, of whom there are only a handful, 'who tell you clearly that there is no God'. There are the *sceptical* atheists, of whom there are a certain number, who do not know what to think of the question and could easily decide it by the toss of a coin. And there are the *fanfarons* (braggarts) who seem persuaded and live as if there is no God.[21] Only one is cited by name in this text – Vanini – and he is not put into any category, though supposedly he falls into that of the true atheist. This categorisation is not helped by a further differentiation, which immediately follows it, between 'the deist, who affirms God's existence, the immortality of the soul and what follows', the sceptic for whom this is not decided, and the atheist that negates them. Diderot, however, seems to closely follow both Bayle and Meslier here – though a direct connection, at least with Meslier, is difficult to prove and only one of Diderot's poems points to a reading of the *curé champenois*.[22] Indeed, Diderot's atheist, in 1746, is Bayle's atheist. It is the one that denies the immortality of the soul. This is clearly shown by Diderot's only named 'atheist' in this text, Vanini, for whom matter was God but who denied the afterlife. Equally, Diderot's classification of the three types of atheists is close to Meslier's, although Meslier had discussed primitive atheists rather than the *fanfarons* who merely live as if there were not a God, as we have seen in Chapter 2. What is interesting in Diderot's classifications is that the sceptic is present at all levels. One can be a sceptic and be in between the position of the atheist and the deist when it comes to the immortality of the soul. One can be a sceptic and be an atheist. One could potentially be a sceptic and a fervent Christian. The sceptic is also portrayed, in this work, as the one that argues against all others, isolated in his position of doubt against all others who believe in something. The atheist, just as much as the Christian, the Jew or the Muslim, believes in his viewpoint, and only the sceptic is left to fight against them all. But reconciliation is not impossible: all can agree on at least one principle: that naturalism is the way forward.

Later in the *Encyclopédie*, Diderot will show that naturalism is now equated with atheism, but that in its beginnings it is merely based on a concern for arriving at conclusions based on the observation of the natural world.[23] The early Diderot thought this naturalism was compatible with most religious beliefs as long as they are ready to follow the lights of reason. It is also the position he defends in his *De la suffisance de la religion naturelle*. Written as an attack on revealed religion, the short text argues that any precepts that contradict natural law and natural religion must be dismissed – irrespective of their supposed authority as divine texts. Natural religion is the one that is in accordance with the goodness and justice of God,[24] portrayed as the first Father of the universe.[25] Ending the short text with a prayer from nature – a literary form that Diderot often adopted – the promise of happiness comes to replace the condition of those who have strayed from natural religion.

In *La promenade du sceptique*, a plethora of characters representing various theological positions are debating one another. Already in this text of 1747, Diderot portrays friends, including atheists, pantheists, sceptics, *fanfarons* and deists, who are arguing about their respective positions in a spirit of tolerance and a genuine quest for knowledge. Diderot clearly had atheist friends whom he enjoyed debating with, although who these friends were at the time is unclear. The style of the work lends itself a lot better than the previous essays to the type of dialogical work Diderot is famous for. Here, he exposes in great detail many contradictory positions, and it is not entirely clear to the reader which he espouses. Though I will argue here that the atheist is not favoured yet by Diderot, it is clear that the position is nevertheless given its full weight, and that despite Diderot's conclusion in favour of the deist, his wavering is already apparent. This is important, because even after 1749, this wavering will never fully go away, and Diderot's position will forever remain a balancing act rather than a mere exposition of a truth.

Comparing the promenade to the ancient Academy, where a diversity of opinions is not an obstacle to friendship and virtue, Diderot inscribes his text in a spirit of toleration.[26] Grouped into cohorts, the characters fall into various categories: the sceptics, the atheists, the deists, the pantheists, and the *fanfarons* or hedonists – closely mirroring his earlier classification, simply differentiating between atheists and pantheists to add some nuance to his tale. Athéos, the main atheist protagonist, is first to defend the position that there is no prince, no court, no need for a particular uniform, and that no blindfold is necessary to guide us.[27] The debate rages on about which system best preserves morals, what is necessary for understanding the world, and what is best in accordance with nature. But the debate is inconclusive. Despite arguments coming from all sides, Diderot does not side with any one in particular. The only one that seems dismissed, at the very end, is the atheistic argument. Athéos, coming home from the debating promenade, found 'his wife kidnapped, his children slain, his house pillaged'.[28] The blind man, with whom he was debating earlier, is suspected of having done the deed, showing that in a world without God, those whose passions are held back by the fear of God will see their actions unbridled – with disastrous consequences for even the best of atheists.

The text that is usually cited in the secondary literature as the culmination of Diderot's journey towards atheism is his *Lettre sur les aveugles* (1749). It was certainly considered an atheist tract by the authorities of his day, as we have seen, and its publication led to imprisonment for the *philosophe*. But the accusation of the *ancien régime* authorities is scarcely proof of Diderot's atheism. In fact, the text itself is highly ambiguous about the supposed atheism of Saunderson, the blind professor of mathematics on whom the treatise is loosely based. It is certainly true that Saunderson, as Diderot portrayed him, uses his blindness to challenge many religious assertions of his contemporaries. But Diderot's overall thesis is not that blindness leads to atheism, but rather that the state in which our organs are has an important impact on our metaphysical and moral principles.[29] In terms of morals, Saunderson had a greater aversion to theft – due to his inability to detect it – and lacks modesty when it comes to covering up his sexual organs, literally seeing no reason to hide them. Saunderson also doubts the justice of a God that has made him blind while giving sight to others. In metaphysical terms, the blind man cannot accept the reasoning that the beauty of nature can act as proof of the existence of God.[30] The argument from design, in other words, lacks potency when one cannot *see* what nature looks like. Saunderson is also closer to believing that matter itself can think, an important theme for Diderot that we will come back to when looking at the

nature of his materialist philosophy. Saunderson defends a radical
sceptical position, comparing Christian theology to Indian cosmology, by ridiculing the myth of the elephant and the tortoise.[31]
'If you want me to believe in God', Saunderson insists, 'you have
to make me touch him.'[32] Yes, this conclusion is not quite atheistic
– Saunderson does at best fit the *sceptical* atheist that Diderot
had categorised and described but is by no means the *true* atheist
that denies outright the existence of God. Furthermore, the dying
Saunderson pleads the God of Clarke and Newton to take pity on
him, rendering him more and more into a deist than an atheist.[33]

What is taken as Diderot's conversion to atheism is actually more typical of his dialogical method. Through a dialogue
between Saunderson and his friend Holmes, numerous challenges
to revealed religion are put forward. Doubtless these were closer
to an atheistic position than previous arguments put forward by
Diderot in his earlier works, and perhaps they do reflect a closer
affinity of the philosopher with the position of atheists. But atheism is hardly triumphant here, and the text provides insufficient
evidence for the conclusion that Diderot was definitely an atheist
when he wrote it. For Diderot's contemporaries, even sympathies
with atheism as a philosophical position were enough to see him
indicted with the crime. But for Diderot, and his closest friends,
the work was about exploring ideas revolving around the link
between our senses and our supposed knowledge of the world (and
of God). Diderot does not seem to be an atheist (yet), as he writes
to Voltaire the same year: 'I believe in God, although I live very
well with atheists.'[34]

We do not know for sure who Diderot's 'atheist' companions
are. Nor do we know if they are the 'true', 'sceptical' or '*fanfaron*' type of the *Pensées philosophiques*. It is likely that there were
some in each category. La Mettrie's *L'homme machine* was widely
attacked and criticised by the philosophes for denying morals –
it seems to fit best in the *fanfaron* category. In the *Encyclopédie*,
Diderot will later definite the *fanfaron* as the one who pretends to
have bravery while having none and is but a coward. But Diderot
quickly relativises the term. A man may be a *fanfaron* for his own
century, but a hero for the next. The *fanfaron* is thus judged to be a
braggard and a coward by his contemporaries, but changing mores

and attitudes may well change the perspective from a historically posterior standpoint.[35] Meslier's work had already circulated in Paris, and Diderot will paraphrase it in one of his poems, so it is likely that he had read a copy (however superficially), and could have considered him a true atheist. Holbach was perhaps not known to Diderot in 1749 as there is no evidence of them knowing each other before 1752. Diderot's later work, however, will clearly use Holbach's *Système de la nature* (among other works) as examples of true atheism. Diderot, then, could still occupy the 'sceptical' atheist position. This would mean, using Diderot's own classification, that the evidence one way or another is rather inconclusive, and that one's atheism may be decided by the toss of a coin. And it is entirely conceivable that for the rest of his life Diderot stuck to that conclusion, and that his 'atheism' won in some circumstances, but that other positions won in others. As we will see, there is evidence that Diderot's atheism, if at times pretty well enshrined, is at other times seriously challenged by at least two other positions: an affective attachment to God, and a hylozoist conception of the universe.

The Hylozoist Challenge

If Diderot is not straightforwardly an atheist, as is often assumed, he is clearly a materialist. There is one strand of philosophy that, although it evolves over time, remains constant in its affirmation: there is only matter and any spiritual realm is pure fantasy. This is the position illustrated in the introduction to his *Pensées sur l'interprétation de la nature* of 1753. There, he warns his young readers who are ready to embark on the study of natural philosophy – what we today call physics – that they must remember 'that *nature* is not *God*, that a *man* is not a *machine*, and that a *hypothesis* is not a *fact*'.[36] Against Spinoza's pantheism, against La Mettrie's mechanism, and against idealism, Diderot proposes that the scientist (he would say, the philosopher) must stick to the interpretation of matter.[37] The surest path to this is not to find answers, but rather to admit the necessity of the sceptical position, and to stick to saying 'I do not know' when we have no explanation of phenomena.[38] While Diderot is certainly a philosophical realist in the sense that he believes that the world exists out there for us to know, he remains a sceptic at his very roots when it comes to our ability to actually get to know the world in a concrete manner. 'Understanding has its prejudices; meaning has its uncertainty; memory has its limits; imagination has its glimmer; instruments have their imperfections.'[39] We are inherently limited in our quest for certainty, and Diderot's materialism fully incorporates these limits on human understanding into its very foundations.

Diderot's scientific method is one of experimental physics, based on careful and systematic observations, as well as the willingness to challenge one's system when new observations come to contradict it. And Diderot is not afraid to apply this method to controversial topics such as the nature of God and the universe. In his work, Diderot first puts forward the hypothesis that we could understand the universe as a 'big animal' that possesses a 'soul'. Building on Mauperthuis's work, which explained sensation in animals in terms of the sensations of the animals' constituent parts and organs, Diderot generalises the principle. If animals feel because their parts have the capacity to feel, could it be that the universe, as a whole, feels because its parts have this capacity? The play on the Latin word for soul, *anima*, and the word *animal* could not have been lost on Diderot, who otherwise simply rejects any spiritualist reading of the soul. 'This soul of the world, could be, though I do not claim that it is, an infinite system of perceptions, and the world could be God.'[40] Diderot, though he had explicitly warned the reader against such an interpretation when opening the work, seems to bring it back through the back door against Mauperthuis's philosophy. Though he does not go so far as to affirm the hypothesis, it comes back again and again in his work, suggesting that Diderot had never quite dismissed its possibility altogether.

In *Le rêve de d'Alembert*, written in 1769 but unpublished in Diderot's lifetime, he further expands on this hylozoist hypothesis that the universe may be comparable to an animal with a soul.[41] This ancient theory of the universe dates back at least to Thales and Heraclitus for whom the substance that formed material objects was considered to be living. The theory was reborn during the Renaissance, particularly in the work of Giordano

Bruno who in the sixteenth century had drawn the consequences of Copernicus's observations about the heavenly bodies to formulate a cosmology in which the entire universe can be considered to be a living creature.[42] Leibniz's thought was often considered, by his adversaries, as a form of justification of hylozoism though he himself never embraced the term or the concept. Kant is most famous for having argued against the poverty of the hylozoist hypothesis.[43] Equated with a rather simplistic conception of matter, where the perfection of the material universe is denied in favour of an organic vision of matter as a whole, it is one of the most far-fetched materialist cosmologies, in that it speculates about the universe as a whole based on a conception of life as we see it on earth. 'Far-fetched' is an adequate description of hylozoism, but in the fictional world of Diderot and in his poetic vision of his own oeuvre, it proposes a radical challenge to anti-materialists.

In *Le rêve de d'Alembert*, Diderot introduces Bordeu, one of the characters of the text, who explains to his conversation partner that this conception of God is the only one that is conceivable. It implies that God is like a living creature, which 'may have been, or have come and gone'[44] – which possesses the attributes of other living creatures. Of course, as with Diderot's other dialogues, it is not entirely clear that this is Diderot's position, rather than that of the character Bordeu, that is being put forward. Yet the fact that it comes fifteen years after the first mention of the hylozoist hypothesis is enough to conclude that it was still something that pressed on Diderot's mind, and that he considered important enough to expose as a serious alternative to other theological positions. A few years later, in 1772, while on route to Saint Petersburg, Diderot will repeat the importance of this position in his *Observations sur Hemsterhuis*. Perhaps the most atheistic of Diderot's texts, it merits special attention when it comes to an analysis of his theological thoughts. Once again, Diderot phrases the hylozoist hypothesis as the existence of one soul, disseminated in multiple bodies. Writing his refutation of Hemsterhuis, he claims: 'It seems to me that all of your objections leave this type of atheism intact.'[45] The hylozoist position, in other words, may well be a type of atheism, perhaps a type of atheism to add to Diderot's earlier classification which included true and sceptical atheism, and the *fanfarons*. Or perhaps Diderot's hylozoist is simply a sceptical atheist, who has maintained the possibility of a type of 'God' that is compatible with a materialist conception of the universe. Certainly, the great animal soul that remains a possibility for Diderot throughout his life is not close to any orthodox conception of God. It does not have any of the attributes of the God of the Christians. It is not eternal, as it lives and dies; it is not all-powerful, as it is limited by its materialist existence; it is not all-knowing, as it merely feels what is appropriate for its constitution to feel; and nowhere is it given any moral qualities. It is, Diderot concludes unashamedly, 'the God of the Stoics'[46]. There is no hope to be got from his existence, and no fear to have if the hypothesis turns out to be untrue. If Diderot can be described as an atheist, it is as an atheist who is always conscious of the limits of the atheistic position. For atheism can only reject particular interpretation of God(s), and Diderot always maintains the possibility that there is one interpretation of God that may be correct – such as the hylozoist position he never fully dismisses.

A second challenge that Diderot proposes to atheism, though it is not a philosophical challenge in the sense of the hylozoist challenge, is that it may well be against our feelings to fully embrace the atheistic position. As James Fowler notes, Diderot's atheism is at best intellectual, but sentimentally he has always had difficulties identifying with it.[47] It may explain why Diderot was never keen on proselytising for the atheistic cause, as opposed to his atheistic friend Holbach, whose work he nevertheless defends on numerous occasions.[48] Though not formulated in great detail anywhere, Diderot's challenge to an affective connection with God is mentioned in passing. For example, in the *Observations sur Hemsterhuis*, Diderot dismisses the role of revelation in religion altogether, admitting that God can 'speak directly to my heart, to my reason'.[49] In his correspondence as well, he labels atheism 'a devil of a philosophy, that my mind [*esprit*] cannot help but approve of, but that my heart denies'.[50] This affective attachment to a belief in a type of God is entirely consistent with Diderot's delicate sentimental character. Writing to his brother the abbot, Diderot denied the labels of atheism, impiety and anti-Christian furies. 'I am not impious, since I believe in nothing. You should have said I am an unbeliever [incrédule]. I do not have anti-Christian furies, since I live with Christians that I admire.'[51] The heart, love and admiration always bring Diderot closer to his fellow human beings, and it is ultimately out of this love of others that Diderot maintains a sentimental attachment to God. This attachment often manifests itself as a prayer, in Diderot's work. In his De la suffisance de la religion naturelle, it is nature's voice that entices mortals to seek their own happiness;[52] while in the Éléments de physiologie a Stoic meditation closes the work, enticing the reader not to fear death, but to seek justice and happiness in this life at all costs. Diderot's materialism is not without a certain spiritual dimension – as long as one understands the human spirit in material terms.

It is when addressing Catherine II of Russia that Diderot seals his position regarding religion and atheism. When discussing the constitution of the state, Diderot asks for the sovereign to ban all notions of God from the laws of the land. This ban would exclude not only theology, but also atheistic positions. For what Diderot is concerned with, as we will see when we come back to his political thought, is fanaticism of every kind. And he explicitly claims that atheism is not immune from fanatical positions.[53] It is only natural for people to dislike positions that are not theirs, and atheists are not immune from this feeling. Whether one believes or does not believe is ultimately irrelevant (at least to the constitution of the state), as both are equally capable of inciting hatred. It is better to stick to natural, material motives common to all humans qua humans, rather than establish official religious positions – or atheistic positions. Diderot is best understood not as an atheist thinker (though he admits he does not believe), but as a metatheist thinker – to coin a neologism I will come back to in the conclusion. All beliefs are worthy of toleration, and only a political position that allows for the greatest toleration is worth defending. This is best achieved, Diderot ultimately defends, by a position that has both embraced the lack of God and moved past it to defend the right of all to come to their own conclusions.

Materialism

One of the constant features of Diderot's philosophy is an attachment to a purely materialistic understanding of the universe. Even his acceptance of spiritual practices, such as prayers, or his affective attachment to certain notions of divinity do not deviate from this focus on the role that matter plays in our bodies. Diderot had, as other learned elites had at the time, accepted the consequences of a Newtonian universe. The largest controversy of his time was perhaps on the notion of thinking matter and, unsurprisingly, Diderot is unwavering in arguing for the sufficiency of matter (without divine intervention) to initiate the process of thought. This is why he rejected the mechanistic account of thinking found in La Mettrie's work, whereby thinking is reduced to a mere process of stimulus and reaction. It is not to say that Diderot rejects a certain deterministic account of the universe – he accepts that all actions create reactions – and his novel *Jacques le fataliste* is the best example to illustrate this point. Jacques, the main character of the book, has inherited a 'fatalism' from his captain when he was in the army. This fatalism is both fatalistic, in that it leads Jacques to believe that there is a bullet with his name on it, but also *deterministic* in that all events are ultimately, in principle, written on a great roll which contains all of the unfolding of the world written on it.[54] But of course, for Jacques and his master, this roll is utterly unpredictable, and leads the pair into numerous adventures and misfortunes. Hence, while we could, with infinite knowledge of the great roll, know the deterministic causes of all actions, in practice human action is utterly incapable of accessing this knowledge, and must resort to judgement to get out of difficult situations. And the act of judgement feels nothing like a mechanistic process. Though we have no free will in the theological sense of the term, we are free in our determinations. Though our determinations are themselves determined by antecedent causes, they are too numerous and complex for us to comprehend, and our choices are no less meaningful because of the nature of this 'fatalism'.

Where Diderot expands significantly on the theories of his contemporaries is when it comes to biology, and in particular the generation of new species, and the changes that occur in species over time. Well ahead of his time, he speculates on the matter on a number of occasions, starting around 1749 and culminating in the *Éléments de physiologie* in 1778. Diderot's biological determinism makes a number of conclusions from observations he had been editing while working on the *Encyclopédie*. In the first instance, he concludes that the animal kingdom derives from the vegetable kingdom, which itself derives from the mineral kingdom.[55] Where matter is in constant flux, the life of plants and animals is a form of resistance against constant decay, a battle between conservation and destruction. While activity is most obvious in animals, and easily perceived in plants, the potential for movement and energy is itself also present in the mineral state of matter. This potential energy, which Diderot names *nisus*, is the basis for all movement of inanimate and animate matter. In fact, inanimate matter does not exist per se for Diderot – if something lacks animation in a particular state, it is not because it does not have the potential for movement, but because that movement is temporarily halted in the form of a *nisus*.[56] Drawing from developments in physics to understand the movement of animals, Diderot exclaims that the laws that determine the movement of inanimate objects are difficult enough to predict movement, and that the laws that predict the movement of objects capable of sensation are not even in draft form.[57] With his usual scepticism, Diderot is thus extremely careful when it comes to understanding what makes animals act in one way or another, as the deterministic laws that underscore this behaviour are extremely difficult to decipher. The life of the animal itself can, however, be broken down and understood through the life of its particular organs (the heart, the lungs, etc.), which in turn can be broken down into the life of individual molecules. Only molecules, Diderot speculates, are unchanging, and the rest of the animal has gone through changes throughout the ages.[58] Though he does not go through the potential changes in species in great detail, it is clear that, for Diderot, species have changed depending on their needs – the eagle and the mole have significantly different eyes based on the respective utility of these eyes in their daily lives. Though he nowhere advances the idea of natural selection, Diderot does put forward a theory of evolution, where species adapt to their environment according to their needs.[59] When it comes to humans, it is clear to Diderot that the monkey is the link between us and the rest of the animal kingdom.[60] As with other animals, humans have features that suit their needs. The large brain, use of reason and perfectibility of humans are all features that depend on their needs. We need large brains as we use our cerebral abilities from the moment of birth to the moment of death; we use reason depending on our particular organisation and how much we have been taught to rely upon it; and we can perfect ourselves because we are born with relatively weak other senses (compared with the eagle's eye, the dog's nose, or the mole's ear).[61] Even our will is subject to the same mechanism. Willpower follows sensation, and we are driven to desire particular things because of our innate desire for happiness.[62] Our highest ideals themselves, such as the desire for liberty, are mere reactions to the bodily needs that constitute our organisation. Instead of drawing conclusions for the existence of a divine architect from the wonders of human reason, Diderot draws us towards a more modest conclusion. We should write an apology of human nature, rather than praise the creator for having made us how we are. 'The human species,' Diderot concludes, 'is but a heap of individuals more or less misshapen, more or less sick.'[63] There is progress to be made, for sure, but perfection is beyond the reach of material beings. If the great animal that is the universe lacks perfection, so does its creatures, be it the most advanced of these creatures: the human being. Diderot's political project will seek to better humans, keeping this general ontological stance in mind. When working with crooked timber, one cannot make straight planks.

Diderot's Political Thought

Diderot took it for granted that religion had often had a nefarious effect on politics. The earliest of his political writings, in the first volume of the *Encyclopédie*, show that quite clearly. In the article on political authority (*autorité politique*), published in this first volume, Diderot clearly divorces political power from its religious roots. Without challenging the divine source of political power overtly, the article is nonetheless clear that any religious claim is to be subordinated to the dictates of reason. 'The prince receives from his subjects the *authority* he has over them, and this *authority* is limited by the laws of nature and the state.'[64] Even his token biblical references clearly subvert the meaning of the Holy Texts, an accusation that was to be brought against him in early attempts to get the *Encyclopédie* banned.[65] This article will be, for twenty years, the most radical political statement that Diderot makes. This is of little surprise considering his imprisonment: Diderot just became much more careful about what he wrote – and most importantly published – to avoid the wrath of the authorities. The article itself makes a number of interesting claims for Diderot's political thought: among these, the claim that liberty is primary, and comes before the claims that authority makes over individuals,[66] the claim that revolutions ultimately are a natural reaction to the abusive exercise of political authority,[67] that a contract made by the nation limits the political power of the sovereign,[68] that only slaves live under political conditions that lack consent and reason,[69] that royal debt should be severely limited,[70] and that though the French monarchy passes to hereditary sons, a lack of heir would instantly see political authority come back to the nation.[71] It is of little surprise that Diderot's work was conceived of as outrageous, both by religious and secular authorities: it openly challenged the order of the *ancien régime* as one lacking proper political foundation. The only concession that Diderot makes at the end of the article is that not even injustice justifies acting against a monarch. Against an unjust king, he concedes, submission and prayers to God are the ultimate recourse of the nation – not revolution. Too little too late, as far as his most critical audience was concerned. Later in the *Encyclopédie*, even the most radical claims will come off as much milder. In the article on citizens, Diderot merely adds that citizens can never fully forfeit the rights they have by nature (against Hobbes's view), and that the closer citizens are to equality, the calmer a state will be.[72] In other words, the advice after 1749 was advice that moderates could accept, and based on observations rather than phrased as normative and imperative bases for politics.

Diderot's political prudence, however, waned over time. When the *Encyclopédie* was reaching its final volumes, and when the workload had lessened for its editor, Diderot came to the defence of his long-term friend Holbach, whose *Essai sur les préjugés* of 1770 had been attacked by Frederick the Great of Prussia. Diderot's text, written in 1771, helps bring together the political thought of the baron, highlighted in the last chapter, and that of Diderot, who comes to the baron's defence against the King of Prussia. Diderot and Holbach agreed on much politically, and it is often difficult to differentiate their positions. In the 1770s, when Holbach is writing his political works, so is Diderot, and thus they are building on each other's work at the time. In the letter of 1771, Diderot fully backs Holbach's claims, and has no reservations in his defence. The world of the *Essai sur les préjugés* is described 'as it is, full of liars, rascals and oppressors', yet describes human beings as those 'who love truth'.[73] This last point, on the love of truth, was disputed by Frederick, who believed that deception was inevitable in politics. The Enlighteners still defended a noble quest for truth, and the Machiavellian ways of a despot were against their taste. Diderot does not shy away from attacking Frederick personally, ending the letter on a call 'for God to preserve us from a sovereign that resembles this type of philosopher'.[74] Diderot's notes, which come with the letter, are ferociously anti-monarchical. It was a form of fanaticism, he claims, that led to the establishment of a strong *stadtholderate* in the Netherlands,[75] and monarchy is only a formalisation of a type of slavery.[76] It may be argued that Diderot did not turn away from monarchy and towards democracy until after his visit to Russia, yet it is clear that in 1771 he already had these sentiments, and that his long talks with Catherine II only strengthened his resolve. This is perhaps the most important difference between Diderot and Holbach. Holbach's scepticism towards democracy is much more muted in the thought of Diderot. That is not to say that Diderot defended democracy all of the time – he sees disadvantages with all forms of government – but he was on the whole a lot more sympathetic to democratic institutions than Holbach was.

Diderot's visit to Russia did serve an important purpose for the formulation of his political thought. He wrote three works that go a long way to explain his political inclinations, and which form the bulk of his political writings: first, his notes for Catherine II, following their time together, which he entitled without much prose *Mélanges philosophiques, historiques, etc., pour Catherine II*; then, his *Plan d'une université*; and finally, his *Observations sur le Nakaz*. The three works really go together, as they are written for the Russian context – though much of Diderot's advice, many of his examples, and the general lessons he draws have an appeal beyond this particular case. For the purpose of this chapter, I will only cover aspects of these three texts that directly shed light on Diderot's religious thought and political thought, confirm this growing inclination towards democratic institutions that Diderot went through in the 1770s, and set up his theory of a social contract, which is complemented by the reading of his contributions to Raynal's *Histoire des deux Indes*, which we will come back to.

Diderot's writings for Catherine highlight the dangers that religion has played in influencing politics. Though he promises the Empress to 'say nothing of God by respect for Your Majesty,'[77] who does not agree with Bayle who claims that atheists can live well in society,[78] Diderot actually spills a lot of ink on the relationship between Church and state. The warnings come in many forms. Catherine will read that priests may be easily corrupted to help sovereigns acquire their subjects' loyalty, but that they will be very difficult to get rid of when they have changed their minds.[79] Catherine will read that religious intolerance has ruined France, by forcing the emigration of great minds;[80] that theology is but a 'science of chimeras'[81] and thus should not be considered a necessary part of a good education.[82] Priests are also not to be trusted, as they more often than not favour ignorance over reason.[83] In his plan for a university, Diderot does not fully exclude religion from education – catechism and good morals are still taught as part of religious studies – but severely limits its scope, in particular forbidding theology from engaging in political speculation.[84] Always pragmatic, Diderot understands that the study of religion is important for most, and thus maintains a role for priests as educators.[85] The spectre of Meslier is not far away. This was, as Diderot relates, a source of disagreement between Holbach and himself, as the former held the view that the belief in a God, even a benevolent God, was ultimately detrimental to morals.[86] Yet disagreement was on religious morality only, for when it came to the morals of Christianity, and more particularly of their contemporary Christians, they agreed that there were detrimental effects, in particular in terms of Christianity's unsociability, uselessness (*inutilité*) and intolerance.[87] Diderot concludes that if religion is to remain a part of public life, it must at the very least be controlled by the state, and subject to its laws. It is the exceptional treatment of churches that he objects to, not their existence per se.

These warnings in mind, Diderot is also adamant that widespread reform is necessary, and that these reforms need to introduce more equality. The levels of inequality present at the time, through serfdom, land ownership, access to education, political power and status are simply not sustainable in the long run – and fundamentally incompatible with the enlightened regime Catherine seems to wish for. Diderot encouraged Catherine to revive the *Nakaz*, a broad statement of political principles she had written in 1767 asking for reform. The way forward, Diderot argued, was to make the *Nakaz* permanent, to reinstate the commission for reform, and ultimately to make this body of representatives of the regions of Russia into a permanent political assembly – a Parliament not unlike that of Great Britain.[88] This political institution, for Diderot, would insert some democratic features into political rule in Russia. Diderot was under no illusions that the British model was perfect – he had been warned by Holbach of the levels of corruption present in London – but he saw it as a step forward in the Russian case. More importantly, it allowed for the combating of a notion that Catherine was too keen to defend: enlightened despotism. Diderot's political advice to Catherine is to limit her own power, to abandon her royal prerogatives wherever possible, and to establish checks and balances by creating other political institutions, such as this permanent assembly. 'The heroic action of a good despot is to bind to his or her heir; it was the first question to pose to the commission [on the Nakaz].'[89] The worst-case scenario for a nation, Diderot repeats on numerous occasions, is to face three good despots one after the other. This would ruin the spirit of independence of the whole people.[90] As he had done against Frederick, Diderot does against Catherine. Monarchy itself is a threat to a good polity, for even good kings and queens are ultimately detrimental to citizens. Catherine, of course, did not follow his advice on the topic.

It is also in his defence of the working man that Diderot pro- motes a democratisation of institutions. The lower classes, he claims, are the wealth of the nation. Habituated to work to get things in life and to better their conditions, men of the lower classes will bring talent, glory and knowledge to their country. It is not only that there are more men of lower standing – although this remains a truism for Diderot – but also that they have an advantage over the wealthy as they have themselves struggled.[91] Perhaps thinking about himself, Diderot defends those who need the support of the state to achieve greatness. Diderot's plan for a university will demand that education be open to all – as a point of principle. Defining the word, Diderot says that 'A university is a school whose door is *indiscriminately* open to all children of the nation, where teachers who are paid for by the state initiate them to elementary knowledge of all sciences.'[92] We are far away from the elitist institutions that Diderot himself attended and gradu- ated from. A concern for the remuneration of all professions will be paramount to this project, starting of course with those who work at universities. They will not only be paid for by the state but given a fair salary and a decent pension after fifteen years of service.[93] Students will compete for scholarships, which must not be given by any particular individual, lest they try to influence the process. Scholarships should be competitive and distributed after an open exam (*concours*).[94] The same applies, of course, to public administration, against the practices of the *ancien régime* to sell positions of authority to the highest bidder. Only this will enable the growth of a class of citizens, who are liberated from their feudal masters, no longer serfs or slaves, and capable of running the state. While Diderot estimates at five percent the number of enlight- ened people in his day, it is clearly his wish for that class to grow, and he proposes policies to that effect.[95]

It is within this context that Diderot reimagines a type of social contract, as Holbach had done at the same time. Diderot had already used the language of the contract in the first volume of the *Encyclopédie*, when he argued that political authority ultimately lay in the consent of the nation.[96] But this point is not developed any further in the article, and is only picked up much later by Diderot, in the 1770s – that is, after Rousseau had published his *Contrat social*. It may be that Diderot was simply too busy with the *Encyclopédie* to respond to Rousseau any sooner, but in any case, his version of the contract is radically opposed to that of the Genevan philosopher. As always with Diderot, though, it is a dialogue between various positions on the state of nature and the social contract that is being put forward, rather than a systematic position. That being said, there is consistency in Diderot's position in at least one way: he believes that neither the condition of man in the state of nature is perfect, nor is that of social man; and he believes that no matter how good the contract is, it cannot possibly last forever. It is a belief in the imperfection of the political order that is the guiding thread of his social contract theory.

When it comes to speculation on the state of nature, Diderot is highly sceptical of our knowledge of it. In the notes he wrote for Catherine II, he clearly states that the 'study' of the state of nature is a matter for the foggy imagination of metaphysicians.[97] Diderot was of course very well aware of the position of others on the matter. He discusses the view that humans are weak in the state of nature, the view of Montesquieu, Voltaire, Jaucourt and other encyclopedists, the view that the family is the cornerstone of this state, as Boucher d'Argis had argued in the *Encyclopédie*, and he even quotes Hobbes directly.[98] Notable by his absence is the view of Rousseau, at least from this particular passage. But Diderot's argument is profoundly anti-Rousseauian. Speculating about what brought the first humans together to get out of the state of nature, Diderot argues that it is a fight against nature itself that created the situation that led to society. Nature is the first enemy, creating need and danger in the form of the harshness of the seasons, lack of food, illnesses and wild animals. The state of nature is not an ideal one, as Rousseau had pictured, but one of strife and struggle. Anything that brings us closer to this state, Diderot continues, is an evil (*un mal*), as it isolates humans and renders them weaker.[99] Typical of Diderot's prose, however, is his warning that we may have gone too far in our uniting against nature. We may have become stronger by grouping together, but we now not only have nature as an enemy, but other groups of human beings. One cannot have progress without further problems. Diderot repeats a similar thesis in his *Observations sur le Nakaz*.[100] In his contributions to Raynal's *Histoire des deux Indes*, Diderot also warns of the corruption of large cities and huge empires, which again go too far in humanity's struggle against nature.[101] Against such a state of corruption, Diderot discusses 'natural societies', where each city is located a safe distance from other cities, and there is no superabundance of population. This thesis is odd, as Diderot is generally a populationist, arguing that growth in population allows for growth in wealth in society. The passage, however, reads as a defence of the new world, where population is still spread thinly, against the old world (in this case including India and China), where large cities abound.

When discussing the revolution in British America in the third edition of the *Histoire des deux Indes*, Diderot further expands on his social contract. Against the thesis that all men are born equal, Diderot defends natural inequality, and in fact goes so far as to argue that tyranny is a direct consequence of this natural inequality.[102] 'The history of civilised man,' he concludes, 'is but the history of his misery. Every page is bloodied, some of the blood of oppressors, others of the blood of the oppressed.'[103] It may have been too early in 1780 to tell which way the American war of independence was headed, but Diderot is ready to jump to one conclusion: revolutions, whether they are successful or not, are the result of inequalities which started in the state of nature, and continue in the social state of human beings. No contract, furthermore, is eternal. All are subject to change, and if they do not change satisfactorily, as in the case of the American colonies, rebellions occur. Admitting the lack of power of speculative philosophy, Diderot concludes that it is self-interest and the ability to achieve happiness that determine whether a nation accepts its current government or attempts to overthrow it. The social contract, in other words, is only valid insofar as it maintains a state of being that the nation is willing to bear. The moment this is no longer the case, rebellions occur, which are a form of 'the legitimate exercise of an inalienable and natural right of the oppressed man, and even of the non-oppressed man'.[104] In perhaps the most revolutionary statement of Diderot's writings, he concludes that every social contract is up for revision, no matter how long-lasting and unchangeable it seems. It is no wonder that this third edition of the *Histoire des deux Indes* was publicly condemned and burned at the stake.

Diderot wrote an addition to the travel account of Bougainville, a French aristocrat who had led a circumnavigation of the globe between 1766 and 1769 and had written an account of his travels on his return. This *Supplément* to Bougainville's travels is to provide the last clues concerning Diderot's social contract theory. Bougainville's famous contribution to the debates about how humans lived in the state of nature was through his description of the inhabitants of Tahiti. By the time the expedition reaches the southern Pacific islands, it encounters dugout canoes, 'some sailing, others paddling',[105] with naked islanders ('savages') on them, brandishing long lances. From the outset of the journey, Bougainville is under no illusion that the natives live peacefully, as he is well aware that the first populated islands he had encountered were hostile to his expedition. Once they reach Tahiti, however, they are welcomed with open arms (and with gifts of animals and fruit) by its inhabitants. In exchange for these gifts, quite necessary for the survival of the expedition, they traded iron and other metals, specifically nails and earrings. The Tahitians, Bougainville notes, were 'giving before they had received, or receiving before they gave indifferently, with a kind of confidence, which made us conceive a good opinion of their character'.[106] They also had no weapons on board their canoes, and started to bring women with them, further convincing Bougainville of their peaceful natures.

But it is certainly the liberality of their sexual mores that most interested the travellers – and the reception of Bougainville's *Voyage*. Once they moored the ship close to the shore, canoes full of naked women approached. They had, Bougainville assures us, 'agreeable features, that are not inferior to most European women'.[107] Notwithstanding a certain 'natural timidity' and 'innocent manner', they offered themselves to the travellers. Or rather, as Bougainville explains, it was the men of the island who explained to the expedition what they were meant to do with the women; 'and their gestures, which were nothing less than equivocal, denoted in what manner we should form an acquaintance with her'.[108] Bougainville found it difficult to contain the French sailors under such circumstances, and notes that he even had difficulty containing himself! This description of the islanders' sexual liberality forms a large part of Diderot's discussion of the inhabitants. The Tahitians, living in a state close to that of nature, have no notion of marriage, or rather have a notion of marriage that is temporary and never permanent. 'Nature, our sovereign master', calls us to enjoy the simple pleasures of the flesh, says Diderot's Tahitian character Orou.[109] In a conversation with the chaplain of the ship, whom Orou had kindly invited to pleasure his daughters and his wife, the debate is around what religion signifies, and what could stop a person from enjoying the pleasures of life. Against a state of nature where women are held in common, or where women are free to choose their sexual partners, the chaplain symbolises the unnaturalness of Christianity and its virtues. In Tahiti, there are still social rules around what counts as a valid relation and what counts as a libertine one. There are rules about the age at which children become adults, for example, but no other penalties for their infringement than social stigma. There are no rules against incest, although it is considered a last resort – if the girl cannot find a partner, her father will provide her with children.[110] That is because children are considered the best gift in Tahitian society. A woman with children, Diderot's Orou tells us, is a good partner for a man, even if the children are not his.

It is not merely the sexual mores that attracted the attention of commentators. Bougainville's description of his expedition's economic exchanges with the islanders is also of interest. On this aspect, Bougainville is a little less perceptive. After the basic exchanges described above, what is of interest to the reader is the economic interactions once the expedition has set foot on the island. In order to treat those affected by scurvy, and to gather wood for the ships, he starts 'hiring' the natives to work. He also sends muskets on shore to defend the encampment, and has a display of fireworks to impress the natives.[111] All of these combined – the introduction of waged labour, the display of technical advances previously unknown to the natives, and the jealous guarding of the camp – disrupted the normal practices on the island, or, as Bougainville notes, 'doubtless their curiosity for new objects excited violent desires in them'.[112] But Bougainville, who noted that the Tahitians did not seem to have notions of property beyond their personal items, is at odds to understand why they suddenly feel the need to steal from the expedition. He lands more guns on the island, including canons, and orders his soldiers to shoot any thieves caught in the act. At the same time, he notes the continued hospitality of the people towards those of the expedition, and the continual invitations into their homes for food and sexual encounters. The disputes around thefts soon turned violent. A number of soldiers attacked Tahitians with bayonets, and the escalation in violence was only avoided when they were put in chains in the presence of the Tahitian chief, as well as the gifting of silks and tools.[113] Bougainville's thought, framed by a concept of private property alien to the communal and hospitable spirit of the Tahitians, is unable to grasp the impact of his economic activity on the natives. As he writes without sensing the paradox of his own sentences: 'in regards to things absolutely necessary for the maintenance of life, there was no personal property amongst them, and that they all had an equal right to those articles. In regard to us, they were expert thieves.'[114] How one can both have no notion of private property and be a thief is never explained by Bougainville. But Diderot had a much clearer idea about the significance of these facts.

Diderot claims that property is the first source of war or discord. 'Savage man' and the tiger have a common pretention to the forest, and this gives them their cruel character.[115] Building on Rousseau's insight that property was the beginning of humanity's stepping out of the state of nature, but refusing the amalgamation of all forms of property, Diderot explains the relations between the Tahitians. An old man – that Bougainville had mentioned – is fictionalised by Diderot, explaining his disapproval at the arrival of the expedition in the *Supplement*. 'We are innocent and happy', because 'we follow the pure instinct of nature', the old man claims.[116] All property is held in common, but the expedition has taught them to differentiate between 'yours' and 'mine'. The introduction of guards for the camp, in other words, challenged the social norms of the Tahitians. In a society where nothing is guarded against others, the introduction of restrictions provoked the Tahitians into curiosity and acquiring the objects so jealously guarded. Diderot notes that the introduction of work was itself a new concept for the Tahitians.[117] It is likely that the introduction of waged labour, paid for in nails, was hardly understood by the Tahitians used to other modes of exchange. A codified economic exchange, in other words, was alien to them, as was the very notion of theft. 'He gave you his fruits, his wife and his daughter, he invited you to his home, and you killed him for a handful of grains that he took without asking you.'[118] Diderot, always perceptive of economic inequalities and their impact on societies, points us to the different economic theories behind the two populations. From the perspective of the Tahitians, it made little sense that Bougainville would give them nails at one moment (as they were helping with cutting trees), and then would shoot at them the next moment when they were merely entering the encampment. There certainly was no notion of land ownership, and given the openness of their own homes, it is certain they would have expected similar hospitality in return. Bougainville had been unable to theorise these economic differences, but they did not escape Diderot.

What characterises Diderot's social contract theory is that he actually does not consider the state of nature to be one that is *prior* to the social state. On numerous occasions in his writings of the 1770s, the condition of men in the state of nature is consubstantial with the condition of social man. It so happens that these conditions are those of colonialism and inequality. Diderot is thus one of the first to theorise that the very speculation of the state of nature is in itself a colonial frame of mind. The conceptualising of land as empty is a direct response to the relative sparsity of population in the new world, when compared to the old world. European nations, he claims, have conceived of America as being in a Hobbesian state of nature, ignoring the local inhabitants who count for nothing, and only considering the claims of other European nations on that land.[119] 'You despise hobbism for your neighbourhood, and this disastrous system acts as a supreme law when you practise it afar.'[120] The state of nature may be a chimera of metaphysicians, but it is also a helpful myth to justify colonial expansion. Diderot, as others have noted,[121] is not strictly speaking an anti-colonial thinker. He considers that colonies are helpful ways to deal with large populations, and that colonies can bring benefits to all, including the native inhabitants. But his utopian colonialism requires a mixing of populations, where the natives are fully integrated into the political community created by the colonists, and is very different from colonial expansion as it had happened by the late eighteenth century.[122]

Diderot's speculations about the interaction of Europeans and other peoples also led him to think deeply about economics. Already in the 1760s in the *Encyclopédie*, Diderot had put forward an economic theory that accepted a form of labour theory of value, when he claimed that wealth comes from man, and more precisely from man's productivity (*hommes industrieux*).[123] It won't be until 1770, however, that Diderot operates a major shift in perspective, by moving away from the physiocratic school of thought (that saw all value come from the land), and starts to diversify his economic position, notably by a defence of manufactories in his *Apologie de l'abbé Galiani*.[124] In the text, he gives a clear example of how someone's labour in a manufactory helps stimulate the labour of others, effectively disputing one of the central tenets of physiocratic economics, and moving close to the labour theory of value as Adam Smith and David Ricardo will later formulate it.[125] Six years prior to the publication of the iconic economic text *The Wealth of Nations* by Smith, Diderot had already contributed to a critique of political economy as found in previous physiocratic texts. In papers written in 1756–7, Quesnay, perhaps the most representative of the physiocratic school of economic thought, had argued that France is an agricultural kingdom whose wealth largely derives from a productive and rich farming body.[126] Quesnay's work was revolutionary in the 1750s, as it proposed a change of policy for the French state, that had hitherto favoured a more mercantilist model of trade, with monopolies and trade companies instead of the free trade model Quesnay promoted. But it had largely ignored manufactories as a source of wealth creation. Diderot further explicitly links the benefits of manufactories and his religious thought. By creating wealth, manufactories contribute to 'forgetting the sky, destroying superstition' and bringing you 'to a state of emancipation', and help combat despotism.[127]

Against metaphysical concerns for the salvation of the soul, in other words, material concerns for the creation of wealth help create a barrier to nefarious religious belief, and the political systems of authority that come with it. Manufactories create material wealth, which in turn allows the labourers to free themselves, not only economically, but religiously and politically. Diderot may have been too optimistic about the role that manufactories could play for human emancipation, but it was a direct consequence of his materialism.

Similar advice is given to Catherine the Great a few years later. Against religious superstition, it is convenient to build commerce and trade.[128] Diderot will go so far as to defend luxury as a means to encourage the liberal arts. Since gold is inedible, Diderot argues, rich citizens will create a need for poets, philosophers and painters – allowing for luxury to morph into virtue. But the bulk of the wealth of nations does not come from its rich citizens; it comes from the ones that need to sell their labour for a living. It is from the *tiers état*, Diderot claims, that come most enlightened men.[129] By opening up all positions of influence to competition (*concours*), Catherine will be able to attract some of these geniuses that just happened to be born poor. In his *Observations sur le Nakaz*, Diderot will further argue for outright emancipation, not only of slaves, but also of serfs whose condition is too miserable to allow for rising through social ranks.[130] Although it will take almost a full century to take effect, the abolition of serfdom was seen by Diderot as an essential economic policy, not just a political policy about freedom over servitude. Serfdom is detrimental to the creation of wealth in the nation, as well as odious to lovers of liberty, and Diderot attempted to convince Catherine that her nation will only get stronger by adopting the policy.

In the *Histoire des deux Indes*, when putting together his opposition to large mining cities, such as Potosí, Diderot still cannot steer clear of his labour theory of value. Mines have created industry, have encouraged growth and have created manufactories.[131] But such advantages are put in the light of a theory of inflation, where increasing the amount of currency available in an economy cannot make the country richer. Never will mines be preferable to agriculture or manufactories, Diderot concludes, industries that create actual wealth instead of adding to the currency supply. His economic theory further sheds light on his social contract. When discussing the disadvantages of social man over man in the state of nature, Diderot claims that it is inequality, alienation (in the sense that men are unable to sense their own oppression), and the distribution of humans into social classes that form the backbone of the disadvantages of man's social condition.[132] It is little wonder that Diderot was named by Marx as his favourite prose writer.[133] Though not a defender of collective ownership of the means of production, Diderot did understand something that was dear to Marx's theory: that wealth comes from labour, and that large inequalities in wealth hurt economic growth.

Conclusion

Unlike Meslier and Holbach, Diderot never openly claims the label of atheism. As I have shown here, it is not because he fully rejects atheism – his beliefs fit at least some of the definitions of the term he gives us – but because he was sceptical that atheism was enough to describe his worldview – or even his religious views. If Diderot maintained the possibility of God, it was certainly not a conventional God, and in fact it was a purely material God that can be described in terms compatible with his materialist understanding of the universe. The hylozoist God, the great animal that is the universe, is one such possibility for Diderot's theistic speculations. In the next chapter, I will expand further on why we can conceptualise this position as metatheistic, as one that both incorporates atheism and attempts to move past it. Diderot is fascinating for a radical understanding of atheism, because he brings the notion to its ultimate formulation – one that we have not surpassed today. Diderot's religious thought, however, had dramatic impact on his political thought. If Diderot is happy to speculate about the nature of a living God, he is not shy of dismissing its utility in the political realm. What matters, first and foremost in politics, is the ability of the political regime to help the material needs of its citizens. Unconcerned with finding the ideal political community, Diderot is fascinated by the ability of different political organisations to contribute to the happiness of their citizens. But some systems are better than others. It is better to have more equality than more privilege, it is better to have more participation in politics than more elite control, it is better to have economic growth than a stagnant economy, better to have a large class of independent citizens than a nation of serfs. Ultimately, Diderot comes the closest out of our four thinkers to defending a vision of democracy that still challenges many of the inequalities and injustices we face today.

Notes

1. Trousson, *Denis Diderot ou le vrai Prométhée*, 31.
2. Ibid. 41.
3. Ibid. 80; Gillot, *Denis Diderot*, 21.
4. Morellet cited in Trousson, *Denis Diderot ou le vrai Prométhée*, 197.
5. Trousson, *Denis Diderot ou le vrai Prométhée*, 197.
6. Ibid. 132.
7. Ibid. 165.
8. Betts, *Early Deism in France*, 76.
9. Trousson, *Denis Diderot ou le vrai Prométhée*, 275–6.
10. Ibid. 276.
11. Ibid. 363.
12. Ibid. 547.
13. Artz, *The Enlightenment of France*, 91.
14. Hubert, *D'Holbach et ses amis*, 27.
15. Wickwar, *Baron d'Holbach*, 46.
16. Hulliung, *The Autocritique of Enlightenment*, 95.
17. Adams, 'Diderot'.
18. Vartanian, 'From Deist to Atheist. Diderot's Philosophical Orientation. 1746–1749'.
19. Diderot, *Pensées philosophiques*, 21.
20. Ibid. 23.
21. Ibid. 26.
22. Wilson, *Diderot*, 600.
23. Diderot, *Encyclopédie*, vol. I, 480–1.
24. Diderot, *De la suffisance de la religion naturelle*, 57.
25. Ibid. 63.
26. Diderot, *La promenade du sceptique*, 102.
27. Ibid. 109.
28. Ibid. 120.
29. Diderot, *Lettre sur les aveugles*, 147; Fontenay, *Diderot ou le matérialisme enchanté*.

30. Diderot, *Lettre sur les aveugles*, 148.
31. Ibid. 167.
32. Ibid. 166.
33. Ibid. 169.
34. Letter from Diderot to Voltaire, 11 June 1749, in Diderot, *Correspondance*, 15.
35. Diderot and d'Alembert, *Encyclopédie*, vol. 6, 402.
36. Diderot, *Pensées sur l'interprétation de la nature*, 559.
37. Wartofsky, 'Diderot and the Development of Materialism Monism', 281–6.
38. Diderot, *Pensées sur l'interprétation de la nature*, 564.
39. Ibid. 568.
40. Ibid. 590.
41. Diderot, *Le rêve de d'Alembert*, 606.
42. Paterson, *The Infinite Worlds of Giordano Bruno*.
43. Wilson, 'Leibniz and Atomism'.
44. Diderot, *Le rêve de d'Alembert*, 639.
45. Diderot, *Observations sur Hemsterhuis*, 711.
46. Ibid. 711.
47. Fowler, 'Introduction', in *New Essays on Diderot*, 2.
48. Versini, *Denis Diderot*, 131.
49. Diderot, *Observations sur Hemsterhuis*, 753.
50. Diderot, *Correspondance*, 979.
51. Ibid. 1146.
52. Diderot, *Éléments de physiologie*, 1317; Diderot, *De la suffisance de la religion naturelle*.
53. Diderot, *Mélanges pour Catherine II*, 271.
54. Diderot, *Jacques the Fatalist*.
55. Diderot, *Éléments de physiologie*, 1262.
56. Ibid. 1262.
57. Ibid. 1266.
58. Ibid. 1275.
59. Taylor, *A Secular Age*, 327.
60. Diderot, *Éléments de physiologie*, 1278.
61. Ibid. 1279.
62. Ibid. 1299.
63. Ibid. 1317.
64. Diderot, *Encyclopédie*, vol. II, 23.
65. See footnote, ibid. 23.
66. Diderot, *Encyclopédie*, 22.
67. Ibid. 22.
68. Ibid. 24.
69. Ibid. 25.
70. Ibid. 26.

71. Ibid. 28.
72. Ibid. 35.
73. Diderot, *Lettre de M. Denis Diderot sur l'examen de l'essai sur les préjugés*, 165.
74. Ibid. 172.
75. Diderot, *Notes écrites de la main d'un souverain à la marge de Tacite*, 177.
76. Ibid. 179.
77. Diderot, *Mélanges pour Catherine II*, 268.
78. Diderot, *Plan d'une université*, 464.
79. Diderot, *Mélanges pour Catherine II*, 207.
80. Ibid. 263.
81. Ibid. 265.
82. Ibid. 289.
83. Diderot, *Observations sur l'instruction de l'Impératrice de Russie*, 509.
84. Diderot, *Plan d'une université*, 484.
85. Ibid. 486.
86. Letter from Diderot to Damialville, end of May 1765, in Diderot, *Correspondance*, 493.
87. On Diderot's views on this, see Letter from Diderot to Vialet, July 1766, in Diderot, *Correspondance*, 657.
88. Diderot, *Mélanges pour Catherine II*, 276.
89. Diderot, *Observations sur le Nakaz*, 515.
90. Diderot, *Mélanges pour Catherine II*, 275; Diderot, *Observations sur le Nakaz*, 514; Diderot, *Contributions à l'histoire des deux Indes*, 660.
91. Diderot, *Mélanges pour Catherine II*, 283, 352.
92. Diderot, *Plan d'une université*, 418.
93. Ibid. 413.
94. Ibid. 494.
95. Diderot, *Observations sur le Nakaz*, 517.
96. Diderot, *Encyclopédie*, vol. I, 24.
97. Diderot, *Mélanges pour Catherine II*, 311.
98. Ibid. 311–12, see also Thielemann, 'Diderot and Hobbes', 221–2.
99. Diderot, *Mélanges pour Catherine II*, 312.
100. Diderot, *Observations sur le Nakaz*, 544.
101. Diderot, *Histoire des deux Indes*, 634.
102. Ibid. 713–14.
103. Ibid. 714.
104. Ibid. 714.
105. Bougainville, *A Voyage round the World*, 102.
106. Ibid. 107.
107. Ibid. 108.
108. Ibid.
109. Diderot, *Supplément au voyage de Bougainville*, 21.
110. Ibid. 42.

111. Bougainville, *A Voyage round the World*, 112.
112. Ibid. 113.
113. Ibid. 116.
114. Ibid. 123.
115. Diderot, *Supplément au voyage de Bougainville*, 9.
116. Ibid. 14.
117. Ibid. 15.
118. Ibid. 17.
119. Diderot, *Histoire des deux Indes*, 696–7.
120. Ibid. 697.
121. Strugnell, 'Diderot's Anti-colonialism: A Problematic Notion'.
122. Diderot, *Histoire des deux Indes*, 693.
123. Diderot, *Encyclopédie*, 48.
124. Diderot, *Apologie de l'abbé Galiani*, 133.
125. Ibid. 141.
126. Steiner, 'Physiocracy and French Pre-Classical Political Economy', 63–7.
127. Diderot, *Apologie de l'abbé Galiani*, 151.
128. Diderot, *Mélanges pour Catherine II*, 240.
129. Ibid. 352.
130. Diderot, *Observations sur le Nakaz*, 534.
131. Diderot, *Histoire des deux Indes*, 607.
132. Ibid. 676.
133. Marx, *Confesssions*.

5

The State of Atheism in France, 1789

Now that we have a clear picture of the atheism and political thought of the four authors of the eighteenth century that best encapsulate a theory of positive atheism, I want to return to a three-pronged approach to the concept of atheism itself. I will show here that understanding atheism as both negative and positive is helpful to appreciating what atheism has contributed to intellectual debates. But I also want to show that a third step was already taken in the eighteenth century: that atheism has moved beyond itself and turned into metatheism. These three movements (negative, positive and meta) are now part of atheism's landscape. Even the metatheist, I will show, which is best illustrated by Diderot, is still a type of atheist. He moved past atheism, but without fully negating it. He incorporated the contributions of negative and positive atheism to make them appeal to those who do not share the same opinion about gods. This movement past the narrow confines of the community of unbelievers is still an important lesson for modern atheism, and one that the eighteenth century has taught us.

I have argued elsewhere for a three-pronged approach to understanding atheism's conceptual contribution to philosophy, so let me rephrase some of this here.[1] I distinguish between three conceptual types of atheism: the negative, positive and meta-atheisms, which can be seen in the history of atheism I have just provided. Though the negative type of atheism often was used as a pejorative term, this need not be the case. Despite the fact that some scholarship, which we have discussed in the introduction, still uses this argument against atheism, I will show here that this is not a fatal limitation of atheism per se. Negative atheism is first and foremost described as reactive. It reacts to theism, as its name suggests, and argues against various religious, mythical, theistic or even deistic and agnostic understandings of the existence of gods. This is often taken as a weakness of atheism, as it depends upon theism for the meaning of the gods that it denies. While there is certainly some truth to that, what those who use this argument imply is that atheism must be able to stand on its own. I argue here that asking atheism to exist in a vacuum is intellectually dishonest. No religion could claim isolation, either. Judaism had the miracles of the Pharaohs, Christianity had Hellenistic gods, Islam had other religions of the Book. All religions of which we have some historical knowledge have had to differentiate themselves from others. In this sense, why should atheism be any different? The philosophy of Gadamer's hermeneutics, which has guided this study, gives us an important sense of why traditions matter and why they are never fully overcome. Atheists themselves, of course, have used this reaction of atheism to other beliefs to their advantage. They are reacting against abuses, errors, corruption, violence and countless other injustices. It is simply intellectually required to engage with competing philosophical claims on the same subject, and this does not make atheism any more parasitic than other beliefs. But negative atheism also negates. It negates particular conceptions, it negates the power of the Church, it negates the political order that comes with a politico-religious alliance such as that which existed in the *ancien régime*, or that still presents in some political systems today. This negationist phase of atheism is inherently limiting of its position, for it may be the only thing that atheists have in common. They may fundamentally disagree with each other on how to bring things forward, on how to build a positive type of atheism.

As we have seen in the previous four chapters, there have been several attempts to build this positive atheism, and these attempts have been varied and plural, and, to an extent, successful in bringing together a coherent worldview without gods. Since one of the largest challenges faced by our four authors, who all defended a conception of positive atheism, was the potential for a society of atheists to exist and thrive, they had to address this point. I will argue in this conclusion that, in a sense, this work was already cut out for them. They could point to concrete examples of virtuous atheists, whether contemporary, historical or removed from us by great distances, as travel accounts had made increasingly clear. But this still needed philosophical justification. The four authors did not agree on all the details for this positive atheism, but they did agree on some of its larger lines. An ethical framework was possible without gods and without the Church, if only based on self-interest, social bonds and utility. Perhaps their utilitarian theories are a little optimistic, and at times naive, but they proposed to answer the challenge that positive atheism was impossible because the doctrine itself was parasitic. They also agreed that politics needed to be reformed, and despite serious disagreements on the details, some form of positive political atheology emerges here – with an emphasis on increased citizen participation, an aversion to civil strife and international conflict, and a concern for the material well-being of fellow citizens.

With Diderot in particular, though isolated passages in all four authors point to this, there is also a desire to move past atheism. What I have called a *metatheism* is a dialectical movement past the limitations of negative and positive atheologies. That is to say that Diderot has not renounced his atheism, but that he sees the logical continuation of his atheism, which essentially denies that religious doctrine is a useful or worthwhile separator of human communities, to its logical conclusion. Diderot is thus both an atheist and a metatheist. He understands that bringing the materialist, secular and emancipatory insights of his philosophy requires cross-belief engagement. He understands that there are voices in the Catholic Church, among the tribes of Tahiti, and among the Orthodox patriarchs of Saint Petersburg who can be convinced to fight for similar goals without espousing his own atheism. Atheism, in a sense, becomes secondary to the values and objectives that became clear through his atheism. This is the dialectic sense of metatheism, that a particular religio-philosophical position (atheism) brought some thinkers to particular conclusions about their values (material well-being, increased political equality) which others from different religio-philosophical positions could come to by a different route. Aware of its existence in a plural world, atheism can cease to be a proselytising enterprise, and attempt to be a bridging enterprise with other belief systems. Diderot understood this, by the end of the eighteenth century, better than anyone else.

The positive conception of atheism was already a problem for Bayle. For him, it was indeed a problem because he had observed the existence of societies of atheists, and the existence of atheist individuals that nonetheless acted morally, and often had a clear advantage over the most zealous of religious believers. Whether it was the Hottentot (Khoikhoi) people of southern Africa, the ancient philosophers who had no knowledge of a monotheistic deity and often doubted the existence of the gods of their contemporaries, or Spinoza, proof was there that one could live a perfectly moral life without God. Bayle came up with an ingenious way to explain this: morality is independent from religious thought. This great ethical split allowed Bayle to conceptualise atheists as being both wrong, in that they did not believe in the existence of something that exists, and good in that they based their behaviour on ethical principles that did not need theological justifications or foundations. There are good reasons why Bayle was read so widely in the Enlightenment, and one of these is that his moral theory proved attractive to an educated public that accepted diversity of religious opinion much more easily because of their interactions with other beliefs. That such ideas flourished particularly well in the Netherlands, where Spinoza and Bayle lived, is of little surprise. There, despite the period of religious turmoil, Calvinists and Lutherans, Catholics and Jews, sceptics and unbelievers lived side by side without fearing for their lives. Social stigma was enough of a deterrent, for much of the history of the United Provinces, for political authorities to see no need for state power to intervene in philosophical speculation.

That is not to say that there was a free circulation of ideas even in the Netherlands. Bayle had to face serious consequences for his work and lost his professorship in the battle against Jurieu. But he could continue to live and write, and flourish, following this episode. The situation in France was very different, as we have seen with the case of Vanini. But in the second half of the eighteenth century, cracks were appearing in the defences of the *ancien régime*. Helvétius's publication of *De l'esprit* characterises this arbitrary character of French censorship. His book, though it denies the existence of God nowhere, was immediately taken as atheistic – as it was largely based on a materialist ontology, a denial of the immortality of the soul, and a morality free of religious authority.[2] The book immediately attracted the wrath of religious authorities, notably the archbishop of Paris, the Pope himself and the faculty of theology at the Sorbonne; as well as of political authorities, such as the Parisian *parlement*.[3] But in the absolutist monarchical state that was France at the time, Helvétius was saved by the clemency of the King – whose mistress and foreign minister were close friends of the *philosophe*. Helvétius had to retract some of his statements made in the book, and apologise, but he got off lightly compared to others with no political connections. This misadventure meant that Helvétius's book had a profound impact on other *philosophes*' methods. Diderot could not hope to get away with similarly radical theories, and hid his most radical political works, which only surfaced after his death. Holbach, whose literary career was just about to erupt, published all of his books anonymously.

The religious authorities, together with the *parlement* that was attempting to assert its own authority, took a much harsher line for years to come. *Tolerantism* was the prime target after 1758. The higher clergy understood only too well that the spirit of toleration pushed by the *philosophes* was a challenge to the Church's authority over secular matters. Toleration had the direct effect of calling for a limiting of religious oversight, over publications notably, and the Church was not ready to let go of its prerogative or of its privileges. Though we scarcely read them today, there was a boom in the publication of anti-philosophical books in that period. Jonathan Israel has documented this important yet neglected social movement of the late 1750s, 1760s, 1770s and 1780s, and there were literally thousands of books coming out of anti-philosophical presses across Europe at the time.[4] Their attacks on the *philosophes* were along numerous lines, but almost all concurred that the new philosophy was dangerous on social and political grounds. It sought to displace the role that religion had traditionally exerted over morals and social order, and it sought to destroy the political foundations of Europe. Tolerance was attacked as a wedge to drive open the floodgates of republicanism, atheism and a complete dismantling of the social order. The full extent of the law had to be used to punish those who transgressed the established order, as the chevalier de La Barre discovered in 1766.

The Abbé Nicolas-Sylvestre Bergier (1718–90) was among the most well known of the anti-philosophes. He is also perhaps the most interesting, as he was a regular participant at Holbach's salon, and knew Diderot very well. His largest anti-philosophical work, the *Examen du matérialisme* of 1771, was a refutation of Holbach's *Système de la nature*. Bergier had even shared an early draft of the book with Holbach and Diderot, both of whom thought it was a well-written critique that would be popular with those of a similar anti-materialist persuasion.[5] His argument was quite simple: the author of the system had misunderstood the thought of moderate English scientists and philosophers, such as Locke, Clarke and Newton, and had radicalised it, thereby losing grasp of reason.[6] Against the empiricist claims of the *system*, Bergier claimed that true knowledge of nature brings one closer to God, not closer to atheism.[7] No doubt Bergier, leading the charge against Holbach and others, saw himself as the true representative of the Enlightenment. He did not share in the hostile anti-tolerance doctrines of others within the Church, but aimed to defend a vision of reason and science that made room for God. This was the struggle of Locke against Hobbes, Bergier further claims – of reason properly moderated by calm and reverence to God, and irrationalism left unchecked. Bayle was also regularly identified as an inspiration for the new philosophy. For without his argument for the toleration of atheists, the new philosophy would not have been possible.

One of the best examples of the inroads that the positive atheism of Diderot and Holbach was making is their friendship with the abbot Morellet. Fresh out of his studies in theology at the Sorbonne, Morellet met Diderot in 1752 at the age of twenty-five, and soon found himself admiring the philosopher's wit and intelligence, while simultaneously disagreeing with his religious position.[8] For Morellet, both Holbach and Diderot were outright atheists, who did not hide their positions in the dinners at Holbach's house. Morellet was among the inner circle there, being among the ten persons that later knew of Holbach's authorship of many works, including the *Système de la nature* and the *Politique naturelle*. Morellet, in memoirs written during the revolution, prides himself on having kept the secret of Holbach's authorship, never doubting the tragic consequences that would have ensued from such a revelation to the authorities.[9] If Morellet never shied away from defending his theistic position at the baron's table, his host (along with Diderot), never tired of listening to him make his defence of religion. Convinced by the need for increased toleration, Morellet himself tirelessly pursued a position that drew a sharp difference between religious toleration, which he rejected, and civil toleration, which he advocated.[10] It is, he argued, the prerogative of true believers to defend their faith against misinterpretations, but this is fully compatible with a neutrality from public officials in matters of faith. The onus for religious conversion is not on those who exercise power, but on those who convince through scripture and faith. Diderot and Holbach could not disagree with such an eloquent defence of toleration from a religious perspective. Morellet relates his unfortunate attempt to make this distinction in the *Encyclopédie*. Tamponet, the *Encyclopédie*'s censor, had made drastic deletions to Morellet's article on Gomarus, which discussed the thought of a Calvinist theologian and his followers. The spirit of toleration that came with Morellet's article was too much for his Catholic censor, and the second half of the article was struck from the printed version.[11] Against the censorship of the Church, Morellet the abbot was ready to side with the atheists. Even when he eventually stopped contributing to the *Encyclopédie* in 1758, following the withdrawal of the royal privilege, Morellet did not stop interacting with the atheists. He did more than merely tolerate their presence, though, as in his *Memoirs* he admits loving them.[12] Their spirit of tolerance, their generosity and their love of truth and philosophy was enough for Morellet to overlook their theological disagreements and establish long-lasting and deep affective bonds with both Diderot and Holbach. Positive atheism meant that one can both be an atheist and love non-atheists; that one can be deeply religious, and love those who are not. Morellet,

Holbach and Diderot shared more in common than they disagreed about. Morellet even goes so far as to absolve his friends of any responsibility for the events of the revolution. They had never advocated civil unrest, and it was inconceivable to see them as forerunners of what unfolded from 1789. If someone was to blame for these events, it was undoubtedly Rousseau.[13]

Revolutionary Ideas

The radicalism of the four authors discussed in this book was certainly subtler than that required for a revolution like that of 1789. They largely shared the prejudice of their intellectual peers against *le vulgaire* – which can be translated as 'the plebs' – and many mentions of the term 'democracy' in their works are still pejorative, especially for Bayle and Holbach, but also, until quite late, for Diderot. Apart from Meslier, whose enthusiasm for political violence is undoubtable, they were sceptical of the power of a revolution to truly effect social change in a positive light. They all saw revolutions as a consequence of bad political leadership, rather than as a source of renewal and an opportunity for change. None of them really foresaw the emergence of large republics, and they still thought about democratic polities on a small scale – that of the *polis* rather than that of the nation-state. But they also thought that political institutions can and should change, and that increased participation in politics was – on the whole – a positive development. They all thought that tyranny and despotism were ills to be remedied, even in their enlightened and philosophical versions. They all argued that a revolution of the mind was needed – and that it was necessary if not inevitable. They all took considerable personal risks to write what they did against political powers that did their best to censor them (or worse), as we have just seen. Their works are the product of periods of intense philosophical, social and political turmoil, and they pointed, calmly yet firmly, in the direction they believed should be taken. They put the propagation of ideas and ideals before their career and personal safety and left a body of work to posterity that we can cherish today. They were true radicals in the sense we discussed in the introduction: they sought to get to the roots of issues, and

never let go of problems until they were solved, sometimes continuing to engage in intellectual debates until their deaths if they
hadn't solved them to their satisfaction. Their determination and
passion are without doubt some of their most noble attributes, and
they merit the praise that only the dead can enjoy – the gratitude
of future generations.

What, then, do our four authors have in common politically?
On the surface, Bayle the absolutist shares little with Meslier the
radical republican, and while Holbach and Diderot shared many
political opinions, the precise nature of their ideal polity is left
vague throughout their works. That is not to say that there is no
political thought there, and I have argued throughout the book
against such a simplification. The four authors' insistence on toleration was as radical as it gets. I have shown in Chapter 1 how
Bayle's conception of toleration, as a universal theory that included
toleration of atheists, went much further than that of many of his
contemporaries, including the more moderate Locke, for whom
Catholics (disguised behind the figure of the Muslim) and atheists
could not be tolerated. Against a non-radical Enlightenment that
defends toleration with severe limits imposed upon it, the four
radicals we have looked at here all had a thorough and powerful
understanding of how important freedom of conscience, freedom
of expression, and religious or philosophical speculation are. The
potency of this radical claim may be lost on some readers today, as
we have come to embrace those principles rather widely, but they
required that initial battle of ideas, formulated in hiding by largely
anonymous authors. The distance covered between the revocation of the edit of Nantes in 1685 and the adoption of the bill on
toleration in France in 1787 was enormous, and it required radicals to push for a settlement of the modus vivendi not only in their
favour, but in the favour of all those who held unpopular opinions.

It was not only the atheists, in other words, that needed toleration, but atheists as the least-liked group in society were the
prime example of citizens whom we could come to tolerate and
learn to live with – or even come to love. The same argument,
of course, held true for religious minorities. Toleration should
logically apply to Jews, Muslims, Hindus, ancestor worshippers,
animists or any other citizen living under the rule of the state.

This was not merely a hypothetical situation, as colonial empires had raised those precise questions. Edmund Burke had made the case for similar religious toleration under very specific circumstances. As Lock, Burke's recent biographer notes, the early East India Company policy towards Bengal was not yet that of later nineteenth-century expansion.[14] Burke saw it as essential to limit the damage the Company did to Indian society; the two pillars of Church and Nobility needed to be preserved for order to be maintained. But Diderot, before Burke, had already made the case that colonial powers had a duty to preserve the societies in which they established colonies. Against Burke, who sees religious freedom as the preservation of a pillar of society, Diderot saw intrinsic value in the cultures which European nations had encountered abroad. Conversion to Christianity was, of course, off the table, but Diderot further believed that an interaction of cultures, and a mixture of peoples, was the way forward. Against Burke who wished to maintain social relations intact whilst profiting from intercontinental trade, Diderot wished for incremental change, assimilation of peoples, and racial mixture.[15] The two could not be further apart – with Burke, unsurprisingly, on the conservative side,[16] and Diderot on the radical side. Toleration was merely a tool to ensure stability, peace and prosperity, but it became a good in itself, something on which increased interaction between cultures could be built.

Bayle was the instigator of a new method of political analysis: critique. It is not an exaggeration to see him as the progenitor of critical theory; he practically invented the literary genre. Where Kantian critique laid dynamite under the entirety of the foundations of Western philosophy, and failed to detonate the trigger (by postulating the immortality of the soul, God and free will),[17] Bayle had already sapped the defences of the canon through his critical approach. The power of critique came through the power of the dialectic. Seen not only as a negative tool, critique acquired a positive dimension as well, as we have seen in the chapter on Bayle. The three other thinkers we discussed here also used this powerful tool to undermine much more than religious authority. The foundations of their political thought, as varied as they are, are all in the profound rethinking of their contemporary condition. It is not quite enough to speculate about the *kalipolis*, or even about the social contract as an ideal, but any political and social thought must be grounded in the here and now. Bayle's concern about and opposition to plans for a Protestant invasion of France, Meslier's rural and local politics, Holbach's ethocracy, and Diderot's critique of colonialism all take part in this important critical appraisal of material conditions for everyday citizens. Without Bayle, such a critique would simply not have been possible.

Meslier, Holbach and Diderot's materialisms made them particularly careful of the impact of political decisions on the material lives of citizens. But Bayle was not unaware of the importance of material needs being met to live a meaningful life – he certainly had direct experience of this himself, and his opposition to the *dragonnades* made this clear. What is striking about the three other authors, though, is that they are pushing for a new direction in political thought that we are still indebted to. They are all materialists who insist on the improvement of material conditions for all. Unlike most of their contemporaries, who were interested in the institutions of the state, such as Montesquieu, or the valuing of a spirit of community over material wealth, such as Rousseau, the focus of our materialists is on concrete improvement in the living conditions of ordinary people. They all defend conceptions of property that make this possible: ownership of your own home, and of a piece of land that allows for subsistence, or fair remuneration in professions and manufactories. This ideal was to be seen by later, Marxist thinkers as desperately bourgeois, reflecting the emergence of the social class they were members of. For all of their differences, and – apart from Holbach – their financial hardships, they were all members of the bourgeoisie. Meslier, who inherited a small rent allowing him to join the priesthood, Diderot, whose father amassed moderate wealth in the provinces and finished his life with a considerable income, and Bayle, who lived modestly from his lectureship and then from his writings, were all relatively well off compared to their contemporaries. That did not make them insensitive to the material conditions of the peasantry, or the emerging working class in manufactories. They knew too well the hardships of peasants with noble landlords, or of artisans trying to make a living in the cities. Even Holbach, a nobleman, had inherited the title from his uncle who had himself bought it following a fortune made on the stock market. Though Holbach's wealth was considerable, he was not a member of the old nobility, and had no sympathy for them. If landlords need to exist, he maintained, they still have a duty to contribute to the well-being of their tenants.

The new impulse of the century was, of course, the notion of utility. All four authors see it as a better guiding principle for ethics and politics than any other principles hitherto used. As I have argued elsewhere,[18] this form of utilitarian thought is not quite the utilitarianism we have come to know and expect. It is neither act- nor rule-based utilitarianism since it still sees utility in vague and imprecise terms. Utility is not an objective measure to be achieved by scientific means, but rather something that must be discussed and debated. Diderot is probably the clearest on this, as it fits with his general writing style, where debate is the norm and conclusions are the exception. But all four authors agreed that utility, arrived at through the communal exercise of reason, was better than other forms of political argumentation. In particular, it was better than revelation, abstract principles or universal claims to be applied irrespective of the situation. Categorical imperatives, as Kant would later formulate them,[19] are a poor guide for ethical and political practice. Better to have a flawed and changing conception of general utility, they thought, which can be challenged and changed as the situation requires, than to stick to one's guns (sometimes literally) and insist on strict principles.

None of these thinkers, therefor, insisted on a political model they thought was best in all circumstances. One does not find the strong defence of democracy that one might expect from having read Jonathan Israel's work, for example. Neither Bayle, Meslier, Holbach nor Diderot believed that we could solve the political situation of a particular country by following strictly the example of another. What works in one context may not work in another, where political culture may differ enormously. In some cases, as Bayle argued, despotism is better than revolution, and although the other three thinkers would have disagreed with him on this point, they accept the underlying assumption that circumstances may require political compromise. None of them strictly rule out monarchical rule, although Diderot and Meslier are particularly virulent in their attacks on even the most enlightened of despots. Certainly, with the possible exception of Bayle, they all favoured increased participation in politics. They all opposed violent revolution, which they saw as a reaction to dictatorial rule rather than real opportunity for change. Diderot, however, came closest to defending revolutionary ideals using political violence in his defence of the American war of independence. Perhaps Holbach shared his view, but he had stopped writing in 1776 due to poor health, so we cannot speculate further with the materials we have available to us. None of them had foreseen the events of 1789, however, as none really believed in large republics. But that did not stop revolutionaries, notably Desmoulins, from arguing that without the radical atheist challenge, the revolution would not have been possible.[20]

When it came to international politics, all four thinkers are very sceptical of the virtues of warfare to achieve useful goals. Bayle is by far the most critical in this respect, arguing that peace is valuable even if it means one needs to tolerate injustices. This is a much more radical position than that achieved, at the end of the Enlightenment, by Kant, and which is the most familiar to scholars and students today. Kant's idea of perpetual peace, in some respects, is utopian — or worse, it requires a religious basis to function.[21] This is worse if only because an international order that requires a common religious heritage is unrealistic even if the common heritage is relatively thin. Kant's argument is deeply rooted in a Protestant ethic, but even a grouping of Abrahamic religions, for examples, would still be too exclusive on the international stage, as it would still exclude a large part of the world whose religious traditions do not fall within such a heritage. Bayle's defence of peace is thus more convincing than Kant's, even if the former is largely unread on this topic today, while the latter is the focus of thousands of studies. But even Holbach, who is the most open to military intervention of the four authors, imposes strict limits on the scope of armed conflict – on utilitarian grounds, but also on virtue ethics grounds, as I have discussed elsewhere.[22] There is thus a strong desire for peace that comes from these four authors, and derives from the rest of their thought. It would be an

overstatement to say that theories of positive atheism lead to paci-
fism, of course, but one may argue that positive atheism, combined
with a careful study of the history of conflict, led our four authors
to believe that humanity was best served by the de-escalation of
conflicts, whether of a religious or political nature.

Similarly, with thinking about colonial enterprises, there is a
tendency towards critique of existing practices. Certainly, the religious conversion of peoples under colonial rule was a strong point
of critique for both Holbach and Diderot. Only the Dutch, they
argued, had held sensible policies in that respect. Though neither Bayle nor Meslier said much of relevance on this topic, they
did portray the attitudes of colonial powers in a negative light.
Diderot is the most accomplished on this topic, notably through
his contributions to Raynal's masterpiece, on which he worked for
until 1780. It is there that one will find the most obvious defence
of the American war of independence, the strongest critiques of
colonial policies; and although Diderot's populationism (the belief
that the wealth of nations comes from a large population and that
the earth needs to be populated further) pushes him to defend
colonies, the restrictions he imposes on them resemble more a
politics of cosmopolitan migration than a firm colonial enterprise
on a national level. Since 'primitive' atheists may still exist out
there, and since forced conversions are the worst of tyrannies, the
positive atheism of our thinkers pushes them to defend the ways
of life, beliefs and practices of the non-European world. Replacing
one superstition with another is never part of their worldview, and
even if they wished to liberate peoples of the world from unhelp-
ful beliefs and practices, it is with a spirit of tolerance that they
wished to achieve these goals.

Moving Past Atheism

By proposing a materialist, utilitarian, republican theory our four
authors did much to build a positive contribution of atheism to
political thought. In some ways, though, they already moved past
their own atheism, and in Diderot's case I have already argued that
he put forward a type of metatheism – past not only theism but also
atheism. This dialectical movement understands atheism as part

of a particular culture and place and attempts to move past it to build a philosophy that is not only reactive or finding new foundations to secularised concepts, but that attempts to move past them altogether, often by engaging with the domain of the spiritual in radically novel ways. Georges Bataille has been a strong defender of a form of 'atheology' that illustrates this movement of metatheology discussed here. Bataille theorised Nietzsche's 'death of God' as a sacrificial ritual that needs to reoccur for notions of the sacred freed from the Christian conception of God to emerge.[23] Bataille's work can thus be understood as an attempt to rescue notions traditionally in the domain of religion, such as the sacred, and to reintroduce them without the religious background they typically come with. As such, he wanted to move past more traditional forms of atheism that reject the sacred altogether with their rejection of God and religion. A metatheology, in this sense, moves past atheism's own rejection of certain concepts and brings it closer to a spiritual understanding of the world.

Holbach's concluding pages of the *System of Nature* are one such attempt to bring about the critique towards atheism itself and rethink the atheist's relation to the spiritual. If there is no god to pray to, what is the point of the prayer? Of course, these prayers are printed, so their primary audience is other human beings, contemporaries of the authors and posterity. They are largely prayers to nature, or prayers of nature to humans. In a world used to praying, such a practice can be difficult to let go of, and natural prayers provide a way of articulating the hopes and wants, the wishes and aspirations of humans who otherwise have little control over their surroundings. Nature is never conceived as a beneficent deity, as a peaceful and cooperative entity. Nature is still often the enemy, full of injustice and in need of domination. Holbach, who lost his first wife, and Diderot, who lost three children, could not have been unaware of how cruel the world before modern medicine could be, even under the mildest of conditions. La Mettrie, who exiled himself to Frederick's court, famously died after devouring some *pâté de faisan aux truffes* while celebrating having cured a patient.[24] Perhaps this is what Diderot and Holbach thought about when they wrote about crimes not going unpunished in nature. But if crimes are eventually punished, not all punishments are deserved. Suffering and pain are often part of daily life without any justification, and no prayer to nature will see it dispense full justice. An atheist can pray, in other words, but any improvement in human condition is always at the aggregate level. If the Enlightenment believed in progress, it did not fool itself into thinking that progress was to be achieved everywhere at once. Progress is a struggle, and one that needs to be kept alive.

Metatheology is thus no longer hostile to the otherness of religious concepts for the atheist, and often attempts to transform and reappropriate them. The 'other' had been used throughout the century as a point of critique. Montesquieu's *Lettres persanes* was a thinly veiled political and religious satire. Although often seen as orientalist works today, the plethora of satirical productions of the Enlightenment were not so much descriptions of the Orient as such, but rather points from which to avoid censorship while still constructing valuable social critiques. Voltaire's *Candide* finds himself in a comical situation with the South American 'other'. Captured by a tribe of cannibalistic locals, he escapes certain death when his mixed-race valet reasons the tribe into liberating them.[25] It is their mutual enmity towards the Jesuits that saves Candide and his valet from the horrible fate, a sign that humanity crosses boundaries and cultures, as long as it combats *l'infâme*. The 'other', no matter how distant or alien, is a potential ally against the worst excesses back home. Holbach occasionally adopts this style, but it is Diderot who truly masters it. His writings on Bougainville's voyage to Tahiti remain one of the most impressive fictional travel writings of the century. Full of social and political flair, Diderot quickly understands that the clash of cultures faced by French sailors with the Tahitians was a productive site for social critique. Whether it is for attitudes to sexual mores or of economic reform, Diderot's supplement pushes the boundaries of the eighteenth century and is a valuable early anthropological work.

Diderot's work is metatheistic, in the sense that it has incorporated the insights of a positive atheism, but also moves past it to formulate a theory that builds something new (in this case, an anthropology) which atheism has opened up a place for. It is of little surprise that anthropology arises as a disciple in these times of colonial expansion and challenge to universalist religion. As a desire to understand the beliefs and practices of other human beings, whether it was from the perspective of the colonial power eager to rule over them, the missionary desperate to convert, or the atheist with a thirst for discovering potential allies against monotheistic belief, the ethnographic study has intrinsic value. Diderot's anthropology is not merely based on the desire to find primitive atheists, or to find additional challenges to Christianity. It is also motivated by the desire to understand the variety of human experience and the way in which the other can help reframe our own prejudices about who we are. The anthropologist here undergoes their own transformation through interaction with the people they study. A metatheology thus also proposes to set limits on one's own beliefs and experience. Atheism itself, it may turn out, is only possible under particular historical circumstances (as a reaction to monotheism in its negative phase, and as a philosophical speculation on an alternative philosophy in its positive phase) that are themselves not unproblematic. Diderot's anthropology sets the limits of his own atheism and brings about the importance of historical and cultural contingency into his thought.

A materialist economic model surfaces in the thought of these authors, also along metatheistic lines. Meslier, though not versed in economic theory, already speculated that a reordering of the feudal model, which he lived under, and the small-scale ownership in which he had stakes as a landowner, needed reform. His communal solution to the problem – that decisions about economic life should be made at the local level by those who work the land – may have been rather unsophisticated, but it pointed to a clear direction of increased democratic control over the means of production. Holbach shared this concern, and although he did not deviate much from a more Lockean theory of property, and did not ultimately undermine the role of large landlords in society, he wished for the emergence of a citizenry that owned its own means of production – the land they worked for a living. This was conceived as the prerequisite condition for a life emancipated from the control of others over one's own economic activity. Their ideals are still agrarian and in line with the physiocratic school, and may seem abstract to us today, who are used to employment contracts, wages and salaries. Diderot was the closest to the developments in economic theory at the time. His defence of a proto-labour theory of value did much to contribute to his defence of the value of waged labour in manufactories. The economic model that was to dominate the nineteenth century was already nascent at the time, and Diderot understood that it was contributing to the wealth of nations and needed the same attention as other productive activities. Though he proposed no concrete conditions for this type of wage labour, he clearly thought that a decent wage was necessary for a fulfilling life, having struggled himself for a long time until the largesse of Catherine II made it possible for him to finally relax his economic ambitions. The economic picture that emerges from the atheists is thus twofold: they insist on the provision of good standards of living and material well-being as an essential part of a fulfilling life, and they argue that productivity is a good, which creates material wealth that then needs to be distributed through citizen control of the economy. They were certainly too bourgeois to argue for seizure of the means of production by the workers, but it would be asking too much of them to grasp the importance that factories and mass exodus from the countryside would bring in the next century. In pushing for these material necessities, however, they were ready to make alliances beyond their doctrinal group. Monasteries could be co-opted to contribute to general utility, nobles could be made to see the benefits of rewarding farmers with their own land to plough, and the King could be seen as an ally to enforce economic reform on the clergy and nobility. In that sense, they were all ready to put their material economic theory ahead of their religious beliefs.

Apart from Meslier, whose writings in terms of proofs reflect a type of self-assured evidence of truth over error, all three of the other authors were enough of sceptics to understand that their philosophical positions were open to challenge and could potentially change as a result of it. That is to say that they treated atheism as a matter of belief, not certainty, and although Holbach was convinced enough of the veracity of his belief to defend it in thousands of pages of illegal manuscripts that could have threatened his otherwise very comfortable lifestyle, he knew that his opinion was not unimpeachable. There were enough theists, deists, sceptics and members of the clergy attending his dinner on a weekly basis to remind him of the fact that his opinions were not shared by all, let alone by the majority of his contemporaries. Even in the educated and literary milieu, many still believed quite sincerely in the religion of their forefathers. Bringing atheism to the realm of *doxa* is an important step in its history. It recognises the contingent nature of the atheistic claims made, it recognises that other opinions differ and are not inferior, and it leaves room for dialogue between beliefs, cooperation and challenge. This radical scepticism, even towards one's beliefs, is the basis for a metatheism as it is discussed here.

Nowhere is this better exemplified than in the work of Diderot, a man who remained sceptical of all of his own positions, including on the non-existence of gods. I have shown in the preceding chapter that Diderot never excludes the possibility of God being a large animal, of which we are mere parts in the universe. This hylozoist perspective shows that Diderot is open to new facts, new arguments and new interpretations challenging his perspective. He can at least conceive of one god that is compatible with this materialist outlook, and though it is far from the god of his contemporaries, he never quite closes the door on that possibility. If one is convinced, as Diderot was, of the contingency of one's own opinion, then there is no room for intolerance. That is not to say that Holbach, or Diderot – or Bayle for that matter – were not convinced of their own opinions. They spent much of their time arguing that their perspective was better than others', and trying to expose more thoughtful, deeper and cleverer ways to understand the world around us. Yet they knew that theirs was not the only way, and that they would need to be convincing to sway others to their own position. The republic of letters proposes not a set of proofs and universally accepted axioms but a battle of wits that each generation is responsible for reproducing. Many of the debates that these four authors contributed to are still alive today and have thus not been settled. One can only hope to convince others of an opinion, not impose a perspective as an ultimate truth.

As we arrive at a metatheistic position by the 1780s with Diderot, it is not because negative or positive atheism have been

superseded. Both the reaction to other positions and the building
of a positive doctrine are needed to be able to move past atheism.
The story here is not one of achieved progress or a finished idea. It
is a constant and never-ending quest for negating errors, miscon-
ceptions and inadequate interpretations, and proposing positive,
better, more adequate and less-flawed conceptions of the world
– and culminates in an openness to the opinions of others over
similar issues. The story of negative atheism, positive atheism and
metatheism is closer to the hermeneutic circle discussed in the
introduction than to a belief in linear progress. John Gray, in his
Seven Types of Atheism, misunderstands this about Enlightenment
atheism.[26] Atheism is not conceived as the ultimate culmination
of the human spirit – all the atheists discussed here had too many
friends who were believers to be so arrogant that they thought
theirs was the only reasonable position on the matter – but is
rather conceived as an informed opinion that can be defended
as coherent, though always incomplete, in one's understanding
of the universe and of our role within it. This is what the story
of metatheism also says: that atheism itself is not a fixed point or
achievement, but something to be defended, expanded upon and
altered continuously. Nietzsche's famous 'death of God' statement
perhaps best encapsulates this maturing of metatheism in the
nineteenth century. The death of God is not a theological statement, nor an atheological statement, but rather an analysis of the
spiritual crisis that philosophy is going through. But this spiritual
crisis is also an opportunity for renewal. As Nietzsche postulates:

Indeed, we philosophers and 'free spirits' feel, when we hear the
news that 'the old god is dead', as if a new dawn shone on us;
our heart overflows with gratitude, amazement, premonitions,
expectation. At long last the horizon appears free to us again,
even if it should not be bright; at long last our ships may venture
out again, venture out to face any danger; all the daring of the
lover of knowledge is permitted again; the sea, our sea, lies open
again; perhaps there has never yet been such an 'open sea'.[27]

A study of later metatheism, as the concept is treated here, would
have to deal with consequences of Nietzsche's thought on the

sociology of religion, though this is beyond the scope of the present book; it has recently been addressed by Peter Watson.[28]

An atheist may have more in common with a devout Catholic (because they both share similar concerns for the material well-being of the poorest in society) than that atheist would have with another atheist who believes the strong take what they can, and the weak suffer what they must. Such is the conclusion of the story of Enlightenment atheism in France: atheists may have more in common with like-minded believers than they have with other atheists. For atheists to be convincing, they had to convince others not only of the validity of their beliefs, but also that if one is to reject their conclusions about god, one can still accept their conclusions about the political and social world. In that they have largely succeeded, for few would doubt that a concern for the material well-being of people comes as one of the fundamental requests of a modern political theory. Atheism's greatest contribution to political thought will be to have made itself unnecessary, for a dialogue between believers and non-believers will be open for all to contribute to. Moving forward in the study of 'atheism', it may be necessary to revise the category itself. Nathan Alexander has proposed one such approach, discussing the merits of using the various terms 'atheism', 'unbelief' or 'nonreligious'.[29] These terms may help us capture more of the phenomenon and find overlaps between those who had a vision of god, albeit a very unorthodox one, those who simply refused to answer the question in the affirmative or the negative, and those who affirmed a type of spirituality without religion. None of the three terms Alexander proposes is without its issues – *atheism* is too close to theism, *non-belief* conforms to a Protestant conception of religion, and *non-religious* ignores the lack of universality behind the concept of religion itself – so perhaps it is time to coin a new term for the study of atheists/unbelievers/non-religious. Historical alternatives have existed, such as naturalists or freethinkers, but they are also not free from their own issues. Some have suggested the term 'bright' to refer to that category of person, in a similar way that homosexuals began to identify as 'gay'.[30] Such a solution is perhaps a little too colloquial and ascribes a little too much common identity to a rather disparate set of persons. I have preferred to stick to the term 'atheist' and have shown that it does not need to stick to its negative connotations. There is a bright future for the study of positive atheism, unbelief and non-religion, and the arguments in favour of such a conception of atheism, which spread for a hundred years between the end of the seventeenth century to the French Revolution, have proven an enlightening foray into the minds of the early thinkers of the concept.

Notes

1. Devellennes, 'A Theory of Atheology'.
2. Smith, *Helvétius*, 1.
3. Ibid. 2.
4. Israel, *Democratic Enlightenment*, 140–72.
5. Kors, *D'Holbach's Coterie*, 116.
6. Bergier, *Examen du matérialisme*, vol. I, 27–8.
7. Bergier, *Examen du matérialisme*, vol. II, 44.
8. Morellet, *Mémoires*, vol. I, 28.
9. Ibid. 134.
10. Ibid. 32.
11. Ibid. 41.
12. Ibid. 130.
13. Ibid. 117.
14. Lock, *Edmund Burke*, vol. II, 30.
15. Diderot, *Contributions à l'histoire des deux Indes*, 729.
16. Robin, *The Reactionary Mind*.
17. Molloy, *Kant's International Relations*.
18. Devellennes, 'Utility contra Utilitarianism: Holbach's International Ethics'.
19. Kant, *Groundwork of the Metaphysics of Morals*.
20. Israel, *Revolutionary Ideas*, 705.
21. Molloy, *Kant's International Relations*.
22. Devellennes, 'Utility contra Utilitarianism'.
23. Bataille, 'The Sacred Conspiracy'.
24. Vartanian, *La Mettrie's L'Homme Machine*.
25. Voltaire, *Romans et contes*, 171.
26. Gray, *Seven Types of Atheism*.
27. Nietzsche, *The Gay Science*, aphorism 343, p. 280.
28. Watson, *The Age of Atheists*.
29. Alexander, 'Rethinking Histories of Atheism, Unbelief, and Nonreligion'.
30. Dennett, 'The Bright Stuff'.

Bibliography

Adams, David. 'Diderot'. In *The History of Western Philosophy of Religion*, vol. 3, ed. Graham Oppy and Nick Trakakis. Durham: Acumen, 2009.

Alexander, Nathan G. 'Rethinking Histories of Atheism, Unbelief, and Nonreligion: An Interdisciplinary Perspective'. *Global Intellectual History*, 2019. DOI: 10.1080/23801883.2019.1657640.

Artz, Frederick B. *The Enlightenment of France*. Oberlin: Kent State University Press, 1968.

Aveling, Francis. 'Atheism'. In *The Catholic Encyclopedia*, vol. 2. New York: Robert Appleton Company, 1907.

Balàzs, Peter. 'Le matérialisme athée d'un "Jacobin" Hongrois: Les *Mémoires Philosophiques ou la Nature Dévoilée* d'Ignace Martinovics'. *La Lettre Clandestine*, vol. 17 (2009), 327–47.

Bartless, Robert. 'On the Politics of Faith and Reason: The Project of Enlightenment in Pierre Bayle and Montesquieu'. *The Journal of Politics*, vol. 63, no. 1 (2001), 1–28.

Bataille, Georges. 'The Sacred Conspiracy'. In *Visions of Excess: Selected Writings, 1927–1939*, ed. Carl Lovitt and Donald Leslie. Minneapolis: University of Minnesota Press, 1985.

Bayle, Pierre. *Avis aux réfugiés. Réponse d'un nouveau converti*, ed. Gianluca Mori. Paris: Honoré Champion, 2007.

Bayle, Pierre. *Dictionnaire historique et critique*, 5th edn. Amsterdam, Leyde, The Hague, Utrecht; 4 vols in folio, 1740.

Bayle, Pierre. *Nouvelles de la République des Lettres*. Amsterdam: Henry Desbordes, 1684.

Bayle, Pierre. *Pensées diverses écrites à un docteur de la Sorbonne à l'occasion de la comète qui parut au mois de Décember 1680*. 3 vols. Amsterdam: Meinard Uytwerf, 1749.

Bayle, Pierre. *A Philosophical Commentary on These Words of the Gospel, Luke 14.23, 'Compel Them to Come In, That My House May Be Full'*. Indianapolis: Liberty Fund, 2005.

Bayle, Pierre. *Political Writings*, ed. Sally Jenkinson. Cambridge: Cambridge University Press, 2000.

Benítez, Miguel. *Les yeux de la raison. Le matérialisme athée de Jean Meslier*. Paris: Honoré Champion, 2012.

Bennett, Jane. *Vibrant Matter: A Political Ecology of Things*. Durham, NC: Duke University Press, 2010.

Bergier, Nicolas-Sylvestre. *Examen du matérialisme ou Réfutation du Système de la nature*. Paris: 1771.

Berlin, Isaiah. *Against the Current: Essays in the History of Ideas*. London: Pimlico, 1979.

Berlin, Isaiah. *Four Essays on Liberty*. Oxford: Oxford University Press, 1969.

Berman, David. *A History of Atheism from Hobbes to Russell*. London: Routledge, 1988.

Betts, C. J. *Early Deism in France: From the So-called 'Déistes' of Lyon (1564) to Voltaire's 'Lettres philosophiques' (1734)*. The Hague: Martinus Nijhoff, 1984.

Bevir, Mark. *The Logic of the History of Ideas*. Cambridge: Cambridge University Press, 1999.

Blank, Andreas. 'D'Holbach on Self-esteem and the Moral Economy of Oppression'. *British Journal for the History of Philosophy*, vol. 25, no. 6 (2017), 1116–37.

Boétie, Étienne de la. *The Politics of Obedience: The Discourse of Voluntary Servitude*. New York, 1975.

Bougainville, Louis de. *A Voyage round the World*. London: J. Nourse and T. Davies, 1772.

Box, M. A. *The Suasive Art of David Hume*. Princeton: Princeton University Press, 1990.

Brykman, Geneviève. 'Bayle's Case for Spinoza'. *Proceedings of the Aristotelian Society*, new series, vol. 88 (1987–8), 259–72.

Buckley, Michael J. *At the Origins of Modern Atheism*. New Haven: Yale University Press, 1990.

Budd, Susan. *Varieties of Unbelief: Atheists and Agnostics in English Society, 1850–1960*. New York: Holmes & Meier, 1977.

Burgess, G. 'The Divine Right of Kings Reconsidered'. *The English Historical Review*, vol. 107, no. 425 (October 1992), 837–61.

Callahan, William J. and David Higgs (eds). *Church and Society in Catholic Europe of the Eighteenth Century*. Cambridge: Cambridge University Press, 1979.

Chisick, Harvey. 'Interpreting the Enlightenment'. *The European Legacy*, vol. 13, no. 1 (2008), 35–57.

Coleman, Janet. *A History of Political Thought: From Ancient Greece to Early Christianity*. Oxford: Blackwell, 2000.

Connolly, William E. 'The Radical Enlightenment: Faith, Power, Theory'. *Theory & Event*, vol. 7, no. 3 (2004).

Cousin, Victor. 'Vanini'. *Revue des deux mondes*, vol. 4 (1843).

Crocker, Lester G. *An Age of Crisis: Man and World in Eighteenth-century French Thought*. Baltimore and London: The Johns Hopkins University Press, 1959.

Delvolvé, Jean. *Religion, critique et philosophie positive chez Pierre Bayle*. Paris: Félix Alcan, 1906.

Dennett, Daniel C. 'The Bright Stuff'. *The New York Times*, 12 July 2003.

Deruette, Serge. *Lire Jean Meslier. Curé athée et révolutionnaire. Introduction au mesliérisme et extraits de son œuvre*. Brussels: Aden, 2008.

Devellennes, Charles. 'A Theory of Atheology'. *Telos*, vol. 166, no. 1 (2014), 81–100.

Devellennes, Charles. 'Utility contra Utilitarianism: Holbach's International Ethics'. *Journal of International Political Theory*, vol. 10, no. 2 (2014).

Diderot, Denis. *Apologie de l'abbé Galiani*. In *Œuvres. Vol. III: Politique*, ed. Laurent Versini. Paris: Robert Laffont, 1995.

Diderot, Denis. *Contributions à l'histoire des deux Indes*. In *Œuvres. Vol. III: Politique*, ed. Laurent Versini. Paris: Robert Laffont, 1995.

Diderot, Denis. *Correspondance*, ed. Laurent Versini. Paris: Robert Laffont, 1997.

Diderot, Denis. *De la suffisance de la religion naturelle*. In *Œuvres*.

Vol. I: Philosophie, ed. Laurent Versini. Paris: Robert Laffont, 1994.

Diderot, Denis. *Éléments de physiologie*. In *Œuvres. Vol. I: Philosophie*, ed. Laurent Versini. Paris: Robert Laffont, 1994.

Diderot, Denis. *Encyclopédie ou dictionnaire raisonné des sciences, des arts et des métiers*. In *Œuvres. Vol. I: Philosophie*, ed. Laurent Versini. Paris: Robert Laffont, 1994.

Diderot, Denis. *Jacques the Fatalist*. London: Penguin, 1986.

Diderot, Denis. *La promenade du sceptique*. In *Œuvres. Vol. I: Philosophie*, ed. Laurent Versini. Paris: Robert Laffont, 1994.

Diderot, Denis. *Le rêve de d'Alembert*. In *Œuvres. Vol. I: Philosophie*, ed. Laurent Versini. Paris: Robert Laffont, 1994.

Diderot, Denis. *Lettre de M. Denis Diderot sur l'examen de l'essai sur les préjugés*. In *Œuvres. Vol. III: Politique*, ed. Laurent Versini. Paris: Robert Laffont, 1995.

Diderot, Denis. *Lettre sur les aveugles*. In *Œuvres. Vol. I: Philosophie*, ed. Laurent Versini. Paris: Robert Laffont, 1994.

Diderot, Denis. *Mélanges philosophiques, historiques, etc., pour Catherine II*. In *Œuvres. Vol. III: Politique*, ed. Laurent Versini. Paris: Robert Laffont, 1995.

Diderot, Denis. *Notes écrites de la main d'un souverain à la marge de Tacite*. In *Œuvres. Vol. III: Politique*, ed. Laurent Versini. Paris: Robert Laffont, 1995.

Diderot, Denis. *Observations sur Hemsterhuis*. In *Œuvres. Vol. I: Philosophie*, ed. Laurent Versini. Paris: Robert Laffont, 1994.

Diderot, Denis. *Observations sur le Nakaz*. In *Œuvres. Vol. III: Politique*, ed. Laurent Versini. Paris: Robert Laffont, 1995.

Diderot, Denis. *Pensées philosophiques*. In *Œuvres. Vol. I: Philosophie*, ed. Laurent Versini. Paris: Robert Laffont, 1994.

Diderot, Denis. *Pensées sur l'interprétation de la nature*. In *Œuvres. Vol. I: Philosophie*, ed. Laurent Versini. Paris: Robert Laffont, 1994.

Diderot, Denis. *Plan d'une université ou d'une education publique dans toutes les sciences*. In *Œuvres. Vol. II: Politique*, ed. Laurent Versini. Paris: Robert Laffont, 1995.

Diderot, Denis. *Supplément au voyage de Bougainville*. Ebooks libres et gratuits, 2004.

Diderot, Denis and Jean le Rond d'Alembert (eds). *Encyclopédie*, *ou dictionnaire raisonné des sciences, des arts et des métiers, etc.* University of Chicago: ARTFL Encyclopédie Project (Autumn 2017 edition), ed. Robert Morrissey and Glenn Roe. http://encyclopedie.uchicago.edu/

Dommanget, Maurice. *Le curé Meslier. Athée, communiste et révolutionnaire sous Louis XIV.* Paris: Julliard, 1965.

Fontenay, Elisabeth de. *Diderot ou le matérialisme enchanté.* Paris: Bernard Grasset, 1981.

Foucault, Didier. *Histoire du libertinage des goliards au marquis de Sade.* Paris: Perrin, 2007.

Fowler, James (ed.). *New Essays on Diderot.* Cambridge: Cambridge University Press, 2011.

Frankel, Charles. *The Faith of Reason: The Idea of Progress in the French Enlightenment* New York: Octagon Books, 1969.

Gadamer, Hans-Georg. *Truth and Method.* London: Continuum, 2004.

Gay, Peter. *The Enlightenment: An Interpretation. The Rise of Modern Paganism.* New York, W. W. Norton, 1966.

Gillot, Hubert. *Denis Diderot. L'homme. Ses idées philosophiques, esthétiques, littéraires.* Paris: Librairie Georges Courville, 1937.

Gray, John. *Seven Types of Atheism.* London: Allen Lane, 2018.

Greig, J. Y. T. *The Letters of David Hume,* 2 vols. Oxford: Clarendon Press, 1932.

Guralnick, Elissa S. 'Radical Politics in Mary Wollstonecraft's *A Vindication of the Rights of Woman'.* In Mary Wollstonecraft, *A Vindication of the Rights of Women,* pp. 309–19. New York: W. W. Norton, 2009.

Haakonssen, Knud. *Natural Law and Moral Philosophy: From Grotius to the Scottish Enlightenment.* Cambridge: Cambridge University Press, 1996.

Hamilton, J. J. 'Hobbes the Royalist, Hobbes the Republican'. *History of Political Thought,* vol. 30, no. 3 (2009), 411–54.

Hampson, Norman. *The Enlightenment: An Evaluation of Its Assumptions, Attitudes and Values.* London: Penguin, 1968.

Hegel, Georg Wilhelm Friedrich. *Lectures on the History of Philosophy,* trans. Elizabeth Haldane and Frances Simson. London: Routledge, 1896.

Hémon-Fabre Catherine and Alain Mothu. 'Un lecteur des curés

Guillaume et Meslier, le Chevalier de la Vieuville'. *La Lettre Clandestine*, vol. 12 (2003), 59–96.

Heyd, Michael. 'A Disguised Atheist or a Sincere Christian? The Enigma of Pierre Bayle'. *Bibliothèque d'Humanisme et Renaissance*, vol. 39, no. 1 (1977), 157–65.

Hickson, Michael and Lennon, Thomas. 'The Real Significance of Bayle's Authorship of the *Avis*.' *British Journal for the History of Philosophy*, vol. 17, no. 1 (2009), 191–205.

Hobbes, Thomas. *Leviathan*. London: Penguin Classics, 2017.

Hochman, Leah. 'The Other as Oneself: Mendelssohn, Diogenes, Bayle, and Spinoza'. *Eighteenth-Century Life*, vol. 28, no. 2 (2004), 41–60.

Holbach, Paul-Henri Thiry d'. *Éléments de la morale universelle ou Catéchisme de la nature*. In *Œuvres philosophiques 1773–1790*, ed. Jean-Pierre Jackson. Paris: Coda, 2004.

Holbach, Paul-Henri Thiry d'. *Essai sur les préjugés ou de l'influence des opinions sur les mœurs & sur le bonheur des hommes*. In *Œuvres philosophiques. Vol. II*, ed. Jean-Pierre Jackson. Paris: Alive, 1999.

Holbach, Paul-Henri Thiry d'. *Éthocratie ou le Gouvernement fondé sur la morale*. In *Œuvres philosophiques. Vol. III*, ed. Jean-Pierre Jackson. Paris: Alive, 2001.

Holbach, Paul-Henri Thiry d'. *La contagion sacrée ou histoire naturelle de la superstition*. In *Œuvres philosophiques. Vol. I*, ed. Jean-Pierre Jackson. Paris: Alive, 1998.

Holbach, Paul-Henri Thiry d'. *La morale universelle ou Les devoirs de l'homme fondés sur sa nature*. In *Œuvres philosophiques 1773–1790*, ed. Jean-Pierre Jackson. Paris: Coda, 2004.

Holbach, Paul-Henri Thiry d'. *La politique naturelle*. In *Œuvres philosophiques. Vol. III*, ed Jean-Pierre Jackson. Paris: Alive, 2001.

Holbach, Paul-Henri Thiry d'. *Le christianisme dévoilé ou Examen des principes & des effets de la religion chrétienne*. In *Œuvres philosophiques. Vol. I*, ed. Jean-Pierre Jackson. Paris: Alive, 1998.

Holbach, Paul-Henri Thiry d'. *Histoire critique de Jésus-Christ, Ou analyse raisonnée des Evangiles*. In *Œuvres philosophiques. Vol. II*, ed. Jean-Pierre Jackson. Paris: Alive, 1999.

Holbach, Paul-Henri Thiry d'. *Le bon sens*. In *Œuvres philosophiques. Vol. III*, ed. Jean-Pierre Jackson. Paris: Alive, 2001.

Holbach, Paul-Henri Thiry d'. *L'esprit du Judaïsme*. Paris: Coda, 2010.

Holbach, Paul-Henri Thiry d'. *Lettres à Eugénie ou préservatif contre les préjugés*. In *Œuvres philosophiques*. Vol. *I*, ed. Jean-Pierre Jackson. Paris: Alive, 1998.

Holbach, Paul-Henri Thiry d'. *Système de la nature ou des Lois du monde physique, & du monde moral*. In *Œuvres philosophiques*. Vol. *II*, ed. Jean-Pierre Jackson. Paris: Alive, 1999.

Holbach, Paul-Henri Thiry d'. *Système de la nature*. In *Œuvres philosophiques*. Vol. *II*, ed. Jean-Pierre Jackson. Paris: Coda, 1999.

Holbach, Paul-Henri Thiry d'. *Système social ou Principes naturels de la morale & de la politique avec un examen de l'influence du gouvernement sur les mœurs*. In *Œuvres philosophiques 1773–1790*, ed. Jean-Pierre Jackson. Paris: Coda, 2004.

Holbach, Paul-Henri Thiry d'. *Tableau des saints*. In *Œuvres philosophiques*. Vol. *III*, ed. Jean-Pierre Jackson. Paris: Alive, 2001.

Holbach, Paul-Henri Thiry d'. *Théologie portative ou dictionnaire abrégé de la religion chrétienne*. In *Œuvres philosophiques*. Vol. *I*, ed. Jean-Pierre Jackson. Paris: Alive, 1998.

Hoogensen, Gunhild. *International Relations, Security and Jeremy Bentham*. Abingdon: Routledge, 2005.

Hruschka, Joachim. 'The Greatest Happiness Principle and Other Early German Anticipations of Utilitarian Theory'. *Utilitas*, vol. 3, no. 2 (1991), 165–77.

Hubert, René. *D'Holbach et ses amis*. Paris: André Delpeuch, 1928.

Hulliung, Mark. *The Autocritique of Enlightenment: Rousseau and the Philosophes*. Cambridge, MA: Harvard University Press, 1994.

Hume, David. *A Treatise of Human Nature*. Oxford: Oxford University Press, 2000.

Hunter, Michael and David Wooton (eds). *Atheism from the Reformation to the Enlightenment*. Oxford: Clarendon Press, 1992.

Hutcheson, Francis. *An Inquiry into the Original of our Ideas of Beauty and Virtue*, 2nd edn. London: Darby, Bettesworth, Fayram, Pemberton, Rivington, Hooke, Clay, Batley, Symon, 1726.

Israel, Jonathan I. *Democratic Enlightenment: Philosophy, Revolution, and Human Rights 1750–1790*. Oxford: Oxford University Press, 2012.

Israel, Jonathan I. *The Dutch Republic: Its Rise, Greatness, and Fall 1477–1806*. Oxford: Clarendon Press, 1995.

Israel, Jonathan I. *Enlightenment Contested: Philosophy, Modernity, and the Emancipation of Man 1670–1752*. Oxford: Oxford University Press, 2006.

Israel, Jonathan I. *Radical Enlightenment: Philosophy and the Making of Modernity 1650–1750*. Oxford: Oxford University Press, 2001.

Israel, Jonathan I. *Revolutionary Ideas: An Intellectual History of the French Revolution from* The Rights of Man *to Robespierre*. Princeton: Princeton University Press, 2015.

Jacob, Margaret. *The Radical Enlightenment: Pantheists, Freemasons, and Republicans*. London: George Allen and Unwin, 1981.

Jacob, Margaret C. 'Radical Enlightenment: Philosophy and the Making of Modernity, 1650–1750 (review)'. *The Journal of Modern History*, vol. 75, no. 2 (2002).

Jansonn, Anton. '"A Swedish Voltaire": The Life and Afterlife of Ingemar Hedenius, 20th-Century Atheist'. *Secularism and Nonreligion*, vol. 7, no. 1 (2018).

Jenkinson, Sally. 'Introduction: A Defence of Justice and Freedom'. In Pierre Bayle, *Political Writings*, ed. Sally Jenkinson. Cambridge: Cambridge University Press, 2000.

Kant, Immanuel. *Groundwork of the Metaphysics of Morals*. Cambridge: Cambridge University Press, 2012.

Kors, Alan Charles. *Atheism in France 1650–1729. Vol. I: The Orthodox Sources of Disbelief*. Princeton: Princeton University Press, 1990.

Kors, Alan Charles. *D'Holbach's Coterie: An Enlightenment in Paris*. Princeton: Princeton University Press, 1976.

Kors, Alan Charles. *Epicureans and Atheists in France, 1650–1729*. Cambridge: Cambridge University Press, 2016.

Kors, Alan Charles. *Naturalism and Unbelief in France, 1650–1729*. Cambridge: Cambridge University Press, 2016.

Kors Alan Charles. 'Radical Enlightenment: Philosophy and the Making of Modernity, 1650–1750 (review)'. *Journal of Interdisciplinary History*, vol. 33, no. 3 (2003).

Kow, Simon. 'Enlightenment Universalism? Bayle and Montesquieu on China'. *The European Legacy: Toward New Paradigms*, vol. 19, no. 3 (2014), 347–58.

Kozul, Mladen. *Les Lumières imaginaires: Holbach et la traduction.* Oxford: Oxford University Studies in the Enlightenment, 2016.

Krüger, Lorenz. 'Why Do We Study the History of Philosophy?' In *Philosophy in History*, ed. Richard Rorty, J. B. Schneewind and Quentin Skinner. Cambridge: Cambridge University Press, 1984.

La Mettrie, Julien Offray de. *Machine Man and Other Writings*, ed. Ann Thomson. Cambridge: Cambridge University Press, 1996.

La Vopa, Anthony. 'Radical Enlightenment: Philosophy and the Making of Modernity, 1650–1750 (review)'. *The Journal of Modern History*, vol. 75, no. 2 (2003).

Labrousse, Élisabeth. *Pierre Bayle. Vol. I: Du pays de Foix à la cite d'Erasme*, 2nd edn. The Hague: Martinus Nijhoff, 1985.

Labrousse, Élisabeth. *Pierre Bayle. Vol. II: Hétérodoxie et rigorisme.* The Hague: Martinus Nijhoff, 1985.

Las Casas, Bartolomé De. *An Account, Much Abbreviated, of the Destruction of the Indies*, ed. Franklin Knight. Indianapolis: Hackett, 2003.

Laursen, John Christian. 'Pierre Bayle's *The Condition of Wholly Catholic France Under the Reign of Louis the Great* (1686)'. *History of European Ideas*, vol. 30, no. 3 (2014).

Lennon, Thomas. 'Did Bayle Read Saint-Evremond?' *Journal of the History of Ideas*, vol. 63, no. 2 (2002), 225–37.

Littré, Émile. *Dictionnaire de la langue française.* Paris: Hachette, 1874.

Lock, F. P. *Edmund Burke.* Oxford: Clarendon Press, 2006.

Locke, John. *Second Treatise of Government*, ed. C. B. Macpherson. Indianapolis: Hackett, 1980.

Locke, John. *Two Treatises of Government.* Cambridge: Cambridge University Press, 2003.

Lough, John. *The Encyclopédie in Eighteenth Century England, and Other Studies.* Newcastle: Oriel Press, 1970.

Lough, John. *The Philosophes and Post-revolutionary France.* Oxford: Clarendon Press, 1982.

Luhmann, Niklas. *Essays on Self-Reference*. New York: Columbia University Press, 1990.

Maritain, Jacques. 'On the Meaning of Contemporary Atheism'. *The Review of Politics*, vol. 11, no. 3 (1949), 267–80.

Marx, Karl. *Capital: A Critical Analysis of Capitalist Production*, vol. I. London: Lawrence & Wishart, 1974.

Marx, Karl. *Confesssions*. Available at https://www.marxists.org/archive/marx/works/1865/04/01.htm (accessed 20 July 2020).

Marx, Karl and Frederick Engels. *The German Ideology. Part One*. London: Lawrence & Wishart, 1999.

McKenna, Antony. *Études sur Pierre Bayle*. Paris: Honoré Champion, 2015.

McKenna, Antony. 'La correspondence du jeune Bayle: apprentissage et banc d'essai de son écriture'. *Revue d'histoire littéraire de la France*, vol. 103 (2003), 287–300.

McKenna, Antony. 'Les manuscrits clandestins dans les papiers de Marc-Michel Rey'. *La Lettre Clandestine*, vol. 23 (2015), 25–45.

Meillassoux, Quentin. *Après la finitude. Essai sur la nécessité de la contingence*. Paris: Seuil, 2006.

Meslier, Jean. *Œuvres complètes*, ed. Jean Deprun, Roland Desné and Albert Soboul. 3 vols. Paris: Anthropos, 1970.

Meslier, Jean. *Testament: Memoir of the Thoughts and Sentiments of Jean Meslier*, trans. Michael Shreve. Amherst, NY: Prometheus Books, 2009.

Moëne, Geneviève. 'Jean Meslier, prêtre athée et révolutionnaire'. *The French Review*, vol. 77, no. 1 (2003).

Molloy, Seán. *Kant's International Relations: The Political Theology of Perpetual Peace*. Ann Arbor: University of Michigan Press, 2017.

Morehouse, Andrew. *Voltaire and Jean Meslier*. New Haven: Yale University Press, 1936.

Morellet, André. *Mémoires sur le dix-huitième siècle et sur la Révolution Française*. Paris: Imprimerie de Fain, 1821.

Mori, Gianluca. 'Pierre Bayle, the Rights of the Conscience, the "Remedy" of Toleration'. *Ratio Juris*, vol. 10, no. 1 (1997), 45–60.

Mori, Gianluca. *Bayle philosophe*. Paris: Honoré Champion, 1999.

Mori, Gianluca. 'Bayle, Saint-Evremond, and Fideism: A Reply to

Thomas M. Lennon'. *Journal of the History of Ideas*, vol. 65, no. 2 (2004), 323–34.

Mossner, Ernest. *The Life of David Hume*. Oxford: Oxford University Press, 2001.

Mortimer, Sarah. 'Christianity and Civil Religion in Hobbes's *Leviathan*'. In *The Oxford Handbook of Hobbes*, ed. Al Martinich and Kinch Hoekstra. Oxford: Oxford University Press, 2016.

Naville, Pierre. *D'Holbach et la philosophie scientifique au XVIIIe siècle*. Paris: Gallimard, 1967.

Nietzsche, Friedrich. *The Gay Science*, trans. Walter Kaufmann. New York: Vintage, 1974.

Nietzsche, Friedrich. *Untimely Meditations*, trans. Reginald John Hollingdale. Cambridge: Cambridge University Press, 1983.

O'Connor, D. J. *John Locke*. New York: Dover, 1967.

Onfray, Michel. *Contre-histoire de la philosophie 4. Les ultras des Lumières*. Paris: Grasset, 2007.

Onfray, Michel. 'Jean Meslier and "The Gentle Inclination of Nature"'. *New Politics*, vol. 10, no. 4 (2006).

Oppy, Graham and Nick Trakakis (eds). *The History of Western Philosophy of Religion*. Durham: Acumen, 2009.

Paganini, Gianni. 'Pour une histoire de l'athéisme à part entière'. *La Lettre Clandestine*, vol. 12 (2003), 7–10.

Pascal, Blaise. *Pensées*. Adelaide: University of Adelaide Press, 2014.

Paterson, Antoinette Mann. *The Infinite Worlds of Giordano Bruno*. Springfield, IL: Charles C. Thomas, 1970.

Pearson Cushing, Max. *Baron D'Holbach: A Study of Eighteenth-century Radicalism in France*. New York: The New Era Printing Company, 1914.

Pellerin, Pascale. 'Diderot, Voltaire, et le curé Meslier: un sujet tabou'. *Diderot Studies*, vol. 29 (2003), 53–63.

Pettit, Philip. *Republicanism: A Theory of Freedom and Government*. Oxford: Clarendon Press, 2000.

Plato. *The Apology*. In *The Dialogues of Plato. Vol. I: The Apology and Other Dialogues*, trans. B. Jowett. Aylesbury: Sphere Books, 1970.

Plattner, M. *An Interpretation of the Discourse on Inequality*. DeKalb: North Illinois University Press, 1979.

Popkin, Richard. 'The Skeptical Precursors of David Hume'. *Philosophical and Phenomenological Research*, vol. 16 (1955), 61–71.

Priestley, Joseph. *Letters to a Philosophical Unbeliever*, 2nd edn. Birmingham: Pearson and Rollason, 1787.

Rex, Walter. *Essays on Pierre Bayle and Religious Controversy*. The Hague: Martinus Nijhoff, 1965.

Riley, Patrick. 'General and Particular Will in the Political Thought of Pierre Bayle'. *Journal of the History of Philosophy*, vol. 24, no. 2 (1986), 173–95.

Roberts, Alexandre. *Justin Martyr and Athenagoras*, trans. James Donaldson. Edinburgh: T. and T. Clark, 1867.

Robin, Corey. *The Reactionary Mind: Conservatism from Edmund Burke to Sarah Palin*. Oxford: Oxford University Press, 2011.

Rosemboim, Or. *The Emergence of Globalism*. Princeton: Princeton University Press, 2017.

Ross, Ian Simpson. *The Life of Adam Smith*. Oxford: Oxford University Press, 1995.

Rousseau, Jean-Jacques. *Discours sur l'origine de l'inégalité parmi les hommes*. In J.-J. Rousseau, *Du contrat social et autres oeuvres politiques*. Paris: J. Ehrard, 1975.

Samuels, Warren J., Jeff E. Biddle and John B. Davis (eds). *A Companion to the History of Economic Thought*. Oxford: Blackwell, 2003.

Sandberg, Karl. 'Pierre Jurieu's Contribution to Bayle's *Dictionnaire*'. *Journal of the History of Philosophy*, vol. 3, no. 1 (1965), 59–74.

Sandel, Michael. *Democracy's Discontent: America in Search of a Public Philosophy*. Cambridge, MA: Belknap Press, 1998.

Sandrier, Alain. *Le style philosophique du baron d'Holbach. Conditions et contraintes du prosélytisme athée en France dans la seconde moitié du XVIIIe siècle*. Paris: Honoré Champion, 2004.

Scarre, Geoffrey. *Utilitarianism*. London and New York: Routledge, 1996.

Schino, Anna Lisa. 'La critique libertine de la religion: mécanismes de formation des croyances et psychologie des masses'. *ThéoRèmes* [online], vol. 9 (2016).

Skinner, Quentin. 'The Idea of Negative Liberty'. In *Philosophy in History*, ed. Richard Rorty, J. B. Schneewind and Quentin Skinner. Cambridge: Cambridge University Press, 1984.

Skinner, Quentin. *Liberty Before Liberalism*. Cambridge: Cambridge University Press, 1998.

Skinner, Quentin. 'Meaning and Understanding in the History of Ideas'. *History and Theory*, vol. 8, no. 1 (1969), 3–53.

Smith, David Warner. *Helvétius: A Study in Persecution*. Oxford: Clarendon Press, 1965.

Steiner, Philippe. 'Physiocracy and French Pre-Classical Political Economy'. In *A Companion to the History of Economic Thought*, ed. Warren J. Samuels, Jeff E. Biddle and John B. Davis. Oxford: Blackwell, 2003.

Stephen, Leslie. *The English Utilitarians. Vol. I: Jeremy Bentham*. London: Replika Process, 1950.

Stephens, Mitchell. *Imagine There's No Heaven: How Atheism Helped Create the Modern World*. New York: Palgrave Macmillan, 2014.

Strugnell, Anthony. 'Diderot's Anti-colonialism: A Problematic Notion'. In *New Essays on Diderot*, ed. James Fowler. Cambridge: Cambridge University Press, 2011.

Stunkel, Kenneth. 'Montaigne, Bayle, and Hume: Historical Dynamics of Skepticism'. *The European Legacy: Toward New Paradigms*, vol. 3, no. 4 (2008), 43–64.

Sutcliffe, Adam. 'Spinoza, Bayle, and the Enlightenment Politics of Philosophical Certainty'. *History of European Ideas*, 34 (2008), 66–76.

Taylor, Charles. *A Secular Age*. Cambridge, MA and London: The Belknap Press and Harvard University Press, 2007.

Thielemann, Leland. 'Diderot and Hobbes'. *Diderot Studies*, vol. 2 (1952), 221–78.

Thomson, Ann. *Bodies of Thought: Science, Religion, and the Soul in the Early Enlightenment*. Oxford: Oxford University Press, 2008.

Thomson, Ann. 'Introduction'. In Julien Offray de La Mettrie, *Machine Man and Other Writings*, ed. Ann Thomson. Cambridge: Cambridge University Press, 1996.

Tønder, Lars. 'Spinoza and the Theory of Active Tolerance'. *Political Theory*, vol. 41, no. 5 (2014), 687–709.

Trousson, Raymond. *Denis Diderot ou le vrai Prométhée*. Paris: Talandier, 2005.

Van der Lugt, Mara. *Bayle, Jurieu, and the Dictionnaire Historique et Critique*. Oxford: Oxford University Press, 2016.

Vaneigem, Raoul. *The Revolution of Every Life*. London: Rebel Press, 1983.

Vartanian, Aram. 'From Deist to Atheist. Diderot's Philosophical Orientation. 1746–1749'. *Diderot Studies*, vol. 1 (1949), 46–63.

Vartanian, Aram. *La Mettrie's L'Homme Machine: A Study in the Origins of an Idea*. Princeton: Princeton University Press, 1960.

Verona, Luciano. *Jean Meslier. Prêtre athée socialiste révolutionnaire 1664–1729*. Milan: Cisalpino-Goliardica, 1975.

Versini, Laurent. *Denis Diderot*. Paris: Hachette, 1996.

Voltaire, *Dieu. Réponse de Mr. de Voltaire au Système de la nature*. Ferney, 1770.

Voltaire, *Le philosophe ignorant*. Paris: Flammarion, 2009.

Voltaire, *Romans et contes*. Paris: Garnier, 1979.

Wartofsky, Marx W. 'Diderot and the Development of Materialism Monism'. *Diderot Studies*, vol. 2 (1952), 279–329.

Watson, Peter. *The Age of Atheists: How We Sought to Live Since the Death of God*. New York: Simon & Schuster, 2014.

White, Reginald James. *The Anti-Philosophers: A Study of the Philosophes in Eighteenth-century France*. London: Macmillan, 1970.

Whitmarsh, Tim. *Battling the Gods: Atheism in the Ancient World*. London: Faber & Faber, 2016.

Wickwar, William Hardy. *Baron d'Holbach: A Prelude to the French Revolution*. New York: Augustus M. Kelley, 1968.

Williams, D. L. 'Justice and the General Will: Affirming Rousseau's Ancient Orientation'. *Journal of the History of Ideas*, vol. 66, no. 3 (2005), 383–411.

Wilson, Arthur, *Diderot*. Oxford: Oxford University Press, 1972.

Wilson, Catherine. 'Leibniz and Atomism'. *Studies in History and Philosophy of Science*, vol. 13, no. 3 (1982), 175–99.

Wokler, Robert. 'Perfectible Apes in Decadent Cultures: Rousseau's Anthropology Revisited'. *Daedalus*, vol. 107, no. 3 (1978), 107–34.

Wollstonecraft, Mary. *A Vindication of the Rights of Women*. New York: W. W. Norton, 2009.

Wooton, David. 'New Histories of Atheism'. In *Atheism from the Reformation to the Enlightenment*, ed. Michael Hunter and David Wooton. Oxford: Clarendon Press, 1992.

Zarka, Yves Charles. 'L'idée de critique chez Pierre Bayle'. *Revue de Metaphysique et Morale*, vol. 4 (1999), 515–24.

Zurbuchen, Simone. 'Religion and Society'. In *The Cambridge History of Eighteenth-Century Philosophy*, vol. I, ed. Knud Haakonssen. Cambridge: Cambridge University Press, 2006.

Index